IMAGINATION

"The power, which a man's imagination over his body to heal it or make it sick is a force which none of us is born without. The first man had it; the last one will possess it. If left to him, a man is most likely to use only the mischievous half of the force—the half that invents imaginary ailments for him and cultivates them; and if he is one of these very wise people, he is quite likely to scoff at the beneficent half of the force and deny its existence. And so, to heal or help that man, two imaginations are required: his own and some outsider's. The outsider's work is unquestionably valuable; so valuable that it may fairly be likened to the essential work performed by the engineer when he handles the throttle and turns on the steam; the actual power is lodged exclusively in the engine, but if the engine were left alone it would never start of itself. His services are necessary. He is the Engineer; he simply turns on the same old steam and the engine does the whole work."

Mark Twain

THE PSYCHOLOGICAL AUTOPSY OF
ELVIS PRESLEY

REVIEWS

Wow! I started the Elvis book last night and just finished it. Except for sleep and meals, I read it straight through. I found it fascinating.

Paul Bergley

In *A Psychological Autopsy of Elvis Presley,* Bill Ronan has created a fascinating vortex of ideas and theories, all of which swirl around the ever-engaging life and death of Elvis Aaron Presley. Ronan posits a set of psychological circumstances as the cause of Presley's death, including issues around self-image, his relationships with others, the death of his mother and twin brother, and his own feelings of detachment and "death" prior to mortality. The author then connects these circumstances to several specific case studies, suggesting ways in which the "deaths of Elvis" can be used to bring the psychological distress of others into focus. Ronan does not shy away from any rhetorical device or from leaps over the intellectual chasms that typically divide fields of inquiry. Hypnotherapy, traditional psychology, social science research techniques, biomedical ethics, and several other disciplines and avocations collide in his work, all casting light on the strange but hardly unique life of Elvis Presley. The book is a journey through original thoughts in original combinations, a journey on which neither the faint of heart nor the hidebound need embark. Even if every hypothesis ends up dismissed, the journey itself is well worth the effort.

Dale Alan McGowan
Ph.D. Music Composition, University of Minnesota (1999). M.M. Instrumental Conducting, with Distinction, California State University, Northridge (1991) Professional Designation in Film Scoring, UCLA (1988) A.B. Music and Physical Anthropology (Honors in Music), University of California, Berkeley (1986) Currently Associate Professor of Music, College of Saint Catherine. Book length works: *Calling Bernadette's Bluff,* satirical novel, 2002; *Why Does Barber's Adagio Break My Heart?,* pending publication

"The points you (the author) makes are valid . . We appreciate and are sure Elvis would have thanked you . . It has taken some time, but then there was a lot to review. We find that it has no commercial value to the public."

Gordon Stoker, First Tenor and Manager of The Jordanaires
(Elvis' back-up group till the late 60's)

Observing this "documentary" does add to my understanding of medical hypnoanalysis and informs me about how MH can be used in the treatment of every person out there who has any kind of problem. It makes you wonder how this therapy could have helped Elvis at any and all levels of chronological growth and development as he progressed throughout his life. MH has a place to changing the world one person at a time.

Tom Zurkowski, MD, Psychiatrist, Batesville, AR

This was an in-depth analysis of Elvis and his problem, how he dealt with it. It was a great demonstration of the Ponce de leon Syndrome and the Walking Zombie Syndrome as represented by Elvis' public and private life. It helped me understand these two diagnoses.

Marge Bauman, RN, MS, LPC, Institute for Motivational
Development, Lombard, IL

It was useful in understanding lots of things—relationships between his mother and his needs to be with her—which triggered the dead part of self. The alive part of Elvis was seen through his music. Temporarily, his wife and daughter filled a need, but finally his death wish to be with his mother resulted in his death.

Marge Harmon, MSW, Private Practice,
Naperville, Lombard, IL

The Elvis "hypothesis" analysis seems applicable on a number of levels and toward other theories. It is a very convincing argument for what we now know about the nature of trauma—how the psychological affects the physiological, how the body then "remembers" even if the brain and heart do not and then how these "memories" continue to "act themselves out" in behaviors—so seemingly bizarre and unexplainable to those watching. The power of an idea to change one's heart, mind, body, and behavior. Bill's work underlines how unawareness of this emotional numbness principle can lead to a low level of self-directedness, and in Elvis' case, a wasteful tragic death. Excellent teaching tool.

**Kade Haviland, MA, CACII, Arapaho House, Inc,
Denver Outpatient Clinic, Denver, CO**

I feel your study was very in-depth. As a documentary, it could be a valuable tool for learning and understanding of the need for medical hypnoanalysis. Elvis clearly had many issues recognizable to us and could have benefited from medical hypnoanalysis.

**Betsy Zurkowski, RNC, Office of Tom Zurkowski, MD
Psychiatrist, Batesville, AR**

I was impressed by the clarity of the diagnosis and the rich evidence carefully compiled to support the medical hypnoanalytic diagnosis.

John B. Hart, D.Min, Private Practice, Bristol, IN

I must conclude that, in my opinion, this book's insightful message illustrates the means by which extreme celebrity combined with emotional instability can cause a person to change from a healthful lifestyle into a narrow corner of life where hope is gone because of the superficial fixes that the extremely famous often obtain in this life. Thus, the person goes through life like the "zombie" that William Ronan speaks about and without coping methods, the person falls ill and sometimes does not recover; the more famous the person, the harder the fall, it seems. Feeling alone in life facilitates illness because of depression and anxiety. That loneliness is well described by Byron in "Childe Harold's Pilgrimage:

> What is the worst of woes that wait on age?
> What stamps the wrinkle deeper on the brow?
> To view each loved one blotted from life's page,
> And be alone on earth as I am now."

Fame does not bring with it emotional fortitude, which is that strength of being which is necessary to keep on striving though life.

**Cheryl A. Gupta, Master of Library Science,
University of Pittsburgh, 1974
Bachelor of Science in Education,
Edinboro State College, 1969**

This was a phenomenal observation, accumulated over a period of years. Bill has done an outstanding job of matching the medical hypnoanalytic process to a regal and very public figure. One wishes if only Elvis could have been introduced to this modality, he might still be with us sharing the gift of his music. Therapy under medical hypnoanalysis is an art. It produces a deep statement from the client with profound change in a short period of time.

Sanded Hobsm, MS Counseling (in process), Memphis, TN

IDEAS

At one of their last meetings, they (Rasputin and Dr. Botkin) had argued about the soul, and Botkin had said, with an air of having completely routed his opponent: "I have performed many autopsies over the years, but I have never located a soul." To which Rasputin replied, "And how many emotions or imaginations or memories have you located?"

Rasputin

". . . speech provides conditioned stimuli which are just as real as any other stimuli which exceed in richness and many-sidedness any of the others, allowing comparisons neither qualitatively nor quantitatively with any conditioned stimuli which are possible in all animals. Speech, on account of the whole preceding life of the adult, is connected with all the internal and external stimuli which reach the cortex, signaling all of them and replacing all of them, and therefore can call forth all those reactions of the organism which are normally determined by the actual stimuli themselves."

IP Pavlov, Nobel Prize winner, summarizing his life's work

According to Paul Martin, in his book *The Sickening Mind,* published by Harper Collins, the number of deaths resulting from shrapnel and physical damage of the actual explosions on the first day of the Scud missile attack on Israel was zero. Statistics would have predicted 89 for the whole day. However, the actual rate for that day was 147. 58 more than predicted. Perhaps death from fear? Perhaps the acceptance of the death suggestion? This is a psychological postmortem of Elvis Presley. The facts have been taken from the many articles, books, pamphlets, etc., written about this man. The analysis has been done entirely from the written and published word for two reasons: (1) to facilitate contextual verification and (2) to prevent researcher bias. The guidelines for following these analyses are as follows: Elvis' birth was reported to have had a "mystical quality" about it. He survived his twin brother, Jesse Garon, who died at birth. Guilt feelings and a feeling of being extra-special were to follow him the rest of his life. These feelings were maximized by the overpossessive, overprotective, almost psychic devotion of Elvis' mother. Elvis devoted his entire life to her, to make up for the loss of his brother.

At the very zenith of his career, Elvis' mother died of a heart attack. This event catapulted Elvis into an overwhelming depression, leaving him functionally and emotionally dead. He became, in essence, a Walking Zombie. Nine years later, he experienced a sort of psychological reincarnation. This preceded his re-entry into live performances. The important turning points were a spiritual vision he feels he received from God, his marriage to Priscilla and the birth of Lisa (making up for the daughter his mother longed for but could not have). Freed from past guilt, but not having adequately dealt with his feeling of having died psychologically with his mother, he began to grow increasingly interested in reincarnation, death, etc. The forces driving these emotions are of a subconscious nature repressed by feelings of guilt and feelings of being extra-special. These feelings led to a belief that he had resurrected. This was too blasphemous for him to acknowledge consciously. His behavior indicated the attitude of one who would believe this.

After his comeback, Elvis lost even more affection from those near him, only to be replaced by the distant affection of millions. Elvis had tried to keep all his friends, coworkers, etc., with him for his life. However, in these last few years, his original backup group left him, he was divorced from Priscilla—a devastating blow—and his friends and bodyguards seemingly turned on him. They wrote a book that revealed, without understanding, some of the strange behavior these emotions would elicit.

During all of this, Elvis felt he was in contact with his dead mother and dead brother. His behavior constantly indicated an extreme overidentification with his mother, which may have led to his death. He died 19 years and 2 days after her death, of approximately the same cause. Having gained weight and dyed his hair black, he even looked like her.

There may be many who will criticize my analysis, just as there may be many who will agree. Both positions are welcome for the sake of clinical debate. If this work does no more than spark thought and discussions, it will have served its purpose.

I hope that this work will serve to illuminate the importance of psychological intervention in human suffering and, by analogy, increase the understanding of those around us. In my opinion, confrontation of an idea such as this serves as a psychological vaccination, hence reducing the probability of repetition. Certainly there will never be another Elvis, but it is equally true that there will never be another you or I. What happened to him is not the most important message of this book—but how and why it happened.

I now present the facts as presented to me.

THE PSYCHOLOGICAL AUTOPSY OF
ELVIS PRESLEY

*The Elvis Analysis:
The Role of Suggestion in the
Etiology of Psychosomatic Disorders*

BY WILLIAM J. RONAN

ACFEI Media Springfield, MO

The Psychological Autopsy of Elvis Presley
by William J. Ronan

© 2005, William J. Ronan,

ACFEI Media
2750 E. Sunshine
Springfield, MO 65804

ISBN: 978-0-9832601-0-3

Printed in the United States. First printing January 2011

SPECIAL THANKS & DEDICATION

A lot of people have helped with this effort. It has been son long since it began that I will undoubtedly leave some people out of this thank you. I apologize for that.

Still some people due deserve mention. My wife of 17 years Deborah L Ronan, who died, suddenly, of an asthma attack, 16 years prior to the publication of this book. She supported me in innumerable ways as I researched this topic. We had discussed often the Walking Zombie Syndrome and I feel that helped me in many ways to not become a WZ and continue living, perhaps even more vigorously as I had then a son aged 4. I did not have the luxury of a depression. Until she died my treatment of what he went thru was purely academic. It was not until I lost the love of my life that I could begin to really feel whet he felt.

Then I would like to thank Linda-Popp Walker, LPCC, who helped very much with the grammar etc. At that time she was new to the field of what is now called Medical Hypnoanalysis.

I would also like to thank Retired Col. Paul LeGolvan, MD, Pathologist, for his support and commentary as this project developed.

"I would very much like to thank, the now deceased, Daniel S. Snow, MD who introduced me to what is now called "Medical Hypnoanalysis" He took me under his wing and guided me. Without him none of this, nor most of my professional life, would not have happened."

Finally I would like to thank the people at the American Psychotherapy Association who took the time to read my manuscript and to help me further with editing etc and their encouragement to finish the book.

PART I
TOOLS FOR UNDERSTANDING

CHAPTER 1

AN OVERVIEW OF MEDICAL HYPNOANALYSIS

There are three basic principles derived from the science of hypnosis that will aid the reader in understanding human behavior. They are as follows:

1. The principle of concentrated attention—when attention is concentrated on an idea over and over again, the idea tends to realize itself.

2. The principle of reversed effect—the harder one tries to do something, the less chance one has of success.

3. The principle of dominant effect—a strong emotion tends to replace a weak one.

CHAPTER 2

EMOTIONS

This is a general model that I use to understand the progress of emotional problems.

1. Initial Sensitizing Event is not recallable by the conscious mind.
    An individual is sensitized by an emotionally powerful incident in the past. "Psychological antibodies" build up against the initial sensitizing event, but no symptoms appear.

2. Symptom Producing Event is recallable.
    A second emotionally powerful event triggers the symptoms into awareness as the psychological antigen meets the psychological antibodies of the previously sensitized individual.

3. Symptom Intensifying Event is again recallable.
    A symptom-intensifying event produces still further difficulties, and this may be the reason for the subject's visit to a therapist's office.

4. The Concept of the Quantity of Power, driving the maladapted

idea as the primary factor to be dealt with in altering the process. The strength of this emotion would later be used to bring about a satisfactory, healthy adjustment.

Medical Hypnoanalysis and the Etiology and Mechanism of Mental Health Issues
As first developed by S.J. Van Pelt

Hypnotic suggestion can play a major role in the etiology and treatment of mental health issues characterized by changes of mood, emotion, and more often than not, by psychosomatic phenomenon. These changes bear a predominantly close similarity to those that can be produced by hypnotic suggestion.

It is easy to suggest to a person in the hypnotic state that he/she is cheerful, gloomy, weary, tired, warm, chilly, muscular, or frail, and acquire the fitting reaction if a satisfactory level of hypnosis has been obtained.

It is equally easy to induce anesthesia, analgesia, hyperesthesia, and a variety of paralyses by hypnotic suggestion, and it is possible to provoke hallucinations of the senses, which may manifest themselves also for the duration of the hypnotic session or posthypnotically.

By way of hypnotic suggestion, a completely ordinary human being can develop a condition in every way identical to that of what may be called a mental health issue. If a person in a satisfactory degree of hypnotic trance is told that in the future he/she will have an uncontainable craving to contact every doorknob he/she sees, then he/she will in fact perform this act just as though he/she were suffering from a "valid" compulsive disorder. Luria, 1932, in Russia, at the State Institute of Experimental Psychology in Moscow, experimented extensively in the production of neuroses by the use of hypnotic suggestion. A conflict was created by suggesting to the hypnotized subject something that was quite contrary to his/her normal behavior, and by suggesting loss of memory, it was possible to bring about a simulated repression. Erickson, 1944, also made numerous uses of an experimentally induced neurosis. Eisenbud, 1937, induced an experimental conflict by hypnosis to show a client the cause of his headaches and loss of memory. Wolberg, 1947, has described how he unintentionally created an experimental neurosis in a medical student by giving him a posthypnotic suggestion to misspell his name. Unbeknown to the operator, the subject had a very entrenched repugnance to misspelling his name, and an artificial conflict was set up. Van Pelt, 1952, recorded 5 cases of neurosis ensuing from thoughtless suggestions given to subjects during stage performances. It is consequently plainly recognized that *a mental health issue can be produced either intentionally for experimental or therapeutic purposes, or it could be accidentally induced by suggestions which arouse conflicts in the subject.*

It is also a recognized scientific fact that the induction of self-hypnosis is quite possible. Estabrooks, 1946 [pp. 85-86], recorded a posthypnotic visual hallucination as the consequence of purposeful self-hypnosis and suggestion, using himself as the subject. Wolberg, 1948 [vol. I, p. 81], states that under certain conditions, the hypnotic state may develop in the absence of a second person. Kroger, 1953, describes how a client was trained to induce self-hypnosis for the use of trouble-free childbirth. Watkins, 1949, records information of two clients who were able to develop self-hypnosis. Therefore, *a condition of hypnosis may be induced either by a hypnotist or by the subject him/herself. In this condition, suggestions can give rise to conditions, which can resemble any of the accepted forms of mental health issues.* Mental health issues (other than those intentionally induced for experimental or therapeutic purposes), that is, the "naturally happening" mental health issues, are the consequence of *accidental self-hypnosis and suggestion.*

The method of this alteration is thought out to be as follows:

Van Pelt's AETIOLOGY AND MECHANISM OF THE PSYCHONEUROSES

1. An event (or series of events), or an idea (or ideas), of *real emotional significance* to the client can, by causing a *concentration* of the mind, induce a condition of *"accidental hypnosis,"* and *any idea fixed in the psyche at this time* will have the influence of a

hypnotic suggestion. The mechanism of this has been illustrated (see below).

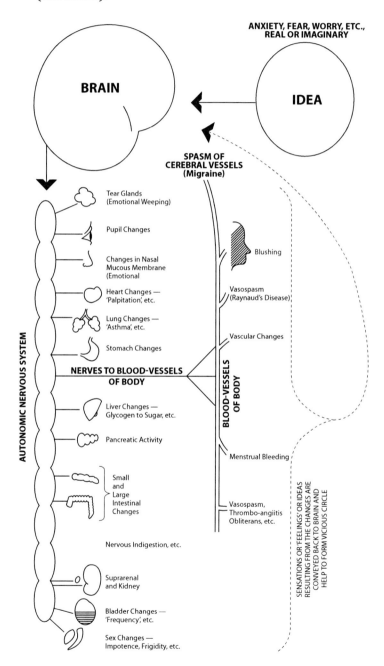

2. The client suffering from a mental health issue behaves in every way as though under the influence of a posthypnotic suggestion. He/she will often affirm that he/she *knows* his/her behavior is irrational, but he/she *feels* he/she must perform the way he/she does. A person who is given a posthypnotic suggestion may declare that he/she *knows* the suggested act is silly, but he/she feels constrained to carry it out, and he/she will in actuality feel everything from indistinct unease to heightened distress should he/she make an effort to defy implementation of the directives.

3. Subjects differ in the level of hypnosis they are able to attain and the phenomena they can develop. This information may account for the variations in mental health issues. Extremely predisposed subjects who are capable of developing a deep degree of hypnosis may display the most fantastic phenomena, while others not so deeply affected may illustrate only milder symptoms.

4. The idea fixed in the mind usually gives rise to secondary symptoms through the action of the autonomic nervous system. Thus an event or idea giving rise to *fear*, *worry*, *or anxiety* of any kind will cause the subject to develop *tension*, as this is the one physical action which is common both to fighting or running away. The *tension*, by interfering with *function*, gives rise to *unpleasant symptoms*. These, by causing more *worry* and *anxiety*, purely generate more *tension*, which in turn generates additional *symptoms*, so that a *vicious circle* is established. The mechanism of this change is shown below. The idea, even if at first *apparently* pleasing, can subsequently cause fear or anxiety. For instance, smoking or drinking may give *momentary* pleasure but eventually cause fear. Other dire habits may give passing gratification but cause anxiety and regret. By the time the client suffering from a mental health issue presents him/herself for therapy, this vicious circle is more often than not well established, and the fear that keeps the situation going or getting worse is *the fear of his/her own symptoms*. The client is frightened of the symptoms of fear.

Original fear (resulting from an event or idea) which starts the problem.

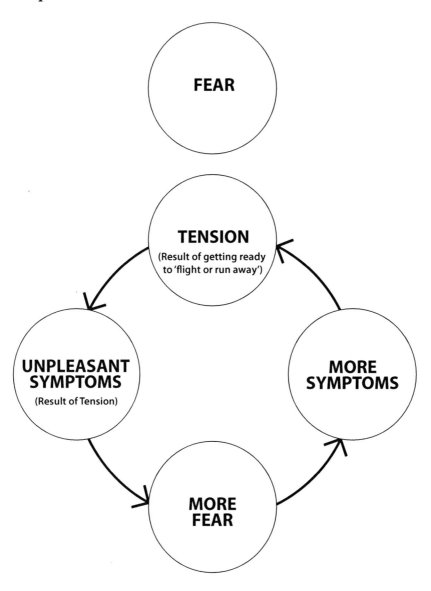

The client becomes so occupied and engrossed with the vicious circle of fear and symptoms that he/she forgets the original cause

The medical hypnoanalytic mechanism of mental health issues.

REFERENCES

Eisenbud, J, 1937, Psychology of a headache, Psychiatric. Quart, 1937, II. 592-619

Erickson, M H, 1944,The method employed to formulate a complex story for the induction of an experimental neurosis in a hypnotic subject, J of Gen Psychol., 31, 67-84

Estabrooks, G H, 1946, Hypnotism, 1946, NY: E P Dutton & Co, Inc

Kroger, W S, 1953, Hypnosis in Modern Medicine, (ed J M Schneck), 1953, Ch, VI 125. Springfield, IL: C C Thomas

Luria, AR, 1932 The Nature of Human Conflicts, New York: Liveright

Van Pelt, S J, 1952, Some dangers of stage hypnotism, Brit J of Med Hypnotism., 3, No 2, Spring, 30-38

Why Clients Can Seldom Remember the Origin of Their Problems

The *original* incident, emotion, or idea which gave rise to apprehension and started the entire problem has typically been *forgotten* for the reason that the client is so engaged and immersed with the vicious loop of fear and distressing symptoms that he/she cannot reflect clearly and coolly. The forgotten event has given rise to the fashionable idea among both professional and lay people that there has to be some deeply obscure "subconscious" repressed event that has caused all the trouble.

No grand "subconscious prying" is needed. The origin of the trouble can be traced very simply in most cases. The event, or events, that produced the idea, or ideas, that led to the vicious circle of fear, tension, symptoms, and further fear and worry, may have taken place in early years. Or they may have occurred at *any time*. A completely normal, healthy individual can, under certain conditions, literally be hypnotized, accidentally or otherwise, into a neurosis. These theories have been confirmed by *experimental proof.*

The symptoms that are so frequently found in cases of mental health disorders can be explained simply when the mechanism of how the disorder develops is considered. *Tension* is very universal and is the common-sense consequence of the client's preparation to fight against, or "run away" from, what he/she imagines to be danger. *Low energy* or *nervous fatigue* is the expected outcome of the attempt to remain continuously tense and/or prepared for action. *Physical symptoms* result if the stress is related to any particular part of the body. For example, tension of the muscles involved in talking can result in stammering. If the tension is involved with the hand, it may be accountable for "writer's cramp." If it is dispersed throughout the autonomic nervous system, all sorts of psychosomatic symptoms are possible. The victim of functional asthma who describes him/herself as being "tight in the chest" and the sufferer of headaches who complains of a "tight head" have each arrived unexpectedly at a diagnosis, which is probably sound both psychologically and physiologically!

Insomnia, which is quite common in mental health clients, results from the client's continuous efforts to stay "on guard" in readiness to battle against his/her ideationally caused dangers. Nature did not design a human being to sleep when faced with peril. The autonomic nervous system (ANS) cannot differentiate between a real danger and an imaginary one. Something may concern the client, which then causes sleeplessness. If he/she worries about lack of sleep and fears it may lead to ill health or nervous breakdown, then this trepidation, by creating tension, keeps the sleepless state going and establishes a vicious circle.

Fear of mental illness is extremely genuine, even if unconscious to the sufferer. The client frequently arrives at the dread conclusion that he/she must be going crazy merely for the reason that he/she is powerless to explain or comprehend how his/her symptoms have come to pass.

Lack of ability to focus is especially frequent in nervous disorders. This in itself is upsetting for the client. From the illustration below, it will be seen that the client becomes increasingly engaged with his/her own objectionable symptoms and feelings. Logically, he/she pays less and less attention to anything else. It is as if the client were *hypnotizing him/herself* and suggesting progressively disagreeable symptoms in much the same way that a hypnotist gains the subject's attention to a greater extent and is able to deepen the trance and achieve phenomena of escalating intricacy.

Deteriorating memory is a familiar complaint—and an especially disturbing one for the sufferer who attributes it to grave mental illness. As the majority of his/her psyche is engaged with disagreeable thoughts of his/her condition, the sufferer takes little notice of anything besides him/herself and his/her symptoms. As he/she takes little notice, he/she absorbs very little, and his/her recall becomes increasingly worse. The state of affairs is comparable to that where a subject pays such great notice to a hypnotist's suggestions that he/she takes little notice of anything else and "forgets" what happened. In mental health issues the client is factually *self-hypnotized*, and becomes increasingly *en rapport* with him/herself!

Psychosomatic symptoms frequently go along with mental health issues and occur in the ANS. Anything that upsets the stability of this delicate, complex system can lead to extensive disorders that envelop the entire range of human problems. The ANS consists of two distinct systems, the *sympathetic* and *parasympathetic*, which are, as a rule, balanced in synchronization. This nervous system controls all the muscles, organs, and glands, which are independent of the will. The *sympathetic* part in general prepares the body for "fight or flight." Under these circumstances, the heart rate is amplified to propel additional blood into the muscles for action. The blood pressure rises; adrenaline is secreted, further stimulating the sympathetic nerve endings; and the liver glycogen is transformed into sugar to make available energy for muscular work. Nature did not mean to have a person process food, have bowel or bladder movements, or indulge in sex when getting prepared for "fight or flight" from some peril. Each is inhibited by the sympathetic nervous system.

This explains why worry can cause digestive disorders, and anxiety may cause sexual impotence. The *parasympathetic* system, in general, produces the reverse action to the sympathetic. What affects the mind can has an effect on the body, and vice versa. Nervous fears and worries can cause physical symptoms, and these physical symptoms, by alarming the client, can cause additional anxiety and so produce a vicious circle. The chart below shows in a simple, illustrative way the extensive ramifications of the autonomic nervous system.

Hypnotic Suggestion
Purely diagrammatic illustration of the way ideas (arising from real or

imaginary things), by causing fear, worry, anxiety, etc., can bring about changes in the organs, glands, and blood vessels of the body through the autonomic nervous system system and gives an idea of the many changes which may well take place as the consequence of any instability of its fragile sense of balance.

S.J. Van Pelt's hypothesis postulates a widespread starting point in some dread- or anxiety-provoking event or idea that concentrates the psyche into a state of adverse hypnosis and acts as a hypnotic suggestion, starting a sequence of thinking leading to a vicious circle. The typical subdivisions, as described in the *Diagnostic and Statistical Manual,* of the mental health issues are consequently regarded to some extent as synthetic and redundant.

REFERENCES:

Van Pelt, S. J. (1956). Hypnotic Suggestion: Its Role in Psychoneurotic and Psychosomatic Disorders. New York: Philosophical Press

Hypnotism is best known for the amazing results achieved through positive suggestions made for the period of the hypnotic trance. More significant to the therapist is the atypical revelation of the subconscious mind of his client during the hypnotic state. Stored in the client's subconscious mind are the details which make a reality out of the client's puzzling problem; we cannot draw conclusions or provide recommendation to the client unless we recognize these experiences and appreciate their influences on the mind of that particular client. In diagnosis, this disclosure of such information stored in the client's subconscious mind may spell the discrepancy between a proper diagnosis and a failure to grasp the importance of the predicament, which disturbs the client. In our search for the beginning of the client's problem, we accept the common sense that states, "There is a universal premise as the basis for each problem." Our clue to the universal premise underlying human illness is found in the oft-repeated question of the therapist, "When did your illness first begin?" We are searching for an event or situation that provides the stimuli which created an adequate hazard to the client's continued existence; an area of anxiety was established in the client's mind called the *initial sensitizing event.*

Once this *initial sensitizing event* has been revealed, we are interested in disclosing all successive events, which helped produce a sense of reality in *this initial sensitizing event*. Afterward, threats to the client's continued existence create greater anxiety in the client's mind and a replication of the emotional discomfort associated with the *initial sensitizing event*. As the sense of reality about these events arises in the client's mind, genuine fear for continued existence is born. The more authentic the apprehensive feeling becomes, the more anxious the client will be made by thoughts associated with these feelings. Instead of revealing these feelings to a rational mental examination, the client buries these thoughts in the subconscious mind.

These problems may be solved by a disclosure of the *initial sensitizing event* and a review of all the succeeding events (threats to security) that lent reality to these feelings. The client will otherwise stay perplexed and disorientated, as he/she is continually faced with this uncomfortable feeling and his/her anxiety will persist or increase. A natural resolution of the anxiety state will happen as the events which shaped a feeling of reality in this predicament are brought to the conscious level of thinking, removing the threat to the client's survival. Once this initial sensitizing event has been exposed, the client and the therapist will be able to explain in a rational way the formerly bizarre pattern of the emotional disorder.

A method of examination that permits a rapid and easy search through the client's subconscious mind is advantageous. Since we know the client's problems are based on experiences that in reality existed in the client's mind, we can trace the painful emotional feeling back through these experiences to its starting point. Once prepared with a comprehension of the beginning of the fear existing in the client's mind, we start with the client's initial contact with this apprehensive feeling and map out its growth up to the difficulty, as it exists at the point of treatment. The *Emotion Regression Technique* is where the painful emotional feeling is recognized and traced back to its start, progressing to the *Emotion Development Technique*, in which we begin with the fundamental fear articulated by the client as it was initially experienced and map out its growth up to the current point in time. The later technique typically follows the *Emotion Regression Technique* as the subsequent part in the client's treatment.

Emotion Regression Technique

In pursuing the procedure of *emotion regression* during hypnoanalysis, the initial step is the creation of a serene condition in the client's mind, at will. This step is most straightforwardly achieved by having the client call to mind some comical happening in his/her life which stimulated his imagination. Early grade school experiences, a pet, the Christmas tree, or a circus represent events that captured the attention of the client and produced in the patient's mind a pleasant state of rapport. Once the client's comfort is secure, the next step involves a careful detection of the distressing emotional feeling as the client experienced it. Such states of anxiety symbolize emotional responses and cannot be voluntarily communicated in words. Then, we ask the client to identity the painful emotional feeling associated with the anxiety, not including reference to any exact feeling as spoken in words. On the initial visit, the client may be in an uncomfortable state of understanding with him/herself, and the painful emotional feeling is by now obvious and recognized without difficulty. On the other hand, a search through the client's history may be crucial under hypnosis to identify the events, situations, or stimuli that created the painful feeling, and it is important to stay attentive and sophisticated while listening to the client's history, alert for the word or phrase that may present a clue to identifying the anxious feeling.

The third step of the *Emotion Regression Technique* involves tracing the painful emotional feeling back through the threatening events that created this response and lent an atmosphere of reality to this warning to the client's continued existence. In retracing each of these events, the therapist is concerned with the point at which the painful feeling was created. These points will stand for a sign leading the client back from one event to the next until the event that first created this painful feeling is disclosed. The therapist must exercise perseverance in retracing these events to their starting point and must not stop his thorough search through these painful experiences until a reasonable account for the basis of the emotional feeling has been reached.

Once these events have been traced back to the *initial sensitizing event*, a spontaneous resolution of the anxiety state can occur. The client is capable, rationally, of looking back now through the entire difficulty and reasonably explaining to him/herself the formerly fear-provoking emotional problem. This disclosure of the source of the client's anxiety is the fourth step in the *Emotion Regression Technique* and, in fact, constitutes a part of the client's treatment since it removes anxiety from the client's mind, destroying the perceived reality of the formerly terrifying events.

Emotion Development Technique

The second technique significant in the resolution of a client's predicament, the *Emotion Development Technique,* is the logical step following the *Emotion Regression Technique.* Once prepared with the understanding of the nature of the fear existing in the personality, we are able to begin at the beginning of the client's contact with this apprehensive feeling and develop a logical explanation for the anxiety that followed. All thoughts surrounding this initial appearance of anxiety in the client's mind must be fully developed so that an intelligent conclusion may be reached, enabling us to adapt posthypnotic suggestions appropriate to the relief of the client's anxiety.

If disclosure of the *initial sensitizing event* has not relieved the client of anxiety, we return to the initial danger to the client's safety and investigate more for deeply hidden material. In this event, we typically discover a more threatening and rational danger than had been formerly disclosed. Since these feelings of lack of self-confidence often involve the crucial notion of fatality, it is vital in the *Emotion Development Technique* to spell out the initial lasting impressions of death that were established in the client's mind.

In all psychopathological and all suspected psychosomatic disorders in which fear surrounding illness, accidents, or deaths is apparent, it is chiefly essential that a search through the deepest areas of the subconscious mind be made to reveal the initial thoughts and impressions symbolizing death to the client. Once this symbol of death has been recognized in the client's thoughts, it will be associated with experiences, which afterward endangered the client, in so doing producing real fear for continued existence.

The concluding step in the *Emotion Development Technique*, as well as the *Emotion Regression Technique*, is the examination of the threatening events in the client's life and the discovery of the point at which the fear-provoking sign was reproduced. This step is significant to the client's treatment, for the formerly unsettling thoughts are out in the open to a rational analysis, and anxiety is detached from the mind by destroying the reality of such terrorization to the client's protection.

In summing up, the *Emotion Regression Technique* is typically employed in the search for the *initial sensitizing event*, which recognized a danger to the client's safekeeping. Once this cause of insecurity has been disclosed, the *Emotion Development Technique* may be employed to shed light on the events that made this warning a reality in the client's mind. The *Emotion Development Technique* may be employed at the start if it is evident that serious illnesses, accidents, operations, or deaths were involved in the introduction of anxiety. The use of the *Emotion Development Technique* is in particular indicated in acute emergencies such as threatened suicides when swiftness in relieving anxiety may prove to be life-saving. The following illustrates in detail the previous theories discussed. The reader will realize Elvis' inability to explain or recall the confusing facts of the history until the *initial sensitizing event* has been disclosed. At this point, the logical explanation of the patient's problem will become apparent.

Lives are full of emotional incidents. The following chart represents some of the factors in a hypothetical life. The bars (------) represent the relative emotional charge

Birth	---	Birth experience: Twin brother dies
10	--	Repeated references to dead brother. Guilt is intensified
	--------------	Puberty
20	-------------------	Career takes off. Guilt feeling intensify over leaving mother.
23	--	Mother dies. Immense feelings of guilt and loss. Becomes a Walking Zombie in some ways and a Ponce de Leon in others. Loses interest in career. Stops performing and makes movies he is ashamed of.
30	-----------------	Marriage to woman who "represents Mom."
	----------------------------	Birth of firstborn. Helps overcome loss but cannot have sexual relations with mother figure. Relationship goes bad
30		
35	---	Has vision. Feels God wants him to do something special. Feels reincarnated. Begins "comeback."
40	--	Father tells him he caused his mother's death by running off into his career. Enormous guilt is magnified.
42	--	Feeling completely hopeless, dies of heart attack. "Broken heart."

Bars represent emotionally significant events occurring during Elvis' life.

CHAPTER 3

WALKING ZOMBIE SYNDROME

The following represent the two theories I feel are most useful in understanding Elvis Presley's pathology. The Walking Zombie Syndrome is the most comprehensive and I feel may have been the cause of death. Therefore, it is given the most attention. The Ponce de Leon Syndrome is secondary, but because of its critical nature, would be taken into account in order to ensure a complete recovery.

THE WALKING ZOMBIE SYNDROME Revisited,
First written about by William Jennings Bryan, MD, PhD, LLD, JD

A word is as real a conditioned stimulus for man as all other stimuli. . .
but at the same time more all inclusive than any other stimuli.
I.P. Pavlov, Nobel Prize winner

Mental health professionals have for years written of the dread of physical termination, and numerous clients complain of an irrational trepidation of passing away. This syndrome has nothing to do with such a fear fixation. In fact, the psychopathology of this situation is purely that the client has previously accepted the fact that he/she is lifeless. For this rationale, the client will clearly demonstrate no apprehension of fatality in view of the fact that psychological death has, before now, arrived. According to John Scott, Ed.D, 1991:

"The death suggestion . . . explain(s) why an individual who is physically sound, socially healthy, developmentally successful from the best of families may become severely depressed. It also explains the depression that occurs in individuals who are inadequate in any of these matters. . . It also provides a specific direction for therapy in each individual case. (In part) for these reasons, it is reasonable to expect that resolutions of the walking zombie syndrome will become more successful than other therapies for overcoming depression."

In a later edition of the journal, 1995, Scott wrote,

"In my opinion, one of the greatest contributions that Medical Hypnoanalysis offers the therapeutic community is the concept of the Walking Zombie Syndrome."

One of the fundamental principles of members of the American Academy of Medical Hypnoanalysis, www.aamh.com, and confirmed by contemporary medical research, is the reality that as soon as an individual accepts a suggestion on an emotional and subconscious or autonomic nervous system level, the client alters his/her behavior pattern so that it conforms to the suggestion that the client has received. For this reason, if a client is told that his/her left arm is paralyzed and the client accepts this idea under hypnosis, the client will perform thus, existing under this posthypnotic suggestion until it is removed. This is true whether the idea was introduced deliberately or unintentionally. T.J. Hudson (1893-1923) described "pseudo death" states that were well recognized in the 19th century, when difficulties in travel made it essential to allow the deceased to remain on dining room tables for numerous days, surrounded by mourners. "Dead" people have been acknowledged to rejuvenate after several days of remaining cold, immobile, and apparently dead. Hudson interviewed such people. All of them responded to the pleas of a friend or relative.

The client pointed out that people in this deathlike state are able to think and to have the sense of hearing. They feel at ease, and they will not suddenly make the endeavor to come back unless someone passionately insists.

Van Pelt confirmed the actuality that the vast preponderance of the psychoneuroses and psychosomatic diseases are, in reality, purely cases of persons who have been inadvertently hypnotized and have received destructive suggestions.

Thomas Ritzman, MD, 1987, defined "accidental hypnosis" as the "implantation of a thought or emotion into the subconscious at any time when the critical factor of the conscious mind is paralyzed by the emotion of the event. When a similar situation arises later in life, the original emotion may be reactivated and result with an inability to deal with the situation in a rational way."

Visualize, then, the odd assortment of symptoms that could be given by a client who felt essentially expired. Such clients give histories like the following:

1. I feel unexciting and lacking energy all the time.

2. I'm utterly detached.

3. Nothing means anything to me any longer.

4. I have no energy.

5. I just don't have any curiosity in stuff to any extent.

6. I feel like I have lost my persona.

7. I just exist; I don't get pleasure out of anything.

8. Existence has been a predicament; I'm very miserable.

This does not mean that every client who reports feeling dreary and lacking energy has accepted the idea that he/she is dead, but several of them are, and this syndrome has only gone on unsuspected.

There are scores of medical physicians nowadays to whom such a history may call for treatment by pep-up medications or tranquilizers. Neither will be of any help to a client who has by now received the thought that the client is deceased and is acting it out.

The Walking Zombie, or client who believes the client is departed on a subconscious or autonomic nervous system level, has no conscious knowledge whatsoever concerning the nature of the dilemma. In fact, if confronted with it, the client would most surely disagree with it, but these very denials would include phrases which, when interpreted analytically, would persuade the medical hypnoanalyst that this was the client's true pathology.

It is, in addition, essential to comprehend that the psychopathology of the Walking Zombie could be manifested by any number of highly diverse symptoms. In some cases, the client may appear in a therapist's office for depression, lethargy, or a general lack of drive and liveliness. In others, the client may show as an alcoholic, drinking himself into nothingness, attempting to corroborate the premise that the client has previously received on a subconscious or autonomic nervous system level.

In still other cases, a sexual difficulty may present itself as the symptoms, the client believing herself to be frigid, when in point of fact the quandary is only that she is dead! In a different case, a person presented himself as an asthmatic, killing himself off in order to act in accordance with the posthypnotic suggestion that the client had by now received in his subconscious mind.

It is imperative that we distinguish these clients when they present themselves to us, and this can only be done by a careful history using hypnoanalytic techniques. Unquestionably, this syndrome should be suspected anytime statements such as those listed above are found in the history, in spite of the symptom presented by the client. Once this process is supposed, it can without difficulty be differentially diagnosed from other problems by testing the premise with the client's history, physical, and actions. The subsequent step involves the right management of such a client.

The client can be told of the suspicion that the therapist feels regarding a possible emotional adaptation the client may have made via Reflective Counseling techniques (Ronan, 1979). The therapist can go beyond what the client has expressed consciously. The therapist can reflect the thematic nature of the now surfacing feelings as they relate to behavior, experiences, or a combination of theses. Once a therapist recognizes the psychodynamics of these themes, his task is to reveal them to the client in such a way that the client can begin to see, understand, and begin to deal with them, or allowing an opportunity for the therapist to better intervene. The clinician can reflect "feeling and content" back to the client during history-taking, saying something to the effect of, "it is not uncommon for people to feel they have emotionally died because of their emotional experiences and subsequently have become like a walking zombie." If the client agrees with this assessment, then the path becomes clearer that this may be the case. Often in a history, there are several times where this kind of reflective statement is possible and allows the possibility of getting confirmations or denials from the client. This author has found this to be a very useful part of the overall therapeutic process. This is in direct opposition to what the originator of this system suggested in his paper on this topic. Essentially, Bryan had stated:

"Under no conditions should the client be told the factual nature of his syndrome, for the reason that the only way the client will be capable to overcome the syndrome is by his own recognition of the trouble on an emotional level simultaneously with the experiencing of a "psychological regeneration."

The therapist should disclose to the client that the therapist knows the client's situation, understands it, and that medical hypnoanalysis can treat it effectively. It is central to keep in mind in taking the history that the client's psychological demise may have occurred at virtually any time during the client's life span. Because youth is a condition of constant hypnosis, and given that one is exceptionally vulnerable throughout the initial years of existence to the planting of such pessimistic suggestions, it is of fundamental significance to investigate these areas comprehensively. Special areas of the history to be singled out for particular consideration are as follows:

1. All acute infectious diseases in which the client has run a high fever, has "been given up" by doctors, or in which the client states, "I almost died" or "I was dead for two days."

2. All accidents or injuries in which the client might have been unconscious mind or the autonomic nervous system or at a low level of consciousness.

3. Any operations during which the client may have received a suggestion from the doctor at the time of the operation that the client would probably expire. This phenomenon has occurred under deepest anesthesia.

4. All war experiences. A typical history might read, "You know I died in Vietnam or the Gulf War, or Operation Iraqi Freedom," and a man can't die twice.

5. All deaths in the immediate family or close friends with whom the client might identify and thereby bring on death to himself.

6. Religious and/or paranormal experiences where the client may have experienced a psychological death and perhaps even a rebirth of sorts.

7. Ego-threatening experiences where the client feels his/her emotional integrity has been shaken.

8. The loss of love can be viewed as greater than the loss of life, as people will sacrifice their physical bodies for it.

By age regressing the client back to the Initial Sensitizing Event (ISE) which was accountable for the client's accepting the idea of being essentially lifeless, the client can experience again the incident all the way through to the conclusion, realizing that the client didn't in point of fact die. Therefore, the client has no need to cling to the symptoms of a deceased man/woman, which continue the client's problem and bewilder the numerous clinicians with whom the client has come in contact. The reality that there are thousands of Walking Zombies on the streets of every city makes it exceptionally critical for us to identify this situation when it occurs and take care of it appropriately. The following are a number of case histories of the originator of this classification, William Jennings Bryan, MD, showing the assorted symptomotology offered to the medical hypnoanalyst, yet the primary origins were constantly the same. These illuminating cases will help to familiarize medical hypnoanalysts who are faced with such a difficulty and ought to assist them in pursuing it to a successful wrapping up, bringing to the client a comprehensive and enduring resolution of the problem.

Mrs. A. K., a 37-year-old white female, had a past history of the usual childhood diseases, jaundice, and rheumatic fever, which she believes left her with a "weak heart Case #1 valve." She also had a uterine suspension operation, in which her tubes were tied. She was married once and had three children. Her physical examination was essentially negative, with no murmurs, thrills, or arrhythmias of the heart being present. Her present illness consisted mainly of "spells" which apparently produced various bizarre manifestations of ravings, and other nervous symptoms. Since this particular case was the first case of the Walking Zombie Syndrom that Dr. Bryan had ever seen, he did not suspect it when he first began treating her but only knew that the spells were obviously psychogenic in origin. She was an excellent hypnotic subject and was age regressed quickly back to an incident of an auto accident, in which she remembered hearing the ambulance siren and was covered with sticky blood. The blood was apparently coming from some area of her face. It was her Dad's birthday, and they were going to the Kentucky Derby at the time the accident occurred. She had amnesia for part of the accident and remembers only that she was looking at a guidebook, and the next thing she remembered was the ambulance siren.

She then regressed to an earlier incident at age 8, in which an earthquake had occurred in the middle of the night, and all the lights went out. She said she felt very, very cold (death), and associated the fact that the lights went out (death) during the earthquake with the fact that the lights went out (death again) as far as she was concerned when she was in the auto accident. She sent back to still another incident in her life when she rolled down a hill in a truck and was thrown out of the truck, suffering injury. Eventually five major incidents in her life developed. They were: (1) The earthquake, (2) The death of her sister's husband, (3) A plane crash and the near death of her husband, (4) The auto accident, and (5) The truck rolling down the hill with her subsequent injury.

She was afraid of hospitals and all automobiles. Despite the fact that the emotions were generally removed from each of these five incidents, she was nevertheless unable to get over her spells. A great many other incidents were then brought out which seemed to have little to do with the general pathology, but were explored fully and thoroughly. She had cried for two days previous to her treatment session, and had hallucinations of undergoing various bloody operations, when the thought came to me to give her a suggestion that she would have a very vivid dream, which would explain the nature of her symptoms. In the middle of the night following her treatment session, I received a telephone call stating that she had a very vivid nightmare, and woke up screaming. Indeed, she had the nightmare twice because the first time she couldn't interpret it, and she went right back to sleep and had the same nightmare again until she did interpret it, and this of course was the catharsis. She was hypnotized over the telephone and told that she would now rest, and that she did not need to dream it again, that it was all over, and that when she came in the next day, she would interpret the dream completely in every way.

The following day, there was a tremendous change in the appearance of the client. The girl was smiling and happy. She felt good, and her whole outlook on life was entirely different. She immediately stated: "I am well, and I know that I am well, and I feel certain that I will never be troubled again." She had had a nightmare about bloody hair being in her face and relived the auto accident in detail. While she was lying in the hospital, her aunt had asked if they could not put a towel over the pillow so that it would not look so bad WITH ALL THAT BLOOD. She said she felt that her mind was elevated from the body (obviously, death), and that she was just lying there dead. The basic principle of this analysis was that if her hair was all matted with blood, and if blood was all over her and all over the pillow, then obviously the blood could not be in her, and therefore she must be dead.

She accepted the fact in her mind that she was dead and that her soul and mind were actually elevated and on their way to heaven. Her trouble was not, therefore, a fear of dying, but that she actually believed herself to be dead. This was such a frightening thing that she repressed it completely, and had been living her life as a Walking Zombie.

Despite the fact that all her previous treatment (which included extensive work with four psychiatrists, including a visit to the Mayo Clinic) had not helped her, she was completely cured once she understood the mechanism of her illness she interpreted from the dream induced by hypnotic suggestion.

Case #2

Mr. K.L.A. was a 65-year-old, white, male real estate broker who was referred to me by a medical hypnoanalyst who had studied hypnosis in one of the classes given by the Institute. The client was the doctor's uncle, and he complained of "swelling muscles which had contracted." He stated: "Nothing wants to move forward." He also complained, "I eat, but I don't know what it is to get hungry."

His physical examination was essentially negative, except for his blood pressure, which was 260/130. High blood pressure had always meant death to him since his father died in 1945 at the age of 72 with a stroke. Furthermore, one of his brothers died with a heart attack in 1952.

In his history, the initial sensitizing incident was diphtheria at age 5 in which he felt he could not last through the night. This was his first experience with death, and he was able to imitate it in many ways following this. His history was simply one death statement after another. He states, "I have had so many operations, I am tired of it." "I contracted gonorrhea at age 34, and after that I became impotent." Obviously by this time, he had developed a reaction pattern of giving up and lying down for death whenever adversity came his way. The particular type of death he underwent depended upon the adversity. For example, as illustrated above, a sexual death occurred following gonorrhea.

Other ways in which he manifested his deathlike existence as a walking zombie are as follows: (1) His nickname was "Grouch" (personality death), (2) My business partner had a fine personality but I had none, (same), (3) He made friends and I lost them. (same), (4) There is always a thin veil between me and happiness (black veil of death), (5) I feel I am just existing (i.e., not really living), (6) I don't get a thrill out of anything, and I haven't for years and years (he died a long time ago), (7) I have dropped one hobby after another (again imitating death), (8) At the present time, I am very much depressed (most dead people are!), (9) Life has always been a problem (obviously if he was dead, "life" would be his greatest problem), (10) How can I make the day pass by being less boring? (11) I remember when I had gangrene and a nurse told me "I couldn't go through what I did and live." (He did go through what he did, but mentally died). (12) I am just getting no kick out of life. (Obviously, because he is not living.) (13) I have the worst kind of insomnia. (Obviously, death is the worst kind of insomnia there is, especially the "living death") (14) Nothing seems to want to register. (Not if you're dead.) (15) The last time I felt anything was in the world of my parents, and when they died, it was as if I was dead too.

Obviously, a history like this tells in many ways over and over that the client has accepted the fact that he has actually already died. Dr. Bryan attempted at first to bring this realization to him by means of suggesting that he was a high diver.

Under hypnosis, Dr. Bryan told him to climb up a very high ladder to the top of a platform. Dr. Bryan's plan was to point out to him when he was on the platform that he had no fear of death in diving down into the water, and hence was probably already dead. As is so often in the practice of hypnosis in medicine, however, the client went me one better. When Dr. Bryan asked him if he had reached the high platform in his own mind, he stated that he was a great deal higher than 100 feet high. Dr. Bryan asked him then how high he was, and he stated "thousands of feet, I am actually in heaven." This realization was almost too good to be true (obviously, if he was in heaven, he must have died first). The client then related many other incidents which had reinforced his belief, including an episode in the war and an episode in which another person had committed suicide with the client's pistol. Unfortunately, the client did not complete his series of treatments. Despite the fact that the diagnosis was clear cut, the client refused to accept the fact that his mental death, which he had inflicted upon himself, was actually the cause of his symptoms. Since he was unable to realize this despite the intensive therapy of the few visits, Dr. Bryan felt very discouraged and counted his case as a failure. However, a number of years later, Dr. Bryan received a letter from the medical hypnoanalyst who referred the case to him. He stated in his letter that while the client had not really accepted the diagnosis in his conscious mind, apparently it had had a tremendous effect for good on his behavior patterns. Instead of killing himself off mentally with his repressed hostility, he was able to take a great deal of it out on me, and thereby take a new interest in life. Indeed, one of his main interests which seemed to give him a great deal of pleasure was his complaining that he had spent such a great deal of money in journeying clear across the nation to be treated by a quack hypnotist who was "unable to do him any good." His improvement was a source of pleasure to his relatives, if not to himself!

Case #3

Case #3 is the case of Mr. H. F. J., age 58, who had unfortunately turned into an alcoholic. He entered the office for treatment of alcoholism. He said, "I am simply unable to accomplish what I intend to do. I have lost all interest in life. I can't earn a dime, and I just don't feel like I am getting anywhere." This client harbored many guilt feelings, because he felt responsible for a great many deaths.

This guilt was heaped upon him when he served in the Marine Corps during World War II. He accepted the responsibility for all the deaths, and punished himself for these deaths by actually mentally killing himself off with the death sentence.

This client has been classified for years as an alcoholic, but actually he should be termed a Walking Zombie. Following treatment by hypnosis, not only was his alcoholism cured, but also his will to live was restored, and his impotency was removed (a by-product of believing himself to be dead).

This is an important factor because contrary to what many medical hypnoanalysts have thought, the mere length of time to which a person has been subjected to suggestion has nothing to do with the ability to cure that client by removing the suggestion. The client may be either 15 years old or 50 years old, and he will get well just as easily once the offending accidental hypnotic suggestion causing the trouble is completely removed.

Case #4

This is the case of Miss B. Z., a 54-year-old, white, female schoolteacher who turned out to be one of the most fascinating cases I have ever seen. In the same manner that alcoholics "bottle up" their problems, Miss B. Z. "sat on hers." Although she described her problem as a feeling of guilt over her conflict regarding sex, it was obvious that it was really her "utter futility of living" that was the basis of her problem. The first statement she made was, "I have down underneath something that is buried." As an unmarried schoolteacher, it is true that she had buried her sexual life, but what she did not realize is that she had also buried the rest of her life as well!

She was age regressed to many incidents in her past, which were traumatic, but the most fascinating experience of all was her regression to the birth experience, which she described as though she felt completely trapped, "like in a cave or something. I must be in the womb, and I want to get out and I can't." After she realized that she was not stillborn and did not die in the birth experience, she was easily and quickly able to rid herself of her other fears and problem. She realized then also that because she felt she had died from birth and that the most traumatic experience of her life was trying to escape from the uterus, she had kept reliving this experience in various ways in later life, trying to escape from her mother. Indeed, in her history under hypnosis, she states that "I always escaped from mother to father. That is why I must have called myself 'Bill' as a child." She explained her fear of water as a fear of drowning in the amniotic fluid. As soon as she gave this explanation, she was able to enter a swimming pool and learn to swim. This was the first time she had ever been in a swimming pool in her entire 54 years of life!

The change in her was remarkable and was observed not only by herself but also by her associates, who described it as "unbelievable." In order to escape from her mother in the birth experience, she had made herself into a male figure, so that positive suggestions were then given her that she was not longer a male, and that actually she was very much female. The most important part of the suggestion, however, was that she was not dead but was actually alive, as this was the very basis of her psychopathology. Later the entire birth incident was verified. She also was intermittently strangled by the umbilical cord around the neck. Subsequent sessions were devoted to straightening out minor deviations, which had occurred because of her original pathology. She is now quite well and happy, feminine in personality and appearance. She is a charming lady with a sparkling personality, taking an interest in life, which she never before dreamed possible.

Case #5
This case is the case of Mrs. E. A. D., a 34-year-old housewife who went into acute depression nine months out of every year. During these nine months, she was unable to do her housework or communicate with anyone. She stated that she was so withdrawn that she could hardly talk and so depressed that she didn't want to face anything. It was eventually revealed that her guilt feelings went back to an abortion, which was forced on her by her mother and husband. She was able to handle this feeling all right until the birth of an unwanted child triggered her symptoms. When she finally realized that the birth from her second pregnancy provided such a lovable and wonderful child, even though previously the child had been unwanted, her guilt feelings were multiplied regarding her first pregnancy, which had resulted in death to the child by abortion.

In her need for self-punishment, she accepted a "Persephone Complex" in which she spent three months of her year above ground and alive, and then the remaining nine months of each year in the deep depression of death. She was unaware of the fact in the waking state that these nine-month periods of depressions were actually atonement for her guilt feelings and represented a pregnancy period. After she had been age-regressed through these painful experiences and realized the scope of her problem, she became well. This, of course, was not a true Walking Zombie syndrome, since the client was only dead nine months out of the year, but because of its similarity to the other cases and because of its fascinating psychodynamic interest, it has been included here.

Case #6

Mr. H. J. was a 50-year-old nuclear scientist who had previously had over two years of psychotherapy for the problem of alcoholism with no results. He also presented a problem of hypertension under stress, which he described as "purely emotional." The initial sensitizing event in his life occurred when he had diphtheria at age 7, and he stated under hypnosis, "I was dead for two days." In going through the experience, he realized that he had actually accepted the idea that he had died completely, and the reason for his alcoholism was merely a desire to imitate the subconscious or autonomic nervous system feeling of death which he believed to be present. This was obvious in his history obtained in the waking state when he said, "I drink for oblivion." He freely admitted that he did not care for the taste or the sensation of alcohol.

For this reason, it is important in treating alcoholics to ascertain the true reason why they drink. Do they drink for the taste? (Are they searching for the bottle?) Do they drink for the sensation? (Perhaps a sexual connotation) or do they drink for oblivion? (Due to a need for death). Many other intensifying incidents were brought to light, but the initial incident was his experience with diphtheria. This serves to point out the importance of severe, febrile, infectious diseases in childhood, and their psychological effect upon the subconscious or autonomic nervous system mind.

Once the treatment was completed, the client's statements were: "I am afraid to believe it, but it works. I have tried it three times and it works. For the first time in my life, I had two drinks and did not feel that I had to empty the bottle. I merely recited the fact that I did not need oblivion, put the bottle down, and rolled over and went to sleep. More and more the desire for alcohol is leaving me entirely, and I am sure it will never bother me again."

It was determined on a word association test given under hypnosis that hypertension also meant death to the client, and therefore as long as he was hypertensive, he was in fact partially dead.

For this reason, when he obtained a cure for his alcoholism, his blood pressure began moving steadily down also and has continued its favorable descent until the present date. This eminent scientist now is living and vital again and is able to contribute a great deal to the betterment of mankind because he has been able to conquer his illnesses through the correct application of hypnotism.

Case #7

Mrs. H. E. was a 50-year old married woman, whose initial complaint was as follows: "I am neurotic, and I just don't like it. Life just isn't any fun anymore, and I think it should be. I feel that I am withdrawn, and for some reason or other, although I have always been a gregarious person, full of pep and life, it has just gone and left me. I just feel very drab and dull, and somewhat like the light has gone out of my life. I suppose this doesn't make too much sense to you, but I am just sort of lost."

Of course, this history makes a great deal of sense once one considers the Walking Zombie Syndrome as a possible basic emotional cause. The client stated that she always felt like she was dead. Then she gave a clue to her initial sensitizing event when she recalled a vivid identification with a storybook character that had died in her sleep as a child. Later on, she stated she actually had to spend one night sleeping overnight in jail when she was arrested late at night for speeding. Under hypnosis, she remembers the painful experience in jail in which she actually "wished I was dead, sleeping there behind bars."

Although her initial sensitizing event had occurred many years before, the symptom-producing event was her overnight stay in jail. This case history adequately illustrates the point that, as is the case with allergies, there is always a sensitizing event. This event may in fact be many years previous to the actual outbreak of the illness as reported by the client.

Case #8

Mr. A. L. was a 60-year-old man suffering from asthma, emphysema, and acute dyspnea as a result. His opening statement to me was, "I have a psychosomatic overlay with every situation that arises, which invariably ends up with a suffocation from emphysema or asthma. I just break out into a sweat and start to suffocate, and then I go into a panic." The key to his opening statement is not that he says he has asthma or emphysema, because he does not. The client is telling the medical hypnoanalyst that what he really has is a psychosomatic overlay that results in suffocation.

Immediately, therefore, the medical hypnoanalyst should realize that some incident in the client's past during which he felt he was suffocated is responsible for the trouble, and such an incident should be looked for and ferreted out by hypnoanalysis. It was just such an incident that proved to be responsible for the damage. His initial sensitizing event occurred early in childhood when a medical hypnoanalyst told his mother that he wouldn't be able to live to be over 11 years of age. He said he felt at the time it was like "taking his last breath." He had difficulty in breathing until, at 11 years old, he sustained a fracture and they took him to the hospital.

On the way, his mother kept saying, " I know he's dead, I know he's dead, I know he's dead." This plus the previous suggestion that he would not live to be over 11 years old fixed permanently in the boy's mind the fact that this was certainly his time to go.

Under hypnosis, he revealed that his biggest fear was the fear of death when the anesthetist lowered the mask over his face and "suffocated him." When placed under hypnosis and a mask was lowered over his face, simulating the anesthetist at 11 years, he went into a very deep trance repeating the words, "I am dead, I am dead, I am dead," over and over hundreds of times. Typical of the Walking Zombie Syndrome, Mr. A. had no fear of death or any will to live. Finally, he was able to reveal to himself the nature of his illness and "live" again. The years of scarring of his lungs from his psychologically induced asthma and emphysema, however, eventually got the best of him, and despite the fact that he temporarily improved, the residual physical damage which he had accrued over the long period of years eventually caused him to expire. It is important to note, therefore, that psychogenic emphysema, like psychogenic ulcers, nevertheless produces a perfectly real physical lesion. The lesion must be treated along with the psychic cause. Sometimes with the best of treatment, both physically and psychologically, the client may expire simply from the physical effects of long-standing psychogenic disease.

Case #9

The next client is a 50-year-old white female, Mrs. M. H., whose present illness is as follows: "My sickness is the way I feel. No matter what I try to do, I get worse. I cannot sleep; I have terrible nervousness that makes me sick to my stomach; I want to die; and I am scared of myself. I hate to be alone, but people annoy me. I was in a sanatorium and had shock treatments, and I have gone to an internist and a surgeon trying to find out what is wrong with me and why I feel so dead. Life is dull and holds no interest for me, and I feel as though I was dead, but I am powerless to resist it. I don't know what it means to enjoy life. I have given up all my activities, and sometimes feel I would just like to lie still like a corpse. I have no strength. I am weak, very weak, and I can't do any work. I want very much to get well so that I can do my work, but I just can't think straight." This is perhaps one of the most straightforward histories of a death suggestion having been accepted that has came to Dr. Bryan's attention.

The initial sensitizing event was brought out later when it was learned under hypnosis that at age 4, the client had typhoid fever "in the stomach" and "they made me a dress to wear in the casket because they thought I was going to die." The client was able to avoid death, however, both physically and mentally, by identifying with her mother. This identification, however, was so strong that when her mother finally died, her subconscious or autonomic nervous system was then left no choice but to die right along with her. It was at this time that the worst of her symptoms began, and they have continued on to the present time. The client is undergoing analysis now, and she should experience a permanent cure once she realizes the psychodynamics of her case.

Summary

The Walking Zombie Syndrome has been described. It does not have to do with the dread of demise but rather is a situation in which the client has received the idea in his subconscious or autonomic nervous system mind that he is deceased. This syndrome is recognized and characterized by case histories which contain statements such as "I feel dull and listless," "I am totally emotionless," "I have no energy or life," "I take no interest in anything," "I am extremely miserable and feel lifeless all the time," etc.

Simply taking a vigilant history can distinguish such clients, using medical hypnoanalytic techniques. The prevalence of the syndrome is extensive, and it ought to be suspected when the history warrants it. The proper management of such a situation involves revealing the Initial Sensitizing Event, in which the client received the idea that he/she was deceased as well as detecting the symptom producing event and subsequent intensifying events, which amplify the harshness of the symptoms.

In order to discover these events in the client's past existence, it is recommended that a number of areas of the histories be searched quite carefully. These comprise every early acute infectious disease, school experiences, accidents, sexual experiences, religious/paranormal experiences, injuries, operations, boot camp experiences, war experiences, and deaths of close friends, pets, and members of the immediate family with whom the client might have identified. And any other area that the clinician might feel could possibly play a role as well as any information volunteered by the client that the clinician might not think of as being an area to consider trauma. Trauma is often subjective.

Case histories are offered which demonstrate the abundant variety of the presenting complaints such as alcoholism, impotence, nerves, psychosis, hypertension, insomnia, sex problems, acute depression, asthma, emphysema, etc. In every case, the underlying origin was the receiving of the death suggestion as a certainty by the client's subconscious or autonomic nervous system mind. The goal is to abandon this incorrect view of life and return to reality (Ronan, 1985). David Leistikow, MD, 1990, noted of the overall therapeutic process:

"This is a rapid treatment modality that anyone can learn to do and apply. It changes core beliefs and the person continues to grow and to change on his or her own thereafter and becomes much more capable of dealing with all of life's challenges.

BIBLIOGRAPHY

(1) S.J. Van Pelt, *Hypnotic Suggestion*, p. 43-48.

(2) S.J. Van Pelt, *The dangers of Stage Hypnotism*, Journal of the A.I.H., summer issue, Vol. II No.3, July 1961.

(3) D. B. Cheek, *Unconscious mind or the autonomic nervous system Perception of meaningful sounds during surgical anesthesia as revealed under hypnosis*, The American Journal of Clinical Hypnosis, Vol.1, No.3., Jan, 1959.

(4) Louis K. Boswell, Jr., *The Initial Sensitizing Event of Emotional Disorders*, Journal of the A.I.H. Winter Issue, Vol. II, No. 1, January 1961.

(5) Hudson, T. J. (1923 *The Law of Psychic Phenomena* (Originally published 1893). Chicago: McClurg

(6) Pavlov, IP, in the book: *Word as a Physiological and Therapeutic Factor: The Theory and practice of Psychotherapy According to IP Pavlov* by KI Platonov, Foreign Languages Publishing House, Moscow, 1959

(7) Bryan, William J, *The Walking Zombie Syndrome*, Medical Hypnoanalysis Journal, p 60 72, 1987

(8) Ritzman, Thomas A, *Accidental Hypnosis*, Medical Hypnoanalysis Journal, p 48-53, 1987

(9) Leistikow, D, *Rapid Therapy*, Medical Hypnoanalysis Journal, p 163-167, 1990

(10) Scott, JA, *Missing links in the treatment of depression part II*, Medical Hypnoanalysis Journal, 45-63, 1991

(11) Scott, JA, *The Walking Zombie- Revised Tape Script*, Medical Hypnoanalysis Journal, p 209-214, 1995

(12) Ronan, WJ, Hypnosis: *An Escape into Reality*, Journal of the Society of Medical Hypnoanalysis,

p 58-61, 1985

(13) Ronan, WJ, *Aspects of Reflective Counseling Techniques and Hypnosis: A Research Essay Submitted to the Faculty of the Gannon College Graduate Programs in Partial Fulfillment of the Requirements for the degree of Master of Science in Counseling,* 1979

Theory of Increased Suggestibility

A study of the illustration below shows that hypnosis is a *concentration* of the mind. In the everyday waking state, the mind is engaged with many diverse impressions so that the "units of mind power" appear scattered. Suggestion in this state will have a modest effect, if any, because it clearly "goes in one ear and out the other." As the client is paying trivial attention (the majority of his/her mind being in use with his/her own "thoughts" and impressions) comparatively hardly any units of mind power are affected by suggestion, and consequently the final creation is weak.

In hypnosis, the mind is *concentrated.* 100% concentration will symbolize very deep hypnosis, in which the subject will be paying attention to the hypnotherapist only. The client in this state would be unmindful of other things—including physical pain—for the entire "mind power" is concentrated on the hypnotherapist's suggestions. There are no "mind units" left to become aware of other stimuli. Hypnosis enables more of the psyche to soak up suggestion. As more of the suggestion is engaged, it is logical to presume that the consequence will be superior to the commonplace waking state. Subsequent to hypnotherapy, each of the "units of mind power" will hold a "dosage of suggestion." Additionally, the client gets the "feelings" that go with, or are associated with, the suggestion.

This notion of hypnosis explains why normal, healthy people with high quality powers of imagination and concentration make the best hypnotic subjects, at the same time as "scatterbrained" people are hard at first but can be conditioned by repetitive sessions. "Deep" hypnosis is not necessary to attain good consequences in psychotherapy, while "light" hypnosis is usually sufficient.

If only 51% of the existing "mind power< can be affected by suggestion, it will surpass the other 49%. It is not possible for the mind to think two contradictory things at one time (it is unfeasible to imagine "I am in good health" and "I am ill" at the same point in time—one idea is constantly prevailing). High-quality consequences will follow as soon as sufficient "units of mind power" have been affected.

Hypnosis is a state of mind resulting from *concentration* on an idea, which may be deliberately or accidentally introduced. This forms the foundation to construct a theory of mental health issues, but also a therapeutic approach. Such concentration of the mind is also expected to take place as the product of an *emotional* incident or idea.

Normal waking state

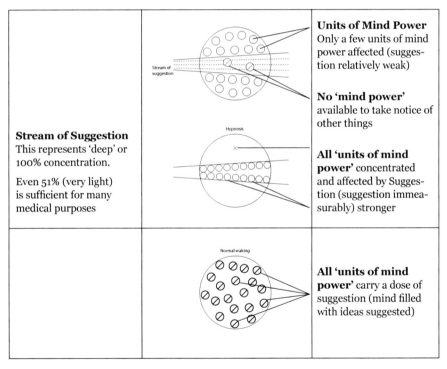

Units of Mind Power
Only a few units of mind power affected (suggestion relatively weak)

No 'mind power'
available to take notice of other things

Stream of Suggestion
This represents 'deep' or 100% concentration.

Even 51% (very light) is sufficient for many medical purposes

All 'units of mind power' concentrated and affected by Suggestion (suggestion immeasurably) stronger

All 'units of mind power' carry a dose of suggestion (mind filled with ideas suggested)

Fig. 1 —The nature of hypnosis, and the explanation for amplified suggestibility in this state.

REFERENCES

Pelt, S J Van, 1956, Hypnotic Suggestion: Its Role in Psychoneurotic and Psychosomatic Disorders, New York: Philosophical Library

CHAPTER 4

PONCE DE LEON SYNDROME

This highly insightful understanding of the human condition was first written about by William J. Bryan, MD, PhD, LLD over 40 years ago. It is still useful today. This paper will introduce the novice to some of the basic ideas involved with this life problem. It was immediately after Juan Ponce de Leon concluded his governorship in Puerto Rico, approximately 1510 or 1512, and was making a contented livelihood on his agricultural estate that a Caribbean woman named La Vieja approached him. Her tale was a bizarre one. She had just come from the island of Guadalupe, where some years back her husband and his brothers paddled away in a canoe to hunt for the mythical Fountain of Youth on Bimini Island. She was certain that her husband had found the fountain, had grown youthful once more, and had forgotten all regarding her. She begged Ponce de Leon to take her to her husband in one of his numerous ships. He himself had heard the legend scores of times from the Indians on Puerto Rico and Haiti. Several swore that the fountain existed. If it did, it could be on any one of hundreds of uncharted islands of the West Indies, contemplated Ponce de Leon.

La Vieja did not know the way but had heard her husband chart the way.

She was sure she could guide de Leon to the island and convinced him to set out in search of it. She just sought to wash in the magical stream in order to recapture her youth and perhaps her husband. Ponce de Leon had zero to lose and conceivably the governorship of Bimini to achieve. He wrote and asked King Ferdinand for a royal grant, but did not reveal the search for the fountain.

Three ships made the journey, passed the Bahamas, and landed close to the later settlement of St. Augustine, Florida. On more than a few occasions, the party encountered intimidating Florida Indians and had to take flight. At last, de Leon and his men reached an island with a fountain, but subsequent to a great deal of dipping, soaking, and lastly drinking the water, they ended up the cleaner for their labors, but that was all.

One story came back that the captain detained la Vieja's head under the water till she drowned, saying, "You may not get any younger, mala, but by all the Saints I'll see to it that you never get any older."

Juan Ponce de Leon, lovingly known as "Father of Puerto Rico," in no way found the Fountain of Youth. It is well that he didn't. His later descendants have found it, and it has proven to be a Pandora's Box for them.

The initial case of the Ponce de Leon Syndrome which William Jennings Bryan, MD, was to recognize was a case of a youthful man 34 years of age, whose life was totally subjugated by the fixation that he was a successor, in actuality the re-embodiment of Ponce de Leon. He lived on "Maiden Lane," professed his love for a girl in Florida bearing the given name Donna Inez (the sane name as Ponce de Leon's spouse), and fashioned page after page of additional data, which he stated decisively proved (at least to him) that he was the recreation of Ponce de Leon. The complicatedness with this re-embodiment was that, not like Ponce de Leon, he had found the Fountain of Youth, submerged in its "psychological waters," and had been incapable to mature any older.

Physically, the youthful man appeared to be approximately 15 to 17 years old and remarkable, as it may seem his assessment of his case was not far-flung from being correct. He had engaged the services of a lay hypnotist who had given him suggestions that he would by no means grow old-er and would not have to partake in the dangers of maturity. The patient was an ineffective photographer with vast aptitude, but pitiable business capability, who exhausted most of his time photographing adolescent girls between the ages of 12 to 15 and dreaming of the sexual contact he was by no means able to take pleasure in.

As soon as he entered Dr. Bryan's office, he stated, "I want to investigate the things I've been writing about and working with in regard to my being the reincarnation of Ponce de Leon, and I want to solve my life problems. The things I am really interested in investigating are integrally bound up with my life's problems." When asked what these troubles were, he declared that, in order of significance, they were as follows:

1. Making an adjustment to the opposite sex. "You see, I have never even started going out on dates. I went out on a date once when I was 15 years old, but that was an afternoon date and not really significant. I know I should have gone to the door with her, but I didn't and I regret it to this day. I have a tremendous desire to go out with women, but I regret that I cannot do it and I feel very frustrated that I can't. You see, it is as though I am just too young."

2. Vocational difficulty. "I have had two years of college, but I didn't finish. I dropped from an 'A' in junior high school to a 'D' at UCLA. It was extremely difficult for me because it was as though I was simply not old enough."

3. "I have occasional stuttering when I attempt to solve adult prob-lems of any kind. It may seem ridiculous, but when I was younger I was obsessed with the idea of the Fountain of Youth, probably be-cause I am a real-life reincarnation of Ponce de Leon. I know this is difficult for you to believe, Doctor, but I want you to consider that although my pattern is abnormal, if you are open minded you may realize how valid it is." When Dr. Bryan reminded the young man that Ponce de Leon did not find the Fountain of Youth but died of a poison arrow inflicted by hostile Indians, the boy said, "That's just it. You see, I didn't want to die of a poisoned arrow and so there-

fore through the aid of self-hypnosis and the amateur hypnotist, a Mr. K., I was able to accomplish what I could not accomplish in my former life. That is to say that I have found the Fountain of Youth. The difficulty with it is that when I became 16, I began feeling bad and very bad from age 18 on. I could make some money, but my business ability remained that of approximately a 15-year-old child. I relate normally to the opposite sex but only in a fashion that a 15-year old boy might relate. The trouble is that I don't get any more confident as I grow chronologically older. I have a real feeling that I am not getting too old at all. In fact, I am becoming less confident as I age chronologically. I don't really know what I want to do, but I am profoundly disturbed. Does any of this make any sense to you, Doctor?"

Of course, it made a great deal of sense. It occurred to Dr. Bryan that many patients might have received some sort of suggestion in the past that they would limit the aging process. Consequently, although they look a great deal younger as they grow older, it actually has an ill effect on the human. Without the natural aging processes, the psychological processes—gaining wisdom as you grow older and learning how to adapt to new situations psychologically—are denied to this patient. He is "out of the stream of life," standing by at age 15 and watching it pass him. He has no desire for homosexual relations, and his only sexual outlet is masturbation, in which he indulges somewhat more than twice a day. He lives in a garage apartment with his mother and grandmother, who is incidentally over 91 years old. In his history, he stated that his father "pulled out" when he was only 19. The parents are divorced, and the father lives in Alaska. The patient spends his time working on his psychological obsession regarding Ponce de Leon and talking to young girls and their parents, photographing them when he can, and selling the photographs at a pittance to photographic dealers. Embroiled in his psychological "research," he sleeps poorly and, as would be suspected by his psychological age arrest, he neither drinks nor smokes.

Apparently, in getting a complete history, the patient had been told that God would punish him if he went to a movie. At age 5 he went to a movie and at that point began developing asthma attacks. These lasted until age

13, when the patient began to masturbate. At age 7 he had a tonsillecto-my and while under the anesthetic had a bad dream that he was swinging from the end of the rope. The swinging rope was a mile in length, and he vowed at that time that he would never *allow himself* to be chloroformed again. (There is some question as to whether ether or chloroform was utilized as the anesthetic.) He is fearful of dogs, loud noises, and women and believes now that he is bathed in the psychological waters of the Fountain of Youth that he will be forever young. He has never grown any older and keeps himself at age 15. He cannot date, hold a job and make money, drink, smoke, or do anything else that might possibly identify him with the adult world. He is so obsessed about growing old and the dangers that are involved that he has made himself forever young, and it has turned into a horrible tragedy. Because of his great fears of grow-ing older, he refused to consent to treatment and the case remained in the same condition as when I first saw it. A subsequent investigation of the patient three years later has shown no change. The real value of this case was to point up to Dr. Bryan that such a syndrome exists and conse-quently that it should be looked for in the histories of patients who came into his office with problems concerned with adaptation to adult behav-ior, especially in the sexual field.

The elderly Caribbean woman, La Vieja, feared that her husband in bath-ing in the Fountain of Youth had turn out to be youthful yet again and no longer preferred the companionship of his older wife. The likelihood she neglected to think about was that her husband might become so childish that he would be incapable of consummating his sexual wishes at all.

Many child-molestation cases can be straightforwardly explained by the uncomplicated recognition of a hypnotic suggestion to the result that the patient is at an age level in which such conduct is okay. In private communication with a number of judges who have tried such cases, sev-eral of them are amazed at the fact that the child molester commonly does not "molest" the child at all. In numerous cases, the children are not ill treated in any way. The man is purely carrying out the same style of exploratory behavior that he might have made at age 6, 7, or 11 which would have been considered typical at that age, but because the man is 39, 52, or 70, is considered definitely abnormal, or even against the law.

The failure to comprehend the origin of such child molestation or such "child-like sexual behavior" has led to the imprisonment of these individuals when in actuality they need medical hypnoanalytic treatment. All of the cases, of course, are not so inclusive as the young man who was illustrated in the preceding case who became so preoccupied with his thought of rebirth that his whole life was so predisposed. Many patients are arrested in their sexual development or in their capability to understand a definite issue only at a particular age level, or at a particular age level in one or multiple fields. The possibilities are just about infinite, and the origin in each case is that the subconscious mind of the individual has simply received a suggestion which if accepted would result in the arresting of some part of the individual's existence at an exact age level. The individual is brainwashed in the Fountain of Youth. (A dreadful bath indeed.)

The paradoxical reality about such cases is that often the patient himself may comprehend the problem and often relates to the therapist, "My friends have all been telling me I have to grow up sometime, and I really know they are right, but I just can't do it."

The trepidation to accept adult tasks may lead the patient to unintentionally agree to a suggestion that he will stay young-looking in order to avail himself of the safety accorded an individual for the duration of this stage of his being. The primary motivation causing each patient to agree to such a detrimental suggestion is that the patient entertains some trepidation with respect to adulthood, which sparks a self-defensive response on the part of the patient, a departure into childhood. In numerous cases, this core apprehension is first and foremost concerned with knowledge and experience. The patient often rationally appreciates adulthood and can converse astutely and often with vast insight concerning the tribulations thereof. The patient, on the other hand, is not disposed to experience these troubles on a personal plane. Patients of both sexes typically avoid the sexual experience and go on to find themselves closer and closer to their parents and other shielding sources. As they turn out to be chronologically older, the public at large demands additional self-reliance of them. Since they have not had the stage during their early years to develop this normally, they become less and less able to grip their own dealings and consequently more and more need the security of childhood, for which they increasingly search. This leads to a vicious cycle arrangement, like that projected by Dr. Van Pelt. The original fear becomes lost in the subconscious mind and the consequential tensions produced go on to generate symptoms, which in turn manufacture more tensions. The vicious cycle continues until, through the process of medical hypnoanalysis, the aberrant fears are brought to light, the suggestions retarding the psychological aging process are detached, and the individual is once more able to experience a typical life.

As you would expect, the earlier the treatment is commenced in cases of this category, the better, for the reason that the individual has a "catching up process" to do over and above what might be predictable from the typical individual. This is not too hard if the phase of time is not too big and if the individual is agreeable to commencing the venture in order to attain his mental health. With the core subconscious fears and suggestions removed and with positive suggestions inserted in their place, the individual is a long way on the road to achieving the condition of independence from psychological arrest at a particular age level. It is vital to bear in mind that degrees of severity of a predicament exist. Immaturity in one form or area is usually there since the patient has received a negative suggestion, which has retarded or arrested his psychological progress in some region at a particular age level.

The subsequent two case histories, by Dr. Bryan, demonstrate to a severe degree the difficulties which the Ponce de Leon Syndrome may present to the medical hypnoanalyst and the methods by which this particular syndrome can be known and fruitfully treated.

Case History No. 1

The case of Mr. F. G., a 40-year-old, well-developed, well-nourished white male who appears to be a great deal younger than his stated age, presented himself for treatment in the office with the following complaint:

"I really don't know what the problem is. Mostly a sense of frustration and anxiety. Now here I am, at my age of 40 and I am still not married and it's preying on my mind. I am anxious and waiting for things to happen that don't happen. I went to a psychiatrist at the..... Clinic for over a year, but all I got out of that was that he brought up to my mind that I was fearful of things because of my mother.

I quit going to him because I wasn't getting any better. I always thought that my father was an aggressive man and that was the cause of my trouble, but the psychiatrist seemed to think that my mother had something to do with it. In any case, he was probably right in the sense that my mother put fears into me by her own actions and insinuations, but he was unable to find out what fears were put into me and he couldn't get them out of me. Also, the psychiatrist said that I don't want to be a man or that I don't want to mature. I suppose that subconsciously that may be true, but what good does it do me if he can't change me? Seven years ago, I didn't want to pass the CPA exam and I had to take it four times. I could have passed it the first time, of course, but I just didn't. It is a difficult exam, but it was not that difficult. And then again this problem where everyone gets married but me. When someone asks me how old I am, I become very upset. You see chronologically, I am 40, but in reality I am much younger than this. I know I am immature. I know I haven't been married and I know that I may have some subconscious fears, but conventional psychiatric therapy, while pointing up the problems, has never been able to come up with any solutions."

The patient in his opening statements voiced many of the objections to conventional psychotherapy which psychiatrists themselves have known for years. Unable to reach the real causes underlying the problems, conventional therapy has at best offered merely an outlet through which the patient may ventilate. Giving the patient someone to talk to, like the relieving of physical pain of the moment, is an important function of therapy, but a far more important function of the therapist is the curing of the disease process which has brought about the symptoms.

Once harmful hypnotic suggestions have been planted in the subconscious mind of the individual, either by design or inadvertently, the disease process cannot possibly be cured by conventional psychotherapy but only through the correct use of hypnosis to remove the harmful suggestions which are present. It follows that to unlock the door that bars the patient's path to health, we must use the same key which first locked the door.

Continuing the history, the patient said, "I have been aware of my illness since 1953 when I was in business for myself. I was all right as long as I was not successful, but when I became extremely successful, I began to feel more and more apprehensive. I finally sold my business to one of my own salesmen and didn't work for a year." When asked what he would do if cured that he could not do now, he stated that he would like to get married, lead a normal life, and be successful. Obviously these are the three things which he fears the most. When asked why he was not married and if his sexual relations were satisfactory, he states, "This is another thing I am embarrassed to talk about. Seven years ago, at age 33, was the first I ever had sexual relations. I had gone out with a woman before then, you understand, but I was frightened to death of sex. I finally got with a girl and she really overwhelmed me. I was sexually aroused. I lost my potency, got sick and threw up out of fear, and had a terrible reaction. But she was so mature and understanding. She went through the entire experience with me, reassuring me at every step. Approximately half an hour later, with her help and assistance, I finally was able to have intercourse with her and reached a climax. Of course, I was terribly frightened and it was not at all satisfactory, but at least I did it. I was even able to do it several times after that, although it makes me very weak and it is quite unsatisfying. Doctor, do you suppose this is because little boys are weak sexually?"

Of course, in thinking of himself as a "little boy," the patient had inadvertently hit the crux of the problem. He was typical of those with Ponce de Leon Syndrome. Because of his fear of adult life, he had bathed in the waters of the Fountain of Youth and only with the greatest difficulty had been able to behave in an adult fashion. His social life had largely been limited to the church of which he was a member. He belonged to a group from the church, many of whose members were much younger than him. He stated that he had a nervous breakdown at age 8 and had to be pulled out of school. He was out of school for over a year and spent one hour each day with a tutor during this period of time. He was very poor in grade school, and the principal thought that he needed some sort of treatment at that time. He was given an IQ test and got the highest IQ in the school, but he was unable to make acceptable grades until he entered college.

At this time they discovered he needed glasses and his grade average raised, but he nevertheless remained "frightened to death." He had a past history of rheumatic fever, rheumatic heart disease, allergies, and the usual childhood diseases. He had a tonsillectomy at age 5 or 6 with ether anesthesia. But one of the major difficulties started in 1953, following a motorcycle accident in which he sustained a severe injury to his nose. It was shortly after this when he became successful and had to sell his business. He has occasional shortness of breath, is "sexually apathetic," and largely impotent when attempting intercourse. His father was quiet in public, but domineering and bossy at home. His mother, just the opposite, was socially very talkative, but at home quiet and meek. They were separated a number of times and at one period for 17 months, but his parents remained married and were apparently not the decisive factor in producing the illness.

The patient described a number of dreams and one particular traumatic incident in which there was an open elevator. He apparently jumped on the elevator while it was moving, barely in the nick of time, and almost got killed in the process. "It was only a split second and I'd have been killed," he said with emphasis. "It was a very frightening experience and I don't know why I did it. I was 21 at the time and should have known better than to attempt it. When asked when his puberty began, he said, "I don't remember." When pressed as to an approximate date he said, "No, it isn't like that; it is sort of as though I haven't reached it yet. You see, I never will forget the one time when I was swimming in the nude at the 'YMCA. My friends had hair and I just had fuzz and they all laughed at me. I started masturbating at 17 or 18 and I used to masturbate at least once daily, but I don't think I have masturbated for a whole month now. I usually masturbate now only several times a month. As I told you, Doctor, I had my first intercourse at age 33 and I have only had intercourse with one girl and this only four or five times. Her name is Mrs. L."

In the word association test, the patient gave many examples of childlike responses. The diagnosis at this time was entertained that the patient was suffering from the Ponce de Leon Syndrome with a psychological age arrest at sometime before puberty, with subsequent intensifying events in 1953 at the time of the motorcycle accident.

In the next treatment session, the patient was encouraged to dream. He eventually dreamt that an old man (his father) was driving a red, low sports car (which the patient eventually stated represented his father's penis) and that he was afraid it might hurt someone. In the dream, the old man looked up at the patient and smiled. The patient interpreted this as meaning we were pretty close to one of the basic problems. Under age regression, the patient went back to his home at age approximately 4 to 5 years.

He was watching the bedroom door where his folks were in the afternoon. Father was trying to get mother to go to bed with him and she was resisting. The patient speaks as follows: "My father is making mother do something she doesn't want to do. Father yells and mother takes her clothes off just to please my father. My father stands there with his clothes on. Finally father takes his clothes off. Father is on top of mother having intercourse. Mother is just lying there and daddy is holding her down. My mother is just lying there like she is dead. No response, no feeling, no nothing.

It's as though my father is killing my mother. Is that why I am so frightened of sex? Yes, that must be it. I remember now when Lois said to me that I was so sexually apathetic and the feeling I had was that I was scared to have sex with her because I didn't want to hurt her. You see, father's penis seemed so big to me at the time, like a big red sports car, I was afraid it would injure my mother, afraid it would kill her. It was as though sex and murder had become associated in my mind. Does that make sense, Doctor?" At this point the interview was interrupted and suggestions were given to the patient that sex and murder were no longer associated in his mind, that every time he felt reticent regarding sex he would see a picture of the incident with the words "sex is good" superimposed over it. He would realize that his father is no longer killing his mother and that this needn't bother him.

He had felt in the past that his penis was a dangerous weapon with which he might injure someone, and was too frightened to utilize it for the purpose for which it was intended. It was because his mother had intercourse only as a duty but not for pleasure that his father became overly aggressive. By becoming mean and over-aggressive, his father sought to stimulate the frigid mother into having proper sexual emotions. However, this only intensified the problem. When the situation was observed by the 5-year-old patient, he accepted the suggestion that to grow older like his father meant that he would have to use his penis as a weapon in the same fashion as his father and that the death of the particular female, being "stabbed by this weapon," might ensue. In fear of being punished for murder, he abstained from all sexual activity and from marriage in particular. The easiest way to accomplish this, of course, was to merely accept the suggestion that he would not grow up at all.

The fact that the patient had accepted this suggestion that it would be "dangerous to grow up" is illustrated by the following dream, which he had on a subsequent session:

"I was watching men competing in sledding down a trail of ice. One after another would come out of a tunnel and shoot down the hill and narrowly missed cars that were also driving across this route." The dream obviously illustrates the persons being born (coming out of a tunnel) and shooting down a hill (growing up) and then encountering the danger (narrowly missing the cars).

A subsequent dream is even more revealing:

"I went into a store to cash a check and while the clerk was getting the money, a man looked up toward the top of something and saw a large deadly snake. People were running about the street describing awful snake bites."

The snake represents father's big penis, which the patient interprets as "evil." The patient then remarked, "My mother always talked against sex. She thought it was very dirty and never let my father kiss and hug her in front of us kids for fear that it would injure us in some way." At the following session, five hours after beginning treatment, the patient reported still a different dream.

"I was in Africa where there was an oasis in the desert. Someone asked me to see if I could find a tree anywhere. I started walking through the sand, but I could see nothing in my direction. I could not find the tree, but I finally came across three people—a man and two women—and they seemed to know where they were going. I said to one of the women that it was certainly difficult climbing uphill, and she said, 'You just have to get used to it.' I didn't climb the hill, however. I came back down the hill and these same people crossed my path, but this time nothing was said. I found myself in the middle of a desert, lost, but I didn't seem upset about it. I just kept walking."

The tree obviously represents the adult penis for which he is looking. He did not climb the hill of life with his classmates and companions but returned back down the hill and met people again. But this time they did not communicate with him because he was actually out of touch with them on a psychological level by virtue of the fact that his psychological and sexual advance had been arrested at a previous age level. He merely remained in the middle of the desert, lost, and just kept walking. He was reassured by suggestions given under hypnosis that the tree was actually there. He had an adult penis. It was not a snake. It was not evil. It had not been cut off or otherwise damaged. It was not a weapon that would be used to injure anyone. In fact, it was a normal sexual instrument.

Although he could get used to his present condition and could continue walking and never finding that, this was not the purpose for which he had entered the office. He would be able to regress to all the incidents which had reinforced the suggestion that he needed to remain youthful, and that he was unable to accept the responsibilities of adulthood. As these incidents were brought out, we would remove the suggestions connected with them. Each time such a suggestion was removed, it would become easier and easier for him to accept the responsibilities of adult psycho-sexual life.

At the next treatment session, he regressed to the motorcycle accident.

He stated that he had never driven a motorcycle before but that he would like to try it. He felt that it would be thrilling to drive one. He got on the three-wheel motorcycle and forgot where the brake was. He stated, "I thought my foot was on the brake and instead of slowing down, I kept going faster and faster. I ran up on a lawn, through a fence and went over on my head. I wasn't really hurt, but my nose was cut up and a lady was more concerned about her fence than she was about me. I went to the hospital and my nose was sewn up." When the patient was asked to interpret this experience, in light of his present difficulties, he stated, "It's as though the motorcycle ride represented sex to me. You see, I had never had sex before either, and I felt sex would be thrilling too and I wanted to try it, and so finally I jumped on the motorcycle as I remember father jumping on mother. The difficulty was, I didn't how to manage it. I didn't know where the brake was, and sure enough, just like father injured mother, I injured the motorcycle, the fence and even cut my nose up in the bargain. You see, it was 'one thing on top of another'."

In rapid succession, the patient recalled other incidents in which his father slammed a car door on the patient's finger and at age 3 or 4 in which the patient's brother had diphtheria. The patient thought the brother had died when a fumigator was thrown out the window. The patient's finger was almost cut off with a butcher knife, but the patient did not feel it. He associated the ether canister connected with his tonsillectomy with the fumigator canister and felt that it was simply not necessary to feel the pain.

This certainly shows the ability of the patient to accept hypnotic suggestions inadvertently. There can be no doubt that the motorcycle accident reinforced the belief that sex was a possibly dangerous experience and that his penis, if allowed to exist at all, would be a dangerous weapon which might inflict great harm on the lady in whom it was inserted. The gravity of it was such that it had to be avoided at all costs, which could be done only by keeping Mr. G. at an age level that would restrict the use of his penis. Subsequent dreams revealed that the patient also had a fear of self-injury and resisted opportunities sexually, socially, and business because of the presence of the syndrome. After removing the harmful fears and suggestions which brought about the syndrome, the patient began to change rather dramatically. He has not been brought up to the age level of his contemporaries, but he is at least dating, having intercourse, and enjoying a more successful period in his business life than he has heretofore been able to allow to exist. He is improving rapidly and growing more and more self-confident and self-reliant.

It is my impression that within the next few months he should be entirely cured. Although he will probably remain on the shy side, he will at least be able to experience a relatively normal life at his own chronological age level.

Case History No. 2

This is the case of Mr. L. E., who is 38 years old and gave a history similar to that of Mr. F. G. Referred by a church counseling service, Mr. L. E. stated that he had a lot of fears. "I am afraid of anything new, a new job, especially when it comes to dating, social gatherings, etc. These things keep me in a panic. I am panic stricken except where I have known everyone from a long time back. I have been having problems of nervous fatigue off and on this year and last year. All the doctors I've gone to say that I am okay physically, but when faced with taking this girl out with whom I wish to make a date, I would become nervously fatigued. I just have to get this problem straightened out. The girl finally didn't go out with me anyhow and, of course, I was relieved that I didn't have to go and the last time I talked to her she was getting married to someone else. But then, after all, I might wish to date some other girls someday." This is another incidence of a 38-year-old, well-developed, well-nourished white male who appears greatly younger than his stated age and whose behavior pattern is that of a small boy, afraid to accept any adult sexual relationship.

It should not be assumed because the three cases involved are all males that this syndrome does not occur in the female. The truth of the matter is that the syndrome occurs far more often in the female than the male. The female, given the nature of our society, is able to excuse herself from the responsibilities of adult psychosexual existence by claiming that it is really a "virtue" that she is protecting (which she zealously protects until her death).

Also, female recluses have been more acceptable or more tolerated by society than the male who fails to become an adult. That is to say, the social adjustment problems are greater for the adult male who washes himself in the Fountain of Youth than for the adult female who does the same.

The syndrome could be disastrous, however, in either sex and the healthy human being continues to grow and mature physically, mentally, and spiritually throughout his or her entire lifetime. The case histories are remarkably similar, but in the present case the Ponce de Leon Syndrome became established at an earlier age than in the case of Mr. G. previously reported. In grammar school, the patient remembered that when he gave a wrong answer, the teacher would "yell at me" and in later years the patient developed a habit of merely answering, "I don't know" to every question so that the teacher wouldn't "yell at me." This childlike response and withdrawal from competition with other students of the same age is one of the first evidences of the beginning of Ponce de Leon Syndrome.

The young girl who constantly refers to her other companions as "too forward or too fast" and "nasty" merely because they are growing up is in fact withdrawing into childhood and setting the stage for the development of Ponce de Leon Syndrome. As with the patient who began withdrawing in grammar school from the competition with his fellow students, this child should be hypnotized right then to find out what fears are present within the subconscious mind which tend to arrest the child's development at this early age. The patient said he had a heart defect (atrial septal defect), which only had been corrected this year. He was always afraid that fights (which he occasionally got into as a child) or sex (which he even less occasionally indulged in) might be the death of him after all. The patient has never had sexual intercourse, and his entire sexual experience consists of light petting, over no more than a half dozen dates with different girls since his early 20s. His last date was September 1961, three years ago.

His only sexual outlet is masturbation, which he began at age 10, and he even developed a fear of a manikin that his mother used for sewing, fantasizing that the manikin, which was stored in the closet, was watching him masturbate through the keyhole. In the word association test, the response "death" was given to the word "kiss" and the patient then said "kiss of death." It should be certainly obvious to every therapist that this patient is not going to indulge in any adult activities, much less intercourse, until the basic fears which have caused his symptoms have been completely removed by age regression and analysis under medical hypnosis.

The patient developed recurring dreams during therapy that he was somewhere without his clothes and was very scared. Another recurring dream he had was that he was in a room that kept getting larger and larger and the door at the end of the room kept getting smaller and smaller in relation to his own size. He also dreamt that he would come out of a tunnel and the tunnel would be wrapped around his shoulders, but just as he is to come out of the tunnel, he turns around and goes back because he feels that the opening is not big enough. Later on, the patient was to interpret this as a fear of growing up. Because of the difficulty in the birth experience, the patient stated that he developed a fear that he was not really born yet and he might have to go through the vaginal opening again. If he grew up and became large, the opening would be too small and he would never be able to make it. This was apparently reinforced by the misunderstanding of a religious experience at an early age in which he was told that he had to be "born again."

It was explained to him that he would not need to be born again "of the water," and under hypnosis the suggestion was removed from his subconscious that he had "better not grow up because he still had to go through the vagina once more." After removing this suggestion, positive suggestions were placed in his subconscious mind that from this moment forward, he would be able to grow up rapidly and completely in every way, for there was no longer any reason to hold him back. The patient realized that the time in his life that he was small, half scared, nude, and had considerable difficulty getting through the small opening from one larger place to another was the birth experience. He no longer had a "fear of being trapped in the tunnel" and he has progressed rapidly since these suggestions have been given. The patient's analysis is not fully complete but inclusion of this case is warranted in order that the clinician will recognize the syndrome when it presents to him.

Summary

This article describes the Ponce de Leon Syndrome. A patient, owing to subconscious fears of the aging progression or some risk that may take place as the patient grows older, essentially arrests his maturity by means of emotional suggestion, either purposefully or unintentionally, and accepts the idea that he is powerless to grow older than some particular chronological age. The patient exhibits behavior of this particular age both physical and mental and is unable to participate successfully with other persons of his/her own chronological age. The symptoms most commonly comprise inability to assume adult sexual behavior, but most frequently consist of the failure to take on any adult behavior or adult behavior in a particular given area. The sexual problems are more likely to come to the notice of the therapist because the disparity between child sexual goings-on and adult sexual goings-on is so much greater than in other areas of development.

Once the core fears are removed and the subconscious hypnotic suggestions which the patient has formerly received are also removed, the patient is then liberated to benefit from a customary aging process and will in the main swiftly catch up to his/her age group. As was assumed by Ponce de Leon from the beginning, the power of attaining everlasting youth lies in the Fountain of the Mind. The consequence of accepting such a suggestion is devastation and an existence wanting contentment and completion. In the vein of the apple tree in the Garden of Eden, the enticement of bathing in the waters in the Fountain of Youth ought to be resisted. Rather the converse, mental health depends on graceful aging, accepting the responsibilities of every stage in one's days, and existing in that time to the fullest.

PART II

BIRTH

CHAPTER 5

BIRTH AND EARLY YEARS (ISE)

The birth as related by Larry Geller, friend and "spiritual advisor."

MISSION TO MAN

They were in the Meditation Garden at Graceland. There were three of them sitting there: Elvis; his father, Vernon; and Larry. The conversation had taken an intimate turn. They were discussing Elvis' birth as a prelude to Elvis having his horoscope done. Elvis' eyes looked beyond his father to the marble, almost life-size statue of Jesus, with its hands outstretched, the recycled water from a fountain splashing in the background.

His eyes came back to his father.

"Daddy," he said, "do you know the exact moment I was born?"

Vernon stroked his chin. "As you know, son, you were born on January 8, 1935. A Tuesday."

Elvis shook his head. "That's not good enough, Daddy. Astrology is supposedly an exact science. An astrologer needs the hour of birth, the minute if possible, to construct a chart accurately."

He had read a book by astrologer Dane Rudhyar, *New Mansions for New Men,* and it had impressed him.

Vernon's mind turned back over the years.

"All I can tell you," he said, "is that it was somewhere between midnight and dawn. It was dark and cold, the dead of winter."

Elvis took a humorous tone with his father. "Daddy, try and remember what you were doing that night. It's all blocked up in your memory. It's there, Daddy, search the old archives."

Vernon smiled quietly, puffing on his cigarette with the relish of a chain smoker. "I'll never forget that house, son. My daddy and me built it ourselves about a year before you were born. We were so poor that we only built two small rooms.

We had no water pipes. If we needed water, we had to go out back and use the pump next to the outhouse. It was a bitter winter, but we couldn't afford a hospital. So it all had to be done at home."

He blew a ring of smoke into the air, watching it slowly dissipate itself. His face clouded for a moment. "Maybe, if we had the money your twin would have lived." He shrugged. "Who knows, maybe it was God's will? I don't know."

Astrology was forgotten, and two men looked at each other and shared their secret sorrow. There was a long silence, each lost in his own little island of thought.

Elvis was the first to come out of it. He leaned forward in his wrought-iron chair. "Well, Daddy, did anything unusual happen? Maybe, if you can remark what you were doing..."

Vernon thought hard for a few moments, lighting another cigarette and pulling on it. Suddenly, a puzzled frown came to his face. "Something very strange and unusual did happen that night, now that I think about it. Like I said, it was bitter cold, and the wind was blowing up a storm. I recall it was way past midnight, a couple of hours past, around three or so, maybe a little later. Because I remember thinking when is that baby coming? I didn't know at the time your mother was carrying twins."

He had gone outside for a moment, for a breath of fresh air.

"As I looked around, son, I noticed something strange. The whole area around the house itself was lit up with a blue light. It seemed to surround the house. And at that very moment, the wind stopped blowing."

There was a long silence, and then Vernon shook his head. "It's funny," he said, "I haven't thought about it for years, and now it's all coming back to me."

Elvis took a deep breath and let the air escape slowly. "Didn't that blue light mean anything to you, Daddy?"

Vernon smiled. "Well, son, it did sort of startle me. But then I heard some commotion in the house, and I ran in. You were born at the very moment the wind stopped howling. A few minutes later, your brother, Jesse Garon, was stillborn. He wasn't breathing. And there was nothing we could do. There was no doctor we could call."

The women of the family and a midwife had delivered Elvis and his twin. They were cleaning up, tending to the mother. It was no time to think of a blue light. Elvis' face, usually so expressive, was now inscrutable. But Larry recalled with a thrill that Elvis had visualized a blue light in his healings and meditations, rather than the usual light.

Father and son mused for a while, the moment so intimate that Larry felt he was intruding. Elvis was the first to pull himself out.

"It's too bad, Daddy, you don't have the exact time, but three o'clock or so might be good enough."

Vernon's mind was still in the past. He turned to Larry now. "This information might be helpful. I know the exact night Elvis was conceived. I knew something special happened because at the moment of conception, my mind blacked out, it went into complete darkness. It was strange, but I knew a child was conceived at that moment. When Gladys told me she was pregnant, I thought back, and I wasn't surprised a bit."

Elvis' face grew solemn. "Daddy," he said, "you never told me that before."

Vernon smiled. "Son, to tell you the truth, I haven't thought about it for years. I guess going back 30 years made me think of it for some reason."

What his father had said fit in with Elvis' notion that his was no ordinary destiny. He could have compared the blue light over the humble house with the star that heralded another birth 2,000 years before. But this would have been sacrilege. And he knew better. But his mind dwelt on the light. He did not know what to make of it. He had meditated blue, and blue was his favorite color, but if the blue light meant anything, it was more than a disposition to a certain color.

He had always thought of it as Christ's color, standing for truth and integrity. "True blue" had been an expression borrowed from childhood.

He couldn't help thinking of the blue light later, and yet he approached its significance cautiously, not wanting to seem vain or presumptuous. He mentioned it half humorously.

"Funny," he said, "how that light meant so little to Daddy."

"He didn't understand it," said Larry.

Elvis gave him a quick look. "What do you think it meant?"

"I have no idea," said Larry, vaguely sensing what he was driving at, "but

I am sure of your mission. I believe you are destined to help millions now lost and troubled."

Elvis' face lit up. "You are right, Larry. That is why I am here. I felt it in that church, when I was only 2 years old, and I feel it now. Only it is more than just my singing."

The following is the birth and early years as related by Dee Presley, Elvis' stepmother.

Unusually large during the last months of pregnancy, Gladys kept telling friends and in-laws that she was carrying twins, but nobody seemed inclined to believe her until shortly after noon on January 8, 1935, when she went into labor and gave birth to identical twin boys. The first child to be removed was Elvis Aaron. The second child was stillborn. Jesse Garon Presley was buried in Priceville Cemetery the following day in an unmarked grave.

A ruthless tornado, one of the worst in history, whipped right through Tupelo during the first year of Elvis' life, taking many lives and sweeping whole houses into its black vortex of destruction. In the years to come, Gladys and Elvis would reminisce about that tornado and consider themselves lucky to have escaped with their lives. Elvis would also remember his twin brother, Jesse Garon. Some people firmly believe that identical twins are joined psychically, like the fabled Corsican brothers, and Elvis would later ponder a sense of incompleteness at having lost a part of himself he could never know.

From Elvis' first moments on Earth until his mother's death some 23 years later, Gladys Presley never stopped worrying about his every waking moment, and when she discovered that her boy was a somnambulist, she worried about his sleeping moments as well. Many of Elvis' fans assumed that Gladys' fear for the safety of her son was a natural overreaction to the loss of his twin brother. But that still doesn't take into account the fact that she was an unusual woman, unusually intuitive about her child. Several people who knew her in those days and in years to come would call her "psychic" about Elvis. Her love for the boy was a fawning, all-consuming emotion that never stopped growing or allowed her a moment's respite. When he turned 5 and started school, Gladys began walking Elvis to school and never stopped until he entered high school. Even then, she insisted that he take his own silverware to school so he couldn't get germs from the other students.

Through all of the hard times that the Presleys faced, Gladys would always go out of her way to make her boy feel that he wasn't as poor as his circumstances would make it seem. Even if his surroundings were humble, she made him feel he was as good as or better than any man.

Elvis heard his first music when Gladys took him to the small, rickety First Assembly of God Church on Adam Street, in Tupelo, and it was the rousing gospel hymns heard there and at revivalist meetings that Elvis first began to sing.

The following is a description of the birth by a friend of the family:

All along, Gladys, Elvis' mother, told everybody she was going to have twins, but the doctor wasn't having any of it. Elvis was borned. They had done washed him and she said she was still in labor. The doctor didn't think so.

Gladys said, "Well, it's the same pain."

Finally, a neighbor said, "Doctor, there's a baby in there that has to come out of there."

The second child was born dead. "We matched their names, Jesse Garon and Elvis Aaron," Mrs. Presley said years later.

All was not well, for Gladys' muffled scream could be heard through the neighborhood as she fought to give birth. There were two babies, twins all right. Both were boys. As Gladys would say later, "If I'd only been in a hospital, Jesse Garon could have been saved. As it was, he died in birth and Elvis Aaron survived. I always think of what just having a little money could have done for us." She would cry herself to sleep years later, remembering the loss of Elvis' twin. She continues, "That's why Elvis is so dear to us. I also knew that I would never be able to have any more babies. He would be our only one."

"Mrs. Presley talked about her twin babies and she just lived for Elvis. Years later, he called her every night when he was touring, for Mrs. Presley couldn't go to sleep until she had heard from him," says Mrs. Ruby Black, a neighbor.

Elvis recalled that his mother walked him to school until he was 15, although to Evan (Buzzie) Forbes, one of Elvis' closest friends at Humes High School, it wasn't all the time. "That only happened same of the time, most of the time he went with us."

The Presleys had no money for movies or any other form of entertainment, except that of church. "We went most every night to church and always on Sunday," Gladys recalled. "Elvis was such a good little boy, kind and considerate from the start. When he'd see me crying sometimes, for I had misery in my body long after his birth, he would hug my knee and say, 'Mama, someday, I will buy you everything and make you laugh and smile.' He was such a little boy, just 2 when he first started talking to me that way. He was an affectionate little boy, so full of love.

One day Elvis asked Gladys, "What is a mama's boy?" She told him it meant that he was good and that he must always mind his Mama, and he must make her happy. That seemed to satisfy him.

"He brought me bouquets of dandelions," said Gladys. "I loved flowers, and he would help me grow a few from slips I'd get from other people's plants. Sometimes they'd grow and sometimes we didn't have enough water for them. Some of the plants would wither and die. Elvis would comfort me, 'Don't worry, Mama, someday I'll buy you a whole rose garden full of flowers,' and he did."

Elvis himself once said, "Mama never let me out of her sight. I couldn't go down to the creek with the other kids. Sometimes when I was little I used to run off. Mama would whip me and I thought she didn't love me. "

"He was," according to Red West, a friend and bodyguard, "more obsessed with making it as a performer for the sake of his mother than running around screwing everything that walked. More than anything, success meant saying thanks to his mother to show her that all the hard work and sacrifice weren't in vain. Elvis' devotion to his mother and her devotion to him constitutes one of the truly great love stories of our time."

When RCA Victor bought Elvis' contract for the fabulous $35,000, they generously threw in a $5,000 bonus for the young singer. The first thing he did was to go out and spend it all on a pink Cadillac for his mother. It was almost as if he'd had a premonition that she would not be with him much longer. Although the money for others was scarce, the dollars were rolling into Presley's account. The first big paychecks were earmarked for something more important. Elvis wanted to buy his mother a home, a real home.

The mother's love as described by Larry Geller:

Elvis was brought up a "mama's boy." And there is no fiercer love than that evolving out of the maternal instinct. It flourishes in women of every age and description, glowing like a beacon in the perilous night. It is fiercely protective, and nobody, not even the scions of the rich and the privileged, was more completely protected by his mother than Elvis.

He was not allowed to play with other children. And this may have been another reason he gave his tricycle away to make friends when he had none.

His mother took him to school by the hand, almost until high school. He was picked up afterward. As he got older, it was a great embarrassment to him. But it unwittingly established a pattern. All his life, the people around him were protective of him, men as well as women. And he took it for granted, for he knew no other way.

His overprotected childhood developed a deep and abiding shyness in him. In high school, he was regarded as an oddball, because he kept to himself and didn't know how to communicate. He had never learned. He had no peers at home, or in the street.

His mother's overindulgence came from a perfectly natural fear. She had lost Elvis' twin, Jesse Garon, and she didn't want to lose him, literally or figuratively. It was not until Elvis began to sing that he opened up and let something of himself come through. It even affected his appearance. As he developed a stage personality, he suddenly became handsome and appealing. Previously, girls had not found him attractive. He was pasty-faced, and his skin blotched from acne, his sideburns came down below his ears. He wore his collar up, as if trying to hide under a hood. He would daydream in school, picturing himself with his idols, Marlon Brando and Mario Lanza. He would relive their greatest roles, seeing himself on the screen. He could never fancy himself in any ordinary job. Even at a time when he drove a truck after school, for $1.25 an hour, he was strumming on the guitar and singing along with rhythm and blues on the radio, in the security of his room.

At 9, he entered a school talent contest in Tupelo and won third place, with his song about a dog, *Old Shep*. History doesn't record who placed ahead of him. He was initially afraid to get up in front of people, but his burning desire to sing overcame his shyness, in a professional way. He had told nobody about his ambition to become a singer, not even his mother, for he knew people would only have laughed. They had always snickered at him, because he didn't seem to have anything to say. Actually, he was too full of his own dreams to think in terms of anything else. There was a single-mindedness about him that none of the other kids had. They couldn't recognize it, for they had never encountered it before. His teachers and his own father couldn't see it. They were concerned about his future. He seemed to have no special talent for anything, and there was nothing, apparently, he wanted to be. When he was 16, his father, and the teachers, urged him to consider his future, to pick out a vocation by which he could earn a living. It didn't seem that he had any serious purpose.

How could this pimply-faced loner tell them that he was destined to sing before the multitudes? He could look out and almost touch the audiences, and hear the ringing applause. It was all the music he needed, and it kept him going.

He made a couple of homemade records and dedicated them to his all-time favorite person, Mama. She kissed her boy and told him how much she liked them. It would be nice to have him singing around the house, and in church, where she liked to have him next to her. He sang so well at all the church meetings. *That's All Right, Mama* started him out of the doldrums of childhood. He began to express himself musically, and the inhibitions began to roll away. He threw body and soul into his songs. As he branched out musically, he began to express everything that had been bottled up all this time.

Elvis remembers his childhood and mother's loss.

"My Mama never let me out of her sight. I couldn't go down to the creek with the other kids. Sometimes, when I was little, I used to run off. Mama would whip me, and I thought she didn't love me.

We were a religious family, going round together to sing at camp meetings and revivals. Since I was 2 years old, all I knew was gospel music. That music became such a part of my life, it was as natural as dancing. A way to escape from the problems and my way of release.

During the singing, the preachers would cut up all over the place, jumping on the piano, moving every which way."

Elvis talks about his Mother after she dies.

"I used to get mad at Mama once in a while. But I guess a growing boy always does. I was the only child and Mama was always right with me. Maybe she was too good.

I could wake her up in the middle of the night if I was worried about something. She'd get up, fix me a sandwich and a glass of milk, and talk to me; help me figure things out."

"My mother, I suppose because I was an only child, and I was a little closer. I mean, everyone loves their mother, but I was an only child and my mother was always with me, all my life, and it wasn't only like losing a mother. It was like losing a friend, a companion, someone to talk to. I could wake her up any hour of the night and if I was worried or troubled about something, she'd get up and try to help me. I used to get very angry at her when I was growing up, it's a natural thing, isn't it? A young person wants to go somewhere, do something, and your mother won't let you and you think well, what's wrong with you? But later on in years, you find out that she was right, that she was only doing it to protect you and keep you from getting into trouble and getting hurt. And I'm very happy that she was kind of strict.

Before his mother's death, he had said: "I want to entertain people. That's my whole life, to my last breath. More than anything, I want to be a good actor, the kind that is around for a long time. But I don't want to ever stop singing."

"When music starts, I gotta move."

"You seem to be popular enough on your singing and appearance alone. Would you stop the wiggling if criticism grew too vast?"

"No sir, I can't. If I don't move when I sing, I'm dead."

PART III

DEATH

CHAPTER 6

DEATH OF GLADYS AND ELVIS' PSYCHOLOGICAL DEATH

The Symptom Producing Event

Dee Presley describes Elvis' mother's death.

What Elvis remained ignorant of during the first two meteoric years of his career was his mother's poor health. Vernon Presley, knowing Elvis' strong attachment to his mother, managed to successfully conceal Gladys Presley's true condition, which had steadily deteriorated. The long years of night work, overtime, and poor nutrition had left Gladys in poor health to begin with, but the pressures created by Elvis' explosion had only exacerbated it. The fans, reporters, and concern for Elvis had taken its toll, and his increasingly long absences from home left her feeling empty and anxious. She channeled much of her nervousness into eating, but the foods she ate—starchy dishes, eggs, fatty meats, and sweets—only bloated her. The weight problems she developed upset her greatly, because she did not think it was appropriate for the mother of a national celebrity to appear unattractive and fat. She wanted Elvis to be always proud of her, so she took diet pills, but only built up a tolerance. The more she took, the less effective they became, and she grew despondent. In her unhappiness, she began drinking. With deep, dark circles under her eyes, a double chin, and ballooning weight, she appeared terrible in her photographs, but then only drank more. As it became worse, she was frequently ill. When Gladys and Vernon accompanied Elvis to Fort Hood, Texas, for his advanced training, Elvis could see that his mother was in poor health and began to worry. Still, he had no idea how bad the situation was. Her death from a heart attack triggered by acute hepatitis on August 14, 1958, was the shock of his life.

Elvis Presley's life can be seen as one long and dramatic unfolding of tragic ironies. You can combine them into a list, a "List of Ironies" which contributed to his career, his divorce, the last devastating period of his life and, finally, his death. The cruelest and most profound irony on that list is that the most important person in his life died at the very zenith of his success and at the threshold of his manhood, when he was in more of a position than ever before to take care of her and give her everything.

Gladys' death came only several months after Elvis received the very first good critical notices for his performance in *King Creole*. The good reviews had filled him with a deep satisfaction and a sense of accomplishment which stayed with him right up until his mother's sudden death. The contrast of the happiness against the shattering tragedy only jarred him more.

From that moment on, Elvis Presley's entire life was shaded by an inconsolable grief. Grief would make itself felt in virtually everything that he did, in his greatest successes and most abysmal moments of despair. Everything that he was to accomplish in the years to come would be fraught with a feeling that it was somehow transitory and fleeting, that it could just as easily be taken or thrown away.

Now that Elvis was a public figure, his mother's death and funeral at Forest Hill Cemetery became a public event to be exploited by mass media and flashed around the world like any other news item. Dee remembers reading about it in Germany and thinking about how she lost her own mother, wondering if Elvis would bear emotional scars that would plague him in later years. He would, of course, and their effect would be profound. Everyone who knew Elvis then or would come to know him understood that Gladys Presley was the most sensitive subject in his life and stay well away unless Elvis brought it up. He never discussed his mother with anyone except his daddy, and for the rest of his life he would refuse to watch his second film, *Loving You,* in which she appears in the audience. "I will spend my whole life through... loving you," he sings in the film, "winter, summer, springtime, too."

Elvis then receded into whatever anonymity the ranks allowed him, becoming an exemplary GI. When the press learned that he was to sail for a tour of duty in Germany, the Colonel informed them that Elvis would surface in Brooklyn, at his point of embarkation, for a brief press conference. On a sunny day in September, amid much hoopla, Elvis, dressed in khakis, deftly fielded questions, flanked by Colonel Parker, Army brass, and a large contingent from RCA who had arrived to record the event for an LP titled, simply, *Elvis Sails.* The troop ship General Randall stood by waiting to transport him to Bremerhaven, Germany.

"One of the last things Mom said was that Dad and I should always be together," Elvis had said. He confirmed it at the shipyard: "My father and grandmother are following me to Germany in a few weeks; they'll be livin' in a house near the post where I'll be stationed."

"I was an only child," Elvis then said to the reporter who asked for a comment on his mother's death. "She was very close. More than a mother...."

Gladys' death is here described by some of his closest friends.

"August was something else. That was when Elvis' world collapsed like a sand castle into the boiling sea."

"His mother had not been well. It had been difficult for her to walk and to concentrate and to carry on a normal life. She had lost most of her enthusiasm and spirit. (It was at this time that Elvis had been taken away by his fans, and now the Army. Elvis had been her whole life; now she was losing him.)

"Elvis and his father decided that she was too ill to remain in Killeen, she should return to Memphis and the family doctor. Which she did, with Elvis driving her to the train on Friday, August 8. In three days, the doctor placed a call to Elvis in Texas. They said he should come home as quickly as possible."

"Elvis obtained an emergency leave and went against his mother's wishes and boarded an airplane. (She worried that he might get killed in an airplane.) He arrived in Memphis Tuesday night and went right to her bedside. The doctor said his presence improved hcr spirits tremendously but didn't affect the odds much. (Such statements, although meant to be consoling, could very easily produce deeper guilt feelings in a sensitized individual).

The doctor's indirect suggestion is that if he had been there right along, her spirits may have improved sufficiently so that she might have survived, thus sensitizing him even more to her upcoming death.

"Her condition remained serious. All through the night and all day Wednesday and Wednesday evening, Elvis and his father took turns sitting at the bedside. At 3 in the morning, Thursday, Vernon, Elvis' father, was in the hospital room and Elvis was asleep at Graceland. Vernon said his wife began suffering for breath and then she died. Vernon called Elvis and told him what happened.

"Elvis arrived at the hospital in a state of shock. He threw himself across his mother's bed and sobbed convulsively. (Imagine how it would feel to throw yourself across the dead body of the person you love most in the world.) The ability to relate to these feelings will help you in understanding the emotional frame of mind Elvis must have been in at that moment. In fact, if there was any single moment when the change took place, it was probably at this moment. The self-fulfilling prophecies could have been "Oh no, not you...me." or "Let me go in your place," or "Mama, I'm still with you, we cannot be apart, we are together." When he emerged from the hospital, he could only mumble answers to newsmen at the scene.

Back at Graceland, he stood for long moments looking up at the building. Elvis then wandered through the house aimlessly.

In the years to come, Elvis gradually grew into a different person than he had been before his mother's death. People close to him couldn't help speculating that her death had more than a little to do with it.

All she really wanted to do was to make Elvis proud of her. And of course, he was proud of her. But she just kept taking those pills, and drinking ... and finally her old heart gave out.

(At his mother's death, he is reported to have said, "Mama's gone, Red. My Mama's gone, Red. What will I do? I've lost everything. There ain't nothing left to live for. She was everything. Without her, I got nothing. It's all over, man.")

Described by friends, "He never forgets ... everybody breaks up when he loses a mother or a father. With Elvis, I think it was a lot deeper. Suddenly he was a ship without a rudder. (On his mother's tombstone it reads, "She was the sunshine of our home." Sunshine is often equated with life, when the sunshine goes, so does life.)

"Elvis was requested to sing when his interview was held before his trip to Germany. It was an absurd suggestion; Elvis had neither plans nor inclination to play or sing, and there was no guitar around anyway..."

"RCA Victor was frantic. They wanted to keep the ball rolling. They wanted him to cut a disc in Germany. When the idea was hit on the head, they even pleaded with him to sing into an ordinary tape recorder, they would do the dubbing and instrumentals back in New York ... Presley would never be pressured or snowed. No matter how he was harangued to cut more discs, he would politely shake his head and say, "Just take it up with the Colonel." (Meaning Col. Tom Parker, his manager.)

"When they sent to Germany, after his mother's death, Vernon organized a place for them to stay in Bad Nauheim. It was a hotel. Now I have read stories saying this was a luxury hotel. Well, it wasn't. It was called the

Grunewald Hotel, and as I saw it, I knew it wasn't a place for me to stay. It was sort of an outpatient's hotel for heart attack victims. There wasn't anyone there under 60, and every one of them had a foot in the grave and the other on a roller skate," says Red West. "Whenever I went downstairs and saw all of those people who looked like they were going to die, I sort of had second thoughts. This was not the place to have fun, although looking back, we did have a ball. All of us, particularly Elvis."

(We tend to associate with people who are most like us...Elvis has begun associating with people who are likely to die from a heart attack. When you are psychologically dead, you cannot be made uncomfortable.)

"Private Presley was assigned to the scouts in the division. If anyone had speculated that he might have gone into Special Services, they were surprised to hear of his posting, which even in peacetime Germany was the least cushy place in the army."

CHAPTER 7

DRUGS AND THE ARMY

Elvis' upbringing and the influence of his mother's strict morality made drugs alien to his world in the early stages of his career. However, when he served his overseas hitch in the Army, he discovered amphetamines. For a GI at that time, such a discovery was natural and innocent enough. During the Second World War, Benzedrine and Dexedrine had become a way of life for many GIs. Pills were dispensed by the millions to soldiers on the periphery and in combat to keep them up, alert, and moving forward. At least covertly, if not officially, they were still being used by the time Elvis was stationed in Freidberg in 1959, when a sergeant would hand them out before maneuvers, not wanting his men to fall asleep in the cold.

"Elvis told me that he brought back two huge trunks of Dexedrine when he came back from Germany," Rick remembers. "He said it was just to be able to stay up and not for the high. When he had that big bus for those cross-country drives during the '60s, he'd use them for the trips. He enjoyed driving long, long distances—20, sometimes 24 hours nonstop— and he'd do it by himself. That was the beginning."

Elvis was a man of boundless ambitions and mercurial energies. Once he found himself sitting on top of the world, it seemed logical to him that he could stay there and keep going even farther for as long as those energies would last. There was a nervous current of power that pulsed through his life and his body. It caused him to tap and drum and pace about, to want to be always doing something or going somewhere. Onstage, he used to perform his shows like a buzz saw cutting steadily through the trunk of a sequoia tree. It never stopped until his body told him in the plain language of overwhelming fatigue that it had to stop. Then, he would sleep.

There were, during this time, reports of Elvis being killed in automobile accidents and all sorts of other facts that the newspapers somehow knew, but which, fortunately, never happened. Elvis and the guys who were in Germany with him managed to find ways to have a good time in the house they rented. Their pranks resulted in their being asked to leave their first German home, a resort for older people. It seems the management didn't think the older guests appreciated some of the fun and games of the guys.

CHAPTER 8

FIRST "LIVE" APPEARANCE

First live appearance after mother's death.

In February, 1961, he makes a personal appearance at two benefit shows in the Ellis Auditorium in Memphis. It is the first time he has done so since his discharge from the Army, but isn't the good sign that it seems. He wears a white dinner jacket, black trousers, and tie, and this time he doesn't even get moist; he is cool and sophisticated.

A couple of weeks later he flies to Hawaii for another public appearance, this time in Pearl Harbor's Bloch Arena. He can't start for five minutes because of the hysteria, but when he gets going he is very smooth indeed...He sings loud and clear, the backup is excellent, but it is all very much tongue in cheek; he is mocking himself.

From this point onward, the course of his career will defy all effective analysis. Certainly for someone so inherently outrageous, he will show a stunning lack of resistance, a mystifying compliance. (A Walking Zombie, by definition, will show no spirit because in a sense he has "given up the ghost.")

Certainly it is true that Col. Tom Parker doesn't read film scripts, doesn't care for the contents, and will only discuss cash at the conference table; he is that sort of manager. But this still begs the question of why Elvis himself, at the height of his success, and with certainly enough drawing power to call his own shots, seems to hand it all over without a word.

No matter how bad the movies, no matter how low his record sales, he lets it happen with no sign of resistance. He is passive, a living ghost...

These films represent the very nadir of his career, but no one ever works out why he does them. He is obviously under the contract and that must account for something—but even starlets have been known to have temper tantrums. What few understand, and what many can't forgive, is that he never steps forward to complain. (It is interesting to note that in the last movie before his mother's death, *King Creole,* he had his best reviews as an actor. It is said that he had more pride in that movie than anything else he had done.) Stories emerge of his boredom and disgust, but no sign of revolt is forthcoming. He flies in for a fortnight, does his bit, and then gets out; back to study the gilt walls of Graceland and remember better days. It is life in a glass bowl. He has lived with the same people for nearly 30 years and anything beyond them is alien, a world he can't handle. Now it is said, he never looks you in the eye, mumbles his words, keeps his glaze on the floor, then drifts away like the ghost in the mansion, just looking for privacy.

CHAPTER 9

GIVING AND JESSE

The seed was always there. For the Christmas when Elvis was 6 years old, his parents, through much scrimping and saving, bought their pride and joy a shiny red-and-gold tricycle.

Elvis loved it. He rode it up and down the street, to the starry-eyed admiration of the less fortunate youngsters on the block. Vernon and Gladys Presley beamed happily at their son's pleasure. It was well worth the sacrifice.

Then one day the tricycle disappeared.

"Where is your bike?" Gladys Presley asked. "Did you loan it to somebody?"

"No," said young Elvis, hanging his head a little. "I gave it away."

"You gave it away?" She was incredulous.

Vernon was equally taken aback. He shook his head. "I don't understand the boy. He loved to ride it, and yet he gave it away." He went off, still shaking his head, and came back in a few minutes with the tricycle.

"The parents were nice about it," he said. "They understood."

Elvis rode the tricycle down the block once more, and the next day, the tricycle was missing again.

Elvis had found somebody else to give it to.

This time, the Presleys, with a sigh, let him have his way.

"We can't punish him," said Gladys, "because he puts others before himself. It is a good Christian trait."

"I suppose so," said a puzzled Vernon, thinking of all the meals he had skimped on and of his own joy in giving—and not realizing then what a headache Elvis' giving would one day be to him.

It was a psychologist's dream. Elvis was plagued by the notion that he had survived at the expense of his twin. The youngsters on the block were of an age with himself and Jesse Garon. It was as if he was giving that tricycle to the twin that didn't live because of him.

All during his life, he reached out for that brother. But generosity was his second nature. The underdogs of the world, the needy, the shut-ins, the crippled, and the infirm, were quick to move him. It was a throwback to childhood. If his parents had not been so poor, his pregnant mother could have been hospitalized, instead of having the twins at home, without a doctor, and proper sanitary facilities. Jesse Garon might have lived, and Elvis would not have been alone.

But Elvis knew exactly what he was doing. He was paving the way for his own salvation, giving for the lost twin who was always just over his shoulder. He gave away houses, cars, trucks, motorcycles, jewelry, furs, clothing, and money as if they were going out of style. He gave to the poor and needy, bolstered by the admonition from the scripture: "If thou wilt be perfect ... give to the poor, and thou shalt have treasure in heaven."

He also gave to the wealthy. Once, he took a $30,000 diamond ring off his finger and gave it to singer-comedian Sammy Davis, Jr.

"Nobody thinks of giving a rich man anything," he explained. "They're people, too. They like to think somebody thinks of them enough to give them something."

CHAPTER 10

DEATH RISKS

Behind Elvis' attachment to cars was something else, something very special they provided him. Thomas Wolfe, in *Look Homeward, Angel,* called it "the dark storm ... the mad devil's hunger, which all men have in them, which lusts for darkness, the wind, and incalculable speed." Elvis Presley loved the exhilarating, gut-shaking burst of speed on a dark highway with his hands fixed on the wheel of the car, his eyes transfixed on the road, the gas pedal floored, and the speedometer buried. You can call his driving machismo, thrill seeking, racing adventure, or just plain madness; for Elvis Presley, the ultimate challenge was to be able to look death right in the chops and grin. "He would take it to the limit," says Rick, "just to see if he could do it."

Billy illuminates this side of Elvis very well. As resident mechanic and kindred car freak (not 25, he has had 26 cars since the age of 14), he and Elvis often shared those moments together. "He would let me work on the car and then he would get out and just run the hell out of it, " he says. "That's what it all came down to the speed." Elvis was a good driver, says Billy, but those moments doing more than 160 miles per hour with the countryside whizzing past in a blur were still unforgettable.

Elvis and Billy almost bought it one night in Elvis' Pantera. Roaring down the highway outside of Memphis at max speed, they suddenly came upon traffic that was blocking the lanes going in both directions at once. Elvis swerved, went around the right side with hardly any room, then almost lost it into a spin. "Oh, shit, I kept saying to myself; he knows what he's doing!"

Elvis also liked to "take it to the max" on a chopper, and Billy often went along. "It was a very hairy feeling, man," he says. "I'd always get on my bike thinking, 'Well, am I gonna die this time or what?' We'd be going down the damn expressway at 120 miles an hour, and that's pretty damn fast for two wheels. Elvis would take his hands off the handlebars—doin' 120—just let 'em go and start flapping his arms up and down real slow like a bird! If you were behind him, it looked like he was flying."

How did the police react when they saw Elvis streaking down Highway 55 at the speed of light? It didn't happen that often, says Billy, because the joyrides took place at night. "When they would pull him over and see who it was," says Bill, "they'd wave and say, 'Oh, that's just Elvis. We let him do what he wants. If he wants to kill himself on the highway, that's his business.'" Sometimes Elvis would be pulled over by a well-meaning cop: "Y'all like to slow down a bit?" "Okay, officer, sorry," would be the Boss's response. Then we'd start busting ass as soon as they left," says Billy.

David remembers Elvis's dune-buggy rides along the silvery beaches of the California coast. Elvis would go full blast up the side of a large dune, shooting the buggy straight into the air at an almost 90-degree trajectory before it would come crashing back onto the sand and racing off, spinning wheels and spewing sand everywhere. He was just as wild on his snowmobiles, gliding across pastures and down mountainsides high above Vail, Colorado.

PART IV
RESURRECTION

CHAPTER 11

MARRIAGE, MOTHER, AND PRISCILLA (SIE)

Larry Geller describes Elvis' attitude about Priscilla, his mother, and polygamy.

Elvis took his father's hand. "Daddy," he said, "I'm glad you're married and aren't alone anymore. It doesn't mean you don't still love Mama. I know you love her like I do, and always will. But Mama would understand. She would want you to marry again, and be happy. She would have been the first to say go ahead. I know that."

Vernon needed to hear that; it made it all right, as all right as it could be, when the wife of 27 years never left his thoughts. Elvis made a discovery of his own. He discovered that the girl one thought of when he was not with her was the one he could not get over. He had nearly every girl he ever wanted, and now he wanted Priscilla.

Elvis was essentially a one-woman man. Which, to Elvis, meant that he had one special girl he could always fall back on, when he was tired of playing the field.

He hadn't been allowed to play with the other kids as a child, and now he wanted to play, but he still needed a mother to go home to.

That mother figure, ironically, had become a now 16-year-old girl—the blossoming Priscilla. Even then they seemed to blend so well. Everybody remarked on their facial resemblance. They were known as the "looka-likes." Elvis gloried in this physical similarity, thinking it showed how much alike they were.

"Things just don't happen without cause," Elvis argued. "There is a reason why people met each other, and why they love one another. Regardless of the age difference, Priscilla and I have a very special influence on each other's lives."

There was a side to him no one woman could satisfy for any length of time. He was like a kid in a candy store, surrounded by an enticing variety of sweets. He could equate polygamy with his new spirituality, pointing out that the elders of Israel had many wives, and Solomon's wives were like the grains of sand. While he thought of Priscilla as his wife in spirit, he showed no haste to get married. First, she was too young to know her own mind, and then he had to be sure, not only for his sake but for hers. He was afraid he would cut himself off from his fans, and, incredibly, from his own entourage.

"After all," he said to Larry, "Jesus never married and he had 12 guys around him, and they wandered all over the country together."

"Besides, I'm committed to Priscilla," he said, "and someday I'll live up to my commitment. Priscilla reminds me of my mom. She wants to be a mother and raise children.

"Yes, Mom would have loved Priscilla. She's her kind of girl, down to earth and practical, who wants nothing more than marriage and kids. " His face suddenly brightened and he took Larry's hand, pumping it up and down. "Just think of having a child, what a blessing that would be. Do you know that Priscilla's the only girl I ever met I would want to have a baby with?" He smiled radiantly. "I want two, a boy and a girl, whichever is first doesn't matter."

They discussed the ceremony. Larry learned to his surprise that he was to be one of three best men, along with Marty Lacker and Joe Esposito. To Elvis, it was just another detail: "Three wise men—an Italian and two Jews."

They were married on May 1, 1967, in a civil ceremony in a Las Vegas hotel, the Aladdin.

Their daughter, and only child, Lisa Marie, was born the following February, nine months later to the day.

Before Elvis married, he said, "Whenever I marry it will be a very sure thing—to be forever, like my Mama and my Daddy. I'll have a big church wedding and do it up proper, with flowers and music and the whole thing. Mama and I used to talk about a big church wedding. She wanted me to have one because she had never had one. She and my Daddy went off and got married by themselves and told their families afterwards. They were all so poor, they didn't want to put anyone to any expense. No one could afford wedding clothes or wedding presents." (Here he clearly states that getting married is important to him, because of a promise that he has made to his mother.) He continues, "Mama realized she'd never have a daughter to dress up and she'd often talk about my wedding and how she'd love me to marry and give her that daughter and some grandchildren." (Here he makes the promise to give her a child.)

"When Elvis met Priscilla, his wife to be, she was quite young, age 15. Elvis thought of her already as one of the family. "She's like the little kid sister I never had." Viewing the relationship this way, it is easy to understand why it began: to give to his mother that which she could no longer have, a daughter. When she became old enough for marriage it would become confusing to Elvis, but he married her anyhow, gave birth to Lisa, and then lost interest in Priscilla, just as if she were put back to the stage of sisterhood again.

The wedding did not take place at all like he had hoped it would. In fact, it began in the middle of the night.

One night, April 30, 1967, and into May l, the next morning, Elvis and Priscilla, her parents, her brothers, and sisters arrived from Palm Springs at 3 a.m. in Elvis' Learjet. At 4 a.m., Elvis got the license at the courthouse. There was no need of blood tests and waiting 24 hours; marriages were instant on request.

In a phone conversation with Red West, he tried to explain why he hadn't invited Red. "That wedding thing, I had nothing to do with that, that was railroaded through. I didn't even know who was there in that little room the size of a bathroom with a Supreme Court justice." (Hardly a church wedding.) "It was there and done so quickly I didn't realize I was married. I could see it back then, but that wasn't my doing." (The decision to marry was made late at night, at least that is when the activity begins. Perhaps Elvis was on one of his nocturnal visits to his mother, he recalls his promise, and is in the process of carrying that promise out.) "I had nothing to do with ... you know. All of a sudden I was getting married. When you go through that you keep your mind on one thing." (Most people would keep their mind on getting married. Was Elvis' mind someplace else, with his mother?)

CHAPTER 12

BIRTH OF LISA (SIE)

When she was born, Elvis said, "The baby's a girl. Lisa Marie. I'm the happiest man in the whole world!" (This part of the promise is fulfilled. You may wonder, but what if it had been a boy? According to Becky Yancey, it would have been named John Baron—which sounds a lot like Jesse Garon.) Now, he will say, "Lisa is my life—my very own. She is all that I have that is personal and private for me. Everything else about me, and including me, is for everyone—for the fans and people who enjoy my work. But for my baby, that's a different matter! Lisa means more to me than life. She is my life."

With the birth of Lisa, Elvis starts to make his comeback and to see less and less of Priscilla. Priscilla was to say that at one point, Elvis looked at her, said that she had grown up, and that she knew it was over. She did not know why, she just knew that it was.

Dee describes the birth of Lisa.

Elvis stayed around Graceland the entire last month of the pregnancy, and on the morning of February 1, 1968, exactly nine months to the day from their marriage, Priscilla was taken to Baptist Memorial Hospital by Elvis and Charlie Hodge, followed in another car by Jerry Schilling and Joe Esposito. Reporters began swarming outside the hospital once they got wind of Priscilla's admission. Inside, Elvis' friends and relatives began to gather. At 5:01 that afternoon, Dr. T. A. Turftan informed Elvis that he was the father of a 6-pound, 15-ounce baby girl. Dee remembers walking down to the maternity ward with Vernon and Elvis for their very first look at Lisa Marie Presley. The three of them stood there for a moment, the two men gazed, as Dee began rapping on the glass cooing, "Well, hello there, little girl ... That is your daddy!"

"She just picked up her head a little and looked at us with those blue eyes," says Dee, "and Elvis' face lit up like a beacon. I've never seen him look like that in all the time I've known him."

CHAPTER 13

THE COMEBACK – REINCARNATION

Shortly after Lisa's birth, Elvis appears at the Hotel International in Las Vegas. At this show, he will say, "This is my first live appearance in nine years. I've appeared dead before, but this is my first live one."

According to Red West, "When Elvis first went to the Hilton International in Las Vegas, there were nights when I sat up all night, just sitting by the window, while Elvis was asleep. I just stayed there because I was scared as hell that he would walk in his sleep and jump out of the window; it was a genuine fear."

PART V

MARRIAGE AND DIVORCE: A CRUSHING BLOW

CHAPTER 14

MARRIAGE AND DIVORCE: A CRUSHING BLOW

Marriage, life, and divorce as described by Marty Lacker.

Elvis and Priscilla seemed to fall more in love each day and after the wedding and the birth of Lisa Marie, he was a very happy man. There is no question in my mind as to how much Elvis loved Priscilla and how much she loved him. They were right for each other and, had Elvis been in another business, I honestly believe theirs would have been a perfect marriage.

The success of the movies and then the tours demanded more and more of Elvis' time. Priscilla would sometimes travel with him, but she didn't want to be a problem and he was really more comfortable being alone when on tour. Lisa, for all the enjoyment she brought, was born a short nine months after the marriage, and neither Elvis nor Priscilla wanted their baby raised in a suitcase.

Even with all his modern music, Elvis was a very old-fashioned man, and he wanted his wife and their child at home when he returned from work. Unfortunately, there were times when there would be six to eight weeks between the time he left for work and when he returned. The long periods of separation began to erode their marriage.

It just wasn't the life for a vibrant young woman like Priscilla. She wanted to see the world, be a part of it and make it a part of her.

Elvis was very possessive and protective when it came to any girl he cared about, and he was especially so with Priscilla. She wanted to be able to get out and do things, but for a while Elvis wouldn't let her, unless he or one of the guys were along.

Things gradually began to change. Priscilla started to take dancing lessons and became quite good at it. Because of her dancing talents and her agility, Elvis suggested that she begin taking karate lessons. She began the karate lessons and started going on shopping trips to New York and Dallas with one of the guys' wives. She was doing anything to break the monotony of being home alone while Elvis was away.

The trips became more frequent, as did the karate sessions, and we began to hear rumors that Priscilla was being seen a lot in the company of Mike Stone, her karate instructor. Elvis brushed off the rumors and didn't seem to think much about them until it became obvious that there was more involved than karate.

The marriage was falling apart without either of them knowing why and without either of them knowing what they would have to do to keep each other. Their love didn't seem to change, but they were unable to go on together.

One night when I was visiting Elvis at one of his California homes, we were standing outside talking. Elvis, almost a broken man, told me, "Moon, Priscilla is leaving me. I love her and she loves me, but she says she isn't happy. She wants to leave and I don't know what to do. I don't want to lose her."

There were tears in his eyes and in mine, when I said, "Elvis, are you going to change? Are you ready to stop traveling and spend more time with her?"

"No," he said. "Moon, I just can't."

"You can't?"

"No, Moon, I can't. I just couldn't live without performing."

"Then you're going to have to accept it, Elvis. You're just going to have to accept it no matter how much it hurts."

I still can't figure it out, and I don't believe anyone else can either, including Priscilla or Elvis, while he was alive. The only thing I know for sure is that they still loved each other when he died.

Elvis after his divorce, as his stepbrother recalls.

Elvis seemed resilient in the aftermath of his divorce, but he had a way of concealing his true emotional and psychological state. Rick's impressions were that he was dazed at first but then found release in his work, throwing himself headlong into a series of 30-day tours. "Elvis seemed like a cat," he says, "who would come back and land on his feet, ready to handle it. He didn't express guilt, but he knew that he blew it, because he did. But he was a man: His attitude was, 'You've got to go on—you can't sit around and feel sorry for yourself.' There were moments when it played heavily on his mind, but as far as letting you know how he felt, he controlled it. He let very few people in on what was really going on inside."

As when he had suffered the loss of his mother, Elvis turned once again to the one person he confided in during a time of inconsolable emotional loss: his daddy. "Don't ask questions" was the order of the day. "Just keep rolling." "Sometimes he'd wake up thinking about her, and you could tell how he felt," David says. "But Elvis and Priscilla were sacred. If Elvis was upset, you knew why."

Elvis was the sort of person who didn't readily allow people into his life to begin with, but once he opened to a person to a level where love was possible, that person became a part of his soul, a permanent part of his emotional life. This is what made the loss of Priscilla so hard to take. Like the tree that is cut down and dragged away, she may have left him, but the taproot still remained. The realization that his wife had left him for another man was shattering to his ego, but the emotional effects of the divorce went far deeper than that. Elvis' dreams for a family and for being a complete father to his daughter had also vanished.

Many people have asked if he loved her so much, how could he have taken her for granted? How could he have defeated himself? Elvis' divorce can only be understood within the context of the devastating effects of his mother's death on his emotional life. Gladys Presley had been the one person whom he'd offered his unfettered love, and her death had taught him the bittersweet truth about love between people, whether they be man and woman or mother and child: There can be no love without pain and loss. When Elvis sobbed, "Oh, God, my whole world is gone!" at his mother's funeral, propped up by friends as the newsmen of the world vied for his statement, he meant it much more literally than one might think. Gladys' death left Elvis with powerful questions, normal enough for a child to feel after the loss of a loving parent. But Elvis lived the rest of his life wary of the vulnerability necessary for true emotional intimacy, afraid to love as fully as he knew he could because he neither wanted to lose that love nor have it rejected. With all of his money, his career, the Next In Line, and his boys to do his bidding, it became all too easy for him to evade this problem and substitute "things" for feelings. He became, in plain truth, a deeply emotional man who became emotionally impaired, constrained, and blocked. He learned to impose his own needs and standards on others, sometimes intentionally, sometimes unintentionally. He hurt many of the people dearest to him because they loved him the most.

The experience of divorce entrenched Elvis more solidly in some of his most basic attitudes about life. Things seemed more transient and expendable than ever to him, but his romantic advice to his brothers smacks of his true feelings. He cared about them and wanted to spare them the same kind of pain. "Protect your heart," he always told them when they sought his advice. "Don't get so wrapped up in one person so that if she leaves you, your whole world crumbles."

With all of its concomitant publicity, people have become used to considering Elvis' divorce as the crucial turning point in his life, as that point when his life and career went into a tailspin and started going to pieces. While it may have removed restraints on his self-destructive behavior, it is unfair and untrue to blame his decline lock, stock, and barrel on his divorce, no matter how convenient it may be for purposes of biography or journalism. It wasn't a precipitous fall, for one thing, but a gradual decline rooted in many complicated factors, done as only Elvis could have done something.

Understanding "what really happened" to Elvis Presley requires looking far beyond and much deeper than the sensationalized outbursts reported by his discarded bodyguards and into his internal life, which he guarded more carefully than anything. Such an awareness, facile as it may seem or sound, is the only thing that can even begin to explain how Elvis Presley, a man who appeared to the American public as the have-not who grew up to have everything, a man of boundless spirit, depth, talent, dignity, and compassion, could spend his last years in unspeakable emotional loneliness, taking drugs, hurting many of those that loved him most; a man who didn't care, as Rick puts it, "if snuff went for nine dollars a dip."

Larry Geller talks about Elvis after his divorce.

Larry could see the mist in his eyes. "When Priscilla left me, it was my lowest point since my mother's death." He pointed to the books strewn over the floor. "Those books saved me from going mad. It was like having my insides torn apart. At first, I blamed others, I screamed and shouted. But I knew I was to blame. A small voice within kept me on the truth. I was shattered. But I retained my sanity. God wouldn't permit me to go over the line. I give all credit to Him."

He reached over and squeezed Larry's hand. "During my darkest hours I thought of you. For, of all the people I know, Larry, you stood for what Jesus meant when He said, 'Seek ye first the Kingdom of Heaven.'"

CHAPTER 15

LINDA THOMPSON EVALUATED

Linda Thompson as described by Dee Presley and her three sons.

"She couldn't have come at a better time in Elvis' life," Rick says fondly. "He was hurtin' from the divorce, needing someone, a kind of woman who could be a lot of different things."

Beauty-queen tall (5'8"), with long, shapely, strong-looking legs and the classic 36-23-36 proportions of the "girl next door" that Hugh Hefner had in mind when he prepared Playboy magazine for the hungry eyes of the American male (she, of course, never posed for the publication), Linda Diane Thompson generated enough force to register a 10 on the Richter Scale. A junior English major at Memphis State, she became the 1972 Miss Tennessee in the annual Miss Universe pageant and then met Elvis Presley; needless to say, she never went back for her diploma.

For close to the next five years, she was Elvis Presley's girlfriend, traveling companion, lover, confidante, comedienne, and co-conspirator in practical jokes. If ever a woman deserved to wear both the TCB and TLC logos on a single chain around her neck, it was Linda.

She is, of course, a beguilingly beautiful woman. Her neck is long and elegant, and the face is that of the model actress with a touch of the farm girl. The cheekbones are high and prominently chiseled, the mouth wide with sensuous, ample lips and perfect rows of pearly teeth. The eyes are a warm, smiling brown and the hair, which has been honey blond at times, is a natural soft brown. With her skin a movie star tan and caparisoned in gossamer blouses or leggy pants and high boots or haute couture dresses with heels, watch out.

Beauty may have brought about her entree into Elvis' life, but beauty alone was never enough to sustain a woman's presence in his life for more than, say, a month.

Linda also had a beauty of the soul and spirit, humor and compassion. Best of all to Elvis, she was a real Southern lady, a Memphis belle with an accent as sweet as honeysuckle who began sentences with things like "Well, bless his little heart" and turned her nose disdainfully away from the unpleasantness of foul language. Rick, who has seen all of them come and go, explains what made her so special: "She was by far the closest to Elvis besides Cilla," he says, "because she was a Southern girl, you know. High morals, but easygoing, and she had a very big heart—that is why Elvis respected her so much. You know, a lot of girls down South still won't go to bed with you unless you promise marriage, and Linda was a virgin when she met Elvis. I really don't know if Elvis promised to marry her; I don't know anything about marriage discussed between them. I'm sure they did, but I don't know what the deal was, but you know, Elvis was brought up in the old school, and he felt very lucky to have somebody like that."

Marriage proposals notwithstanding, Linda moved into Graceland with Elvis and became his steady, live-in girlfriend. For quite a while, the relationship suited them both perfectly. Linda had aspirations of her own; she wanted to break into the movie and television labyrinth of Hollywood. Elvis, of course, showered her with credit cards, cars, clothes, a home, anything else that she my have wanted. Linda was certainly aware of the benefits afforded by her relationship with Elvis. But unlike scores of other girls who have known him (carnally or otherwise), her opportunism and knowledge of how he could open doors for her was always tempered by a very deep love that she developed for the man. Like all of the other women in his life, at first she aroused the suspicions and mistrust of those around Elvis. Their first inclination toward any new woman in his life was to see her as an empty-headed, gold-digging chick with plenty of looks but only a credit-card mentality who was using Elvis —"going for a buck"—and would be discarded in several weeks' time like a used Kleenex tissue. Linda was very different, and she proved it.

"She was a fantastic woman and still is," observes Rick, "loved and re-spected by my family, by Cilla, by just about everybody. Linda stayed with Elvis even more than his own wife, and it was a good thing because she was really good for the man. You know, she could have had what she wanted and pulled out long ago, but she hung in there because she cared, and let me tell you something, being Elvis' girlfriend is heavy. You do what he does and that's it. She did it for five years—traveled with him, took care of him, and a lot of credit has to go to that girl, because she would have done anything for him."

Linda was a Gemini lady like Priscilla, Dee, and Grandma Presley, but her personality was markedly different from Priscilla's in that she was more easygoing, less strong-willed (Dee's opinion), had more of a sense of humor (David's), and was, on the whole, much more flamboyant in dress and appearance. She came along at a time in Elvis' life when he needed a woman who could play many different roles, determined by his mood of that particular moment. She fit the bill. She could cheer him up when he was down, mother him when he needed solace, indulge him, sit and discuss books and religion, share his interests, and then, like a chameleon, transform herself from a buddy into a sexy, mature woman to become his lover. Her awareness of his drug problem caused her to guard him when he took his sleeping medication at night. If he got up, she got up, and if something was wrong, she was always there. Linda also loved Lisa and they got along beautifully whenever she visited; the feeling was quite mutual on Lisa's part, and Linda and Priscilla became good friends.

Aside from being with Elvis, which was sometimes as much a job as a pleasure for her, the most obvious reciprocation of all that she put into their relationship was Elvis' offer to buy her parents a home in White-haven, which he did, and his invitation to her brother Sam to become one of his personal bodyguards. She was also written up and photographed, traveled, vacationed, bejeweled with beautiful stones, and outfitted with a wardrobe that rivaled any woman's. But was she happy? When it came to the emotional bottom line of their relationship, Elvis bridled at commitment and sought safety, once again, in numbers. He felt most comfortable leaving their relationship in that ill-defined state between a commitment and a more "open" relationship. "Elvis told me that he wanted to start dating other chicks," says Rick. "He was going to get Linda her own home so he could have whatever chicks he wanted over to his house in Memphis. I think he really loved her in his way, but you know, one of Elvis' theories was that you gotta get away. Women can't understand things like that, and I don't think Linda could either."

Whether she could or couldn't, she swallowed her pride and sometimes came along on the dates with other women as his friend before she, too, began to stray. After so many years, the relationship began to meander. "Linda really loved Elvis," offers Dee, who also harbors a strong love for her. "I think she would have loved him even if he hadn't been 'Elvis,' the great star. I think the reason they split up is because she saw that they would never get married, and after all those years, she gave up hope."

"Linda was getting into that same cage that Elvis was in," elaborates Rick. "You know—withdrawn, not getting out much, just falling into the same thing as the guy. She's a young, beautiful woman—26, 27 years old—and she needed to get out and see what was going on in the rest of the world instead of getting locked in by Elvis. She'd been around for five years and she really cared, but she had to get out, and you know what? It's a good thing that she did, because nobody can live like that. No woman could live up to the standards that Elvis wanted; they'd go nuts. They'd get to that point where they didn't know what day or city it was anymore, where they weren't able to even get out for a walk."

Gradually, though they remained the best of friends, Linda and Elvis phased each other out of their lives. "It was no real big traumatic breakup thing," says Rick. "They both just kind of bowed out gracefully." But with Linda gone, Elvis seemed more alone than ever before. Another very special woman, she ended up being taken for granted just like Priscilla. The friendship, warmth, and understanding she added to his life were gone, abandoned for the Next in Line. She had no choice but to move on. Had she stayed in his life as his girlfriend or maybe even his wife, she might not have been potent enough to turn his life around (he was already falling into the bad patterns when they met), but David and Rick both think that she would have made a big difference on that fateful August morning when Elvis rose from his bed and stumbled into his bathroom to meet his Maker.

The Boss seemed to age more rapidly after Linda's departure, which also seemed to coincide with an upswing in health problems and drugs. There were still women to occupy his time, but they lost meaning quickly and rarely held his interest for long. It was as if someone had pulled the plug on his libido. Sure, there were still brief flings, affairs galore, flirtations and encounters both during and after Linda. Elvis was spotted with the likes of blond and willowy Cybill Shepherd and a gorgeous model from Chicago named Sheila Ryan, who later became Mrs. James Caan. Then Ann Pennington and Mindy Miller waltzed forth, performed a brief fandango with the Boss, and twirled away, as did many others. "He was lonely," says Rick, "He tried to kill it with companionship. He may have been 40, but he was pushing 70 and just wanting to relax. If there was any way he just could have lived comfortably, it might have added years to his life, but you've got to realize how much he loved his work. "

As written in the July 1980 issue of McCall's Magazine:

His whole life had been a study in irony. He was the man who stood for rebellion, yet worshiped his mother with such intensity that at her funeral, when he was 23, he had sobbed inconsolably, saying, "My whole world is gone." And he had been desired by millions of women, yet loved just two women for an enduring time, and both had left him. Priscilla Beaulieu had been his wife. Linda Thompson lived with him after his marriage, for four and a half years. She left him eight months before he died and moved to Los Angeles to begin the acting career she had put aside, at his request, when they met in 1972.

As a rule, Linda Thompson says little about Elvis Presley. "People aren't interested in what they can learn from life," she says. "They're more interested in the sensational aspects, in saying, 'Oh, Elvis Presley, he did that?' But, there are some lessons to be learned from Elvis' life that might benefit other people and, in that sense, it's worth talking about him."

She was not prepared for Elvis' humor, which was sharp, continual, and often self-directed. "I was also touched by his spiritual sense. He realized there was a purpose to our existence, that we weren't just here by chance. And he felt that he had a special spiritual mission. We had a real camaraderie. And I adored him. I don't think there'll ever be a meeting of souls like it, because there's not another soul like that."

He never chose his own movies, those 31 versions of what was essentially the same story. They were, he once said, movies in which "a Southerner beats up a guy, and then sings to him."

Galvanized perhaps by his marriage in 1967, and the birth of his daughter nine months later, in June 1968, he walked out in front of an audience for the first time in eight years.

He wore gold-lined capes. He was preceded onstage by a chorus of heavenly voices and the theme from 2001. In another performer it would have been pretension bordering on the delusional. But he was the King.

Then his wife, Priscilla, left in January 1972. He told a friend, "Entertaining is my life. I thought she understood that when she married me. I love making people happy, and here my own life is going to be wrecked and unhappy." While his analysis neglected to mention the numerous other women he had made happy while not onstage, it was entirely accurate in terms of what it said about Elvis Presley and entertaining. To perform was reinforced by his fans, who loved to see and hear this man who loved to sing. He had come to depend on receiving this love as much as he depended on giving it, and there are those who maintain that all the things performing entailed kept him alive and then, finally, killed him. But in

July 1972, on the night he met Linda Thompson, he was, to all appearances, still a graceful rider of the wave.

Yet he was already taking those pills he got from doctors' prescriptions which were euphemistically described by everyone around him as his "sleeping medication." In early 1972, his pill taking increased, the dissolution of his marriage seeming to dissolve also whatever restraints he may have previously placed on his behavior. He had had a mother who wanted him to be good, and a wife who needed him to be. Along with his daughter, they had been the most important people in his life. Now they were all gone, and though he would continue to see his daughter for long and frequent visits and to adore her, it would never be quite the way he must have wanted it to be. Until then, he had controlled his use of drugs, but now he may have felt, Why try anymore? In any case, he was soon to find his drugs controlling him. In that sense, by the time he met Linda Thompson, it was already too late. And three years later, two years before he died, he would record a song he may have understood all too well. The song was *Pieces of My Life.* It goes: "I found all the sad parts, but I guess I threw the best parts away."

Later, when he was performing infrequently, they were often alone for weeks at a time. They would stay in his room and talk about their thoughts and feelings. "On stage I might be this sex symbol, " he said, "but when I close the door, I'm just a little baby, I like reverting back to just being a child." He called her Mommy. She called him Buntom. Sometimes she called him Baby.

While they were upstairs in his room, his friends were always downstairs. These were the men called "The Memphis Mafia," and they were, Linda says, "his social friends and family, but he didn't discuss things with them. He did that with me. I think I was his best friend in the world. He unloaded everything on me, even his anger." Often, when he was upset, he would rant at her. But then he would say, "I'm sorry, honey, it's not you I'm angry at." And he would explain a complaint he had against a friend or his manager, Colonel Tom Parker. After that he would say, "You always hurt the one you love, the one closest to you. But I know you'll love me and understand."

"When I was a boy," he had said in 1971, "I was the hero in the comic books and movies. I grew up believing in a dream. Now I've lived it out." But a year later he said, "The image is one thing, the human being is another… It's very hard to live up to an image."

Throughout his life he had been overly protected and sheltered. From the moment he was born, his mother had showered him with love. She had walked with him to school every day. She had insisted he carry his own eating utensils. He had slept in the same bed with his parents until he was grown. A few years after that, he had become a 21-year-old millionaire and a star. "After he got rich," Linda says, "he let his daddy take care of everything, so he never even knew how much money he made. 'Daddy'll handle it. Daddy'll take care of it, Daddy'll fire him,' he always said. He just put it all in his daddy's lap. In so many ways he never did grow up. He remained a little child, and he really did need a mother."

"He was acutely sensitive to life," she says, "so much so that it was difficult for him to filter out thoughts and ideas and feelings. When he wanted to go to sleep, he couldn't shut his thoughts off. I think what he tried to do with the sleeping pills was just dull his mind."

In an interview on Elvis' 40th birthday, she had said, "There have been heartless, cruel, vicious rumors that have persisted about Elvis using drugs. Why, Elvis is a federal narcotics officer! Three years ago former President Nixon issued Elvis a federal agent's badge." At that same time, in private, she would tell him, "You're taking too many pills," and then she would cry and say, "You're going to kill yourself." "Mommy, just relax," he would answer. "I want to see Lisa grow up and to watch her little kids, and I'm going to live to be an old, old man."

But then one day she said to him, "What do you think your biggest failing is?" He said, "I'm self-destructive." "You do recognize that?" she asked. "I recognize it," he answered, "but there's not a lot I can do about it."

Two weeks after his 40th birthday in January 1975, Elvis went into a severe depression. For four days, he seemed barely aware of his existence. His eyes were badly swollen. Once or twice he managed to get out of bed and stumble downstairs. At this point, Linda says, "I literally felt responsible for his life. Because when you take sleeping pills it's easy to wake up in the middle of the night and not realize you're still essentially asleep even though your mind is working. You think you're awake and you reach over and take another sleeping pill. So every time he rolled over in bed, I had geared myself to wake up and make sure he was okay. I didn't ever sleep well at night. It was like caring for a newborn baby."

Linda was asked to give a deposition in his favor. Despite the arguments she had had with him, she had liked Dr. Nick, as he was called, and felt sorry for him. She felt he had loved Elvis and had thought he was helping him by dispensing drugs to him and, in the process, ostensibly keeping an eye on every drug he took. But she could not give testimony that would help him. And she told Dr. Nick's lawyers that she would not testify for him, because she did not want to hurt him.

When she began to live with Elvis, she had gone one Sunday to the Pentecostal Church of which his family had been members. "I wanted to discover more fully where he had come from," she explains. She had been shocked by what she found there. "These people would get up and literally wallow in the aisles. He was used to that sort of freedom, to that explosion of the senses. Elvis' moods were intense. He ran the emotional gamut over and over—the highest highs, the lowest lows, and you ran it with him.

"He was a complete paradox. He was either like a little angel that had dropped out of heaven or like the devil incarnate. There was very little in between. He could be the tenderest soul, and then turn around and just be wicked and cruel and devastating." Once, when she had seen him do something spectacularly generous for a stranger and then, just afterward, begin to berate a friend viciously, she had thought, Is this the man I just saw buy that woman a house and cry with her?

During that period he had begun to say repeatedly: "I feel intensely lonely at heart." Then she would say, "But, honey, think of all the people in this world who adore you. They know who YOU are, and they love you." "Not in a personal way," he would say. "Not like Grandma loves me or

Daddy does or you do. They love Elvis Presley with all the sequins." She didn't agree. "I think they saw in him a real depth of character."

"My heart used to bleed for him," she says. "He was so vulnerable, so tender, he had such a terrific capacity for love. And I felt very protective of him. I felt he needed me so much and was so dependent on me. After a while it drained me. I was really depleted. In the beginning we had an all-encompassing relationship: We were lovers, friends, brother and sister, daddy and little girl, mommy and baby." But now she woke up each time he moved in the bed, and had to care for him in the most basic ways. "I felt more and more that he depended on me for his very existence. I felt the mommy-and-baby relationship starting to take over."

It was not a surprising transition, for he had always had one form or another of such a relationship in his life. The first had been with his own mother, and he had, of course, been the baby. Then she had died, and shortly afterward he met the woman he would marry. At the time, he was 24 and she was 14, and accounts of their relationship indicate that at first, at least, he had very much wanted to be her parent. With Linda Thompson, he was the baby again.

It had not always been that way. In 1968, when he was fighting to be taken seriously again, after the years of silly movies, the Colonel had wanted him to do his comeback television show clad in a tuxedo and singing 25 Christmas songs. The producer had wanted a more abrasive, sexier show, and he got it, because Elvis had sided with him. Now it seemed that conviction and spirit had left him. Later, many people told Linda that *A Star Is Born,* which had the strong, dramatic part Elvis had always said he yearned for, might have put some challenge back into his life. But he was not willing to fight for it, and that seems ominous to Linda now. "It makes me think that Elvis had really just given up a long time ago."

In February 1976, Elvis Presley walked into the recording studio he had set up in his home in Memphis. It was to be the last time he would record enough material for an album. He recorded 12 songs in a week. One was *Danny Boy,* which had been his mother's favorite song. There was a similarity among the other 11 songs, and it may be significant because, although he did not write his own material, the songs he chose to sing often reflected his state of mind. Some songs recorded in those sessions were *Hurt, I'll Never Fall in Love Again, The Last Farewell,* and *Blue Eyes Crying in the Rain.*

"I knew he was very much a victim of life, but even if we are victimized, that's our own burden to carry, our own load to bear. I couldn't live his life for him."

"He had grown so used to his ways, to the strange hours and to darting in and out of service elevators and garbage routes, that it had become a normal way of life for him. He didn't see it as bizarre, so he saw very little reason to change it." There had been a time, not long before she decided to leave, when she said to him, "I'd just like to whisk you up in my arms and take you away to the country." He had laughed and said, "Well, what the hell for?" "To get you away from all this." He had turned serious. "Hey," he had said, "it's my life." She didn't trust her ability to tell him she was leaving. And so to say goodbye she wrote him a long letter, explaining why she felt she had to go. Then she wrote, "I don't think I'll ever love this way again, but in all honesty I don't want to. I've already known the pain of too much tenderness."

His drug taking increased after she left. And so, apparently, did his depression. Still, in those last eight months of his life, he continued to perform. His health was failing. He had eye trouble, colon trouble, and a severe water-retention problem. His father's health was failing, too, and it frightened him. A book about him, written by three of his former bodyguards, was soon to be published and would reveal details of his drug taking. What seemed to concern him most about the book was its potential effect on his daughter. In his last month, Ginger Alden recalled that Elvis spoke of Jesse Garon, his twin brother who was born dead. Elvis had said that sometimes when one twin dies, the survivor takes on his mental power and becomes twice as powerful as he might normally be. One night Elvis had gone to the closet and taken out a large picture of his parents with himself, at the age of 3, standing between them. He had placed the picture on a chair, then asked, "Does that bother you?" When Ginger said it didn't, he had left it there day and night.

She remembers his apprehension about the tour in August, the tour he never made. He had not performed since June. He had been heavy then; now he was heavier. He talked about going to a spa, but didn't. "I'm lazy," he had said, "unless someone kicks me." Then one day he was looking through his costumes, none of which fit. He had said, almost to himself, "I've been off too long."

She also remembers when he took her to his trophy room, which contained, among other things, the gold records he had been given for each of his songs that had sold over a million copies. He had been awarded so many that they were just scattered around, and he had long ceased counting them. She remembers his looking slowly around the trophy room. "Sometimes," he had said, "it's like all this happened to somebody else." Linda Thompson was in her Los Angeles apartment when her phone rang that afternoon; the caller was Elvis' daughter, Lisa Marie. Lisa was out of breath, sobbing. "My daddy's dead. My daddy's dead." "No, honey, he's not." "Yes, he is, he died in the bathroom. No one knows about it yet except us here at Graceland." Someone took the phone from Lisa. It was Linda's brother, Sam. He said, "You better come back here." She said, "He's just sick, isn't he? He's just sick and they took him to the hospital and he's not really dead." "No," Sam said, "he's gone."

She dropped the phone and screamed. Then she remembered Lisa. This little nine-year-old girl is still sobbing and in shock, she thought. If she loves me enough to call me now, I have an obligation to her. She talked to Lisa for what seemed to be a long, long time.

Linda returned to Graceland the next day. Elvis' father, grandmother, aunts, his doctor, and his friends told her that had she been there, she might have saved him. "I think they had just grown so accustomed to my caring for Elvis that they felt I could have done something miraculous." She didn't agree with them. She said nothing, but she thought to herself, "Fate has a way of working itself out, no matter who's there."

CHAPTER 16

WORK = LIFE

Work represented life to Elvis.

Work for Elvis had also become like an anodyne, a panacea for his ills and problems, which ironically reflected them all right back at him when the quality of his shows started to decline. The satisfaction and sense of accomplishment that the love and admiration of his fans provided him in those last years was so great that it's difficult to measure. To slow down would have gone against the grain of everything in his character; it would have been an admission of defeat, of not being what he once was, of playing it safe. Almost as if to leave himself no choice in the matter, he spent his money more recklessly than ever, as fast as he seemed to make it. The Colonel set up the dates, and for Elvis not to fill each and every one of them would have been unthinkable. Work meant life to Elvis, and too much was never enough. Refusing to set limits for himself, he would die before slowing down.

CHAPTER 17

GINGER ALDEN

Elvis' later years and relationship with Ginger Alden, as described by Larry Geller.

Elvis had grown philosophical with the years and his studies, and the fierce thrusts of his youth appeared to be blunted. Not through any lack of vital energy or virility on his part, he was quick to note, but through a wish to sublimate the unselective sexual drive of youth into higher spiritual channels. He meditated for hours at times, making a supreme yogic effort to raise the energies of the body's gonadal area to the higher sphere of the thyroid and the pituitary.

"I am as capable as ever," he assured Larry, "it just isn't that important." He was presumably in love with Ginger Alden, yet he could confide to Larry that he had never consummated the relationship. It was a radically new departure for him, and he attributed it to an access or excess of spirituality. He vowed his celibacy up and down. "It's not easy for me," he said, "but this one is special." He was waiting, like the greenest sophomore, for the day they married.

Larry was well aware of the temptations flung at Elvis, and what his self-denial must cost him. In some way, Elvis had persuaded himself that sexual abstinence and morality went together.

He quoted from Corinthians in a soulful voice: "Flee fornication. Every sin that a man doeth is without the body, but he that committeth fornication sinneth against his own body.'"

Like so many reformers, Elvis' remorse sprang from his own excesses. In the early years of his fame, he had enjoyed an excess of what he was now denying himself. And as with that wastrel-turned-reformer, the saintly Augustine, venerated doctor of the Catholic Church, it contributed to his awakening.

"Man," said Elvis, "I had to see the pits before I could see the top."

In 1958, after Elvis learned he was going into the Army, he spent every available moment having sex with every girl he could find. He was soon totally fatigued, confined to bed, alone, in a hospital. It was a valuable lesson.

"I needed that experience. I realized then that sex without love or affection is a waste."

He was aging visibly when he met Ginger. He lacked his old drive but compensated by dramatizing the relationship. He was obviously a man looking for a dream to take substance. As usual, the maternal sanction was sought.

"When I look into Ginger's eyes, I see my Mom's eyes. She is a youthful version of my mother."

He never chose a girl without "checking" with his mother. "I ask myself how Mom would like her, and a tiny voice would always respond."

"I've never been with a girl that meant anything to me," he told Kathy Westmoreland, "that I didn't see something of my mom in her."

"I didn't understand my first attraction for Priscilla then, but I see it now, having learned about reincarnation. How else would a grown-up man feel so attracted to a 14-year-old girl?"

Linda and Elvis remained friends. "Once Elvis Presley touched your life," she said, "you were never the same."

Ginger made a striking impression on Larry. She was younger than springtime, tall at 5 feet 8, slender, dark-haired, brown-eyed. Larry saw a certain resemblance to pictures of the young Gladys Presley.

As Ginger entered his hotel suite, Elvis seemed like a small boy. He took her hands, almost clumsily, and said, "I'm glad you're here." She replied uncertainly, "So am I. I never thought I'd get here."

The next morning, Elvis sent for Larry. He was in the bedroom, alone.

"Larry," he said, "we talked for hours, and that's all we did. I asked her if she would go to Las Vegas with us and finish off the tour, and she said she would." He grinned sheepishly. "You may not believe this, but I didn't even kiss her." His face took on a faraway look. "You know, Larry, I was looking at Ginger and I saw my mother's face in hers, when I was a kid. Maybe she's my soul mate."

His thoughts of marriage had a lot to do with a desire to have a son. He longed for somebody he could project himself in, another Jesse Garon, all his own this time, whom he could raise in his own image, play and shoot with, teach karate.

"I don't want him growing up afraid of anything," said Elvis. "I don't want them putting fear in him like they did to me. I don't want the Cross to be his symbol of life. I want it to be the Resurrection."

He thought Ginger would make a good mother. But he had his doubts of an unequal relationship.

"What's wrong with me?" he said to Charlie Hodge. "Why do I feel this way about a girl who's so young she can't begin to know what I'm all about?" "There's nothing wrong with you," said trusty Charlie. "Your heart's involved, Elvis. It's got nothing to do with reason or logic. Do what your heart tells you."

CHAPTER 18

ELVIS' LAST FEW YEARS

Rick understood the step up from capsule to ampule and hypodermic needle better than anyone else around Elvis Presley. By the time Elvis started seriously abusing his sleeping medications, he had already run the gamut himself—painkillers, opium-based drugs, Dilaudid, Demerol, morphine, and finally heroin. By the time it started getting bad with Elvis, Rick had already kicked, and it hadn't been easy. He became frightened when he saw how Elvis was using drugs, knowing where it was heading. "I've never seen anybody who could take it like that," he says. "You just don't do dope like he did and live through it."

Rick's time in the rehab hospital taught him how hard it was to get rid of a habit. "I was very lucky, man," he says, looking back. "I really enjoyed getting off on the drugs and I was getting more used to it, but I wasn't all the way to the point of my body craving it if I didn't have it, so I wasn't totally addicted yet. But it was starting. I knew it because I would be pissed off and irritated more often when I didn't have it. When I started to get strung out, my girlfriend, Jill, put it to me. 'It's either the dope or me.' She was right. I committed myself to the drug rehab program at the hospital.

Nobody talked me into it; I did it of my own free will. But I was lucky."
The power and nature of Elvis' drugs was what worried Rick. "It was
all prescribed narcotics, no black-market stuff, and he was heavily into
it for about five or six years, but it started getting bad in 1972 to '73.
That's when he started getting into needles. Wow, man, that's when I
really started to worry—when he became a needle head. His body began
to look like a pincushion. He never stuck anything into his veins because
they were too shallow—he'd go into the muscle, and it wasn't only drugs.
Sometimes he'd shoot vitamin B-12, but mostly it was the same drugs I
did—Tuinal, Demerol, and Dilaudid. He was addicted, for sure. He enjoyed the high."

The World Health Organization defines drug dependence as "a state of
psychic or physical dependence or both on a drug arising in a person following administration of that drug on a period or continuing basis." Over
the years, Elvis had built up both kinds of dependencies. Apart from psychological or emotional reasons that may have motivated the upswing
in his drug taking, there was danger in the drugs themselves. If the narcotic user discontinues the intake of the drug he has become dependent
on, the effects are unpleasant; if totally cut off, the user can experience
anxiety, nausea, weakness, tremors, confusion, disorientation, hallucinations, or convulsions. Moreover, if the dosage is decreased in strength
or frequency or tolerance is built up and the drugs are not increased
sufficiently to bring about the same results, the same symptoms can occur. The symptoms may be milder, perhaps, but still very unpleasant,
tempting the user to increase oral dosage or to administer the drugs by
injection. The result is a vise which only turns tighter with the passing of
time. Rick knew the symptoms and tried his best to dissuade Elvis from
continuing, to step back and take a look at himself. It was a touchy issue.

"Hey, Elvis," he said one afternoon, broaching the subject, "I gave it up,
man, and you're a much stronger man than I am. Why can't you do it, too?"

The Boss's reaction was contingent upon his mood. If he was feeling receptive to the advice, he could say, "I am, man. I know exactly what I'm
doing," as he did to Rick that day. "That was the one answer you wanted
to hear from him," Rick says, "so you wouldn't pursue it anymore be-

cause he'd get pissed. You just hoped that he meant it, but he never did. I just couldn't see hope for him if he didn't get it together."

Elvis seemed bent on the drugs for many reasons. He searched for rationales and found them when he needed to. Health problems and muscular aches and pains from performances became a convenient excuse. "He was like a hypochondriac sometimes," Rick continues. "He enjoyed the feeling of the relief of pain. If he had a little pain from something, he'd try to get rid of it by taking something strong—every bit of it—and if he thought he might have more pain later on, he'd take more drugs then, before it happened, to prevent it. See, the man actually thought he was benefiting himself by some of the things he did. There were times when he'd realize what he was doing to himself, though. He'd get mad at himself and say, 'Man, what the hell am I doing!' But that last year, he just didn't care anymore."

The others around Elvis were as powerless as Rick to influence Elvis' behavior, because if they tried, he could become incensed, feeling that they had no right to meddle in his personal affairs. Joe Esposito, Rick, and Dr. Nick all successfully infiltrated his bottles of medication to decap the barbiturates and substitute harmless mixtures of vitamins, but that proved ineffective because he usually knew or had too many sources. Rick was in a precarious position because he had been a fellow drug user and Elvis never liked to use a needle himself. He knew all about Rick's experiences and entrusted him with the job of administering the drugs. The contradiction of trying to stop or at least cut down his boss's drugs and then help him shoot up is evident, but that's the way it was for everyone else around Elvis. The dope became, like everything else, an outgrowth of Taking Care of Business.

"Sure," Rick sighs with a straightforward honesty that doesn't hide the sadness and regret in his voice. "I did it for him all the time. David did, too. A lot of people will say, 'Well, if you loved the man, how could you have done it? Why didn't you try to tell him?' I'll tell you why: After a while, he just didn't want to hear it. He'd say, 'Cool it. I don't want to hear it.' You could not penetrate. He'd been up there for so long that nobody could talk to him."

The issue of guilt did not enter the picture. "Look," Rick points out, "he was going to do it anyway, whether I did it for him or not. There were times I protested, but in the long run I was devoted to the man—to doing his bidding—and I would do whatever he wanted me to do. Whether or not it was good for his health didn't make much of a difference. People were thankful that I was around most of the time because I knew what was going on and half the tine nobody else did. Many times I had to do things to pull him through and keep him alive when we thought he wasn't going to make it. He'd fall asleep sometimes in the middle of eating and nearly choke to death on his food."

Another problem was when Elvis would wake up, forget that he had taken his medication, and then take more. "Sometimes I'd find him on his back on the floor," says David. "I'd carry him to his room. We'd pull the covers over him and stay with him."

As the problem worsened, Joe Esposito became more crucially important to Elvis' life and the TCB operation than ever before. According to Rick, he was the one man who could come closest to really reaching Elvis. "Joe would get angry at him whenever Elvis would pull something bad," Rick says. "Elvis would have to answer for his actions more to Joe because he respected him so much. Many times he answered for Elvis' actions, and every time something went wrong, he was trapped in the middle but always kept his head. Elvis couldn't have made it without him because there's no earthly way that the things that went on in that group could have continued without someone like him at the helm. Vernon couldn't have done it—he would have snapped under the pressure."

It was Joe, Rick, and Dr. Nick who convinced Elvis to enter the hospital and dry out. There were two weeks in October of 1973, two weeks in January and February of 1975, and two more weeks in August and September of that year when he was admitted to the hospital in Memphis. Reasons of health were released to the public—fatigue, enlarged colon, stomach inflammation, gastroenteritis... "Every time he went in was to dry out," says Rick. "You can cover it up as much as you want. They would slowly and surely try to cut him off his medication. I thought it was ridiculous because they'd cut him off but still give him small amounts. If they wanted to dry him out, I didn't understand why they couldn't cut him off completely just like they did me when I went in. Blam! That's it. It's rough, but it's the only way you can do it." With all of the doctors and employees involved, it is still both unwise and unjust to blame anybody but Elvis for his drug habits. He was the sum total of his life and times, of his lifestyle, his psychology, and character, of the world that he created for himself; those that did his bidding were only a part of that world. His efforts to dry out and detox in the hospital were only partially successful. Even if he had achieved 100 percent success, he might very well have gone back to the drugs.

"As he started to do more drugs, he became more withdrawn," says Rick. "He only confided in a *few* people—me, David, Esposito, Billy Smith, Charlie, Larry." "Withdrawn" in this case meant seclusion, "hibernation" in TCB lingo. Elvis would disappear into his room for longer periods of time. "Somebody would always see him, though," says David. "I saw Elvis three times a week on a normal basis, even if he was in so-called seclusion. I was allowed, so was Ricky, Charlie, and Larry Geller. See, Elvis really liked his room. I loved his room. I could sit there and listen to music with him all night. He would just read, watch television, relax. He was fortunate enough to like seclusion. Anybody who says, 'Well, I feel sorry for Elvis because he wanted to get out' is off the mark; he liked that way of life. He could always get out if he wanted to, and if he did we went to Vail or Hawaii if he felt like it."

Elvis remained astonishingly calm and composed about himself those last few years. Like always, he still had his emotional moments. "He was into controlling his emotions for sure," David says, "but many times I've seen him break down and cry. We had an expression that we liked to use: 'Your eyes are the mirror to your soul,' and sometimes it's good to cleanse things by just letting go, because that's what a man is." Elvis still became angered by bad service at hotels and had fights with his girlfriends, but, says Rick, "I think he more mellowed than got angered those last years. The only things that got to him were the really bad things and the pressure, but he started laying back and taking it easy."

Loneliness could set in, unexpectedly. "Sometimes Elvis would want to be left alone," says David, "but sometimes we'd leave him alone too much, and he'd let us know about it. I'd say, 'God, Elvis—I'm sorry I thought you wanted to be alone now,' and he'd say, 'No, I want you guys to talk to me...' I'd love it, you know; I wouldn't go to bed even if I had to be up and going at 6 in the morning."

But even with all of this wealth and the devotion of a few close friends, the one almost constant condition of that last year was an overwhelming, crushing, damnable sense of ennui, a total apathy and acquiescence; nothing could hold his attention. "He'd had it all," says Rick, "and it seemed that he was just tired. People will say, 'Oh, if only Elvis could have gotten out and done this, if only he could have done that.' He'd already done what he wanted to do—the women, the bikes, the cars, jets —that was the last kick, and he got three of them. 'Elvis Presley Airways.' He always tried everything and then got burned out on it and just moved into bigger things when it wasn't fun anymore. I guess to a certain extent, he felt that he'd done it all."

This feeling of profound apathy and aimlessness rubbed off on the boys. "We were really getting depressed," Rick remembers. "When Elvis got down, I got down; if he had that I don't-give-a-shit attitude, that's the way I would react and just slough everything off with a 'big deal.' If he couldn't get excited about anything, neither could we."

The impression one would conjure of Elvis during this final period of his life seemingly illustrates a man reclusive, paranoid, insecure, and unsure if he had a friend left in the world. A man so whacked out and screwed up on narcotics that he didn't know what was going on anymore. On the contrary, things just plowed right on: business as usual. The Boss functioned enough to work and live his life, although the pace became more difficult when he did work. "He knew exactly what was going on at all times," Rick says. "I never saw him freak out or just lose it. He always kept his wits about him no matter what; it's just that he stopped caring."

To the TCB boys closest to him, Elvis Presley would remain "Boss"— benefactor and manipulator—the most sincere friend and advisor who couldn't follow his own good advice and a man of supreme contradiction to the very end of his life. He lived more and more in a world of I, Me,

Mine but stayed a child of hard times, recklessly generous one moment, cruelly selfish the next, a man who would graciously offer you a home and then become furious if you took a french fry from his plate.

Yet his feelings about death remained a paradox even as he flirted with it. By 1976, after his last attempts to dry out failed, he did more drugs than ever before. "I just said, 'God, if Elvis keeps up like this he'll never make it,'" David remembers. "You just don't do barbs like that every night. You know, it's a strange thing about Elvis: I don't think he intended to live long, but I also don't think he killed himself on purpose."

David's last observation puts the paradox of death in Elvis' life more sharply into focus and brings to mind a particular incident. The Boss was sitting in front of his television when the news of Freddie Prinze's suicide came on. Prinze, a young, brilliant comic from New York and star of *Chico and the Man,* had also been catapulted suddenly to fame and fortune at a young age. He was idolized by kids everywhere, guaranteed a sellout on the nightclub circuits, and a hot property for television and movies. While it was all happening, he got married, had a child, and seemed to have become engulfed by his instant celebrity, by the pressures, the money, the drugs. One evening, after his wife left him and took their child, he loaded himself up, as usual on Quaaludes, coke, and booze, stuck a gun to his head, and blew his brains out.

"Jeez!" Elvis said, turning away from the television in disgust. "That's really the chickenshit way out!"

Prinze's suicide had affected the Boss because somehow he recognized the similarities in the pathology of their despair. Elvis extracted one important lesson from the death, which was a strongly felt religious resistance to out-and-out suicide. "'The Lord's way would never be to kill yourself," he said earnestly. Also, his sense of manhood and dignity would never allow him to take the "easy" way out. His intricately constructed mechanisms of rationale, which still allowed him to fall back on the belief that he wasn't doing anything wrong by his actions, helped him to survive whatever impulses he may have had to pull a Freddie Prinze on the world. Had you suggested to him that he was doing with drugs, diet, and overwork over a long period of time what Prinz managed to accomplish with a bullet in a split second, he would have scoffed.

Elvis Presley surely wanted to live, but on many levels, he just as surely prepared himself for the inevitability of his death. He clung fast to life even in the atmosphere of lethargy and listlessness that pervaded the final year of his life, when he became bereft of his most powerful motivations to live and could feel the specter of his death creeping closer. Like black and white knights, his life and death impulses vied for power over him, jousting on the fields of his conscious and subconscious.

He talked about it more and more. "He told me that he began to accept death right after his mother died," Billy says. "He said, 'Death is the hardest thing for anyone to accept,' and anything hard to accept was a challenge for Elvis."

"Death never scared Elvis because he had to conquer every fear he had of it," says Dee Presley. "Elvis couldn't live with fear. I think the final fear in his life was to walk out on that stage and no longer be 'Elvis Presley'." Apart from challenge and the question of exceeding limits, the promise of peace and release in death became more important to him. "I guess in the end he was just as much aware of death as life," Rick says. "A lot of people will get up and think about how the day is going to be. They're really in tune with life itself, thankful and in praise of it. Elvis remained thankful for life, but he became more aware of death. It was more on his mind than living."

Sometimes, at night, he would ride south from Graceland on Highway 51 to the Forest Hill Cemetery to visit the grave of his mother. With the vast, empty real expanse of the night sky stretched above and the moon and stars beckoning to him, he would stand there, somberly and respectfully, his hands at his sides, his eyes turning from the sky to the grave marker.

GLADYS SMITH PRESLEY
APRIL 25, 1912-AUGUST 14, 1958
BELOVED WIFE OF VERNON PRESLEY
AND MOTHER OF ELVIS PRESLEY
SHE WAS THE SUNSHINE OF OUR HOME

Then he would turn to the figure of Christ with the two angels at His feet, feeling, during those moments of communion with her spirit, closer than ever before to peace, to the answers he sought, feeling the imminence of reunion. He spoke of her more often and reflected on how different his life might have been had Jesse Garon lived and Elvis Aaron not been an only child.

People closest to Elvis were still refusing to acknowledge the truth about him, even though the signs were everywhere. He now lived the nocturnal life of the bat, never seeing the sunshine, taking the fresh air more rarely, shunning most exercise. Racquetball became a travesty. "He'd get out there and just walk over to the ball and take one swing," Rick says. "It was killing us all because we wanted him to do things."

As performance time neared before his Las Vegas shows, the Boss now rode the elevator down the 30 floors from his suite to a golf cart, which transported him through the backstage corridors to the stage so he would no longer have to walk. With cops jogging alongside like Secret Service men around a presidential limousine, the hotel employees would stop and stare at him with their trays in hand as he rode impassively by.

"It got to where he was totally bedridden during the days that last year," Rick recalls sadly. "We'd fly into a city and he'd get right into bed as soon as we got there. We'd have to get him up to do the show. Back on the plane, he'd get right back into bed."

Back at Graceland before a tour, the boys had their hands full just rousting him out to get his circulation going and his energy up. Rick would burst into his room. "Hey, Elvis, we just went motorcycle ridin'! Come on! It's a beautiful day!" Someone else would offer, "Hey, man, have you been doin' your exercises, come on, man! Get up! Get out of bed!" If they could even get him out of bed, they considered it an accomplishment.

The public was getting hip. Lyrics were slurred more often and forgotten. His puffy appearance, so terribly hard to abide for those who knew how magnetically handsome Elvis had been in his late 30s, began to rankle fans and critics alike. The punch left his stage movement, but usually his superbly gifted voice, which could seem remarkably intact on a good night, and his pure musical canniness were enough to carry him through. On nights when they were failing and when his energy ran out, he subsisted on guts, willpower, and the ragged edges of his emotions. Whatever else he lacked, he could always compensate for by simply riding on the coattails of the most mythic and archetypal of his stage qualities. Incredibly, there were still moments of pure brilliance in his performances.

Critics savaged him. "That was his livelihood, the most important thing he had done all his life," says Rick. "He was still a perfectionist. When people said that he did a lousy show, it was like a slap in the face. See, he stayed confident of himself and maintained his self-respect. Elvis knew that he was slurring words, but he didn't want to admit it to himself. He knew what kind of condition he was in, but he was trying to instill in his mind; you know, 'Hey, man, watch this, I'm still going to go out there tonight and do this show and—you know what?—it's gonna be good, too!' He would get out there and do it, but bless his heart, man, he just couldn't. He was beginning to realize that."

Simple problems of health sometimes held him back. "God, if Elvis was sick on tour, we'd all cry," remembers David. "If he couldn't give 100 percent, he was very upset because he had to deliver."

It was during this period that Elvis began singing *My Way*. "That was his song," Rick says. "He always knew about it and liked it, but he never started doing it as part of his show until that last year. Of all the songs he did, that one meant the most to him. It was so dramatic for us and for other people who really knew him and understood what was happening to see him get up there and do it, because he did, man... he took the blows, and he still did it his way."

The song became Elvis' statement on his life for anyone who cared to listen, his comment on the pleasures, pains, price, glories, and failures of being Elvis Presley. Perhaps Sinatra had done the song better, but the emotions of triumph and tragedy that Elvis filled into Paul Anka's lyrics, culled from the experience of his own life and replete with all of his ironies and contradictions, made the song, for all who knew him, as poignantly real as an open wound.

"I'd like to do this song for you, ladies and gentlemen," he'd say into the blinding lights at the end of his shows, mopping the sweat, catching his fading breath and picking up the sheet with the lyrics. "Don't know all the words ... but I'm gonna read 'em off this sheet ... hope y'all don't mind," while behind him the slow, wistful piano introduction led him slowly into the song as James Burton haunted the melody with bitter-sweet guitar notes like a whippoorwill on a lonely summer night. Elvis sang slowly and simply, without being fancy or showy, concentrating hard on his breath control so he would be sure to deliver the crescendo, carefully mouthing and enunciating the words, sometimes failing. Coming close to the finale of his show, his audiences would sit, drained like Elvis, unusually silent but raptly attentive, aware that they were seeing something special and that somehow Elvis was finally spilling the beans. He sang the words, his breath tremulous, the phrasing unsteady: "And now the end is near, and so I face the final curtain..." and his voice would quaver slightly on the word "curtain." When he came to "I've lived a life that's full, I've traveled each and every highway," the voice would clog once again with emotion on the final word as Elvis freed himself to tell the world that he could still laugh at it all. Even if the price he had to pay would be his life, he was still his own man, a true believer in himself.

And when it was over, he'd say almost ruefully, "And now I'd like to sing the saddest song I've ever heard in my life, ladies and gentlemen," and he'd sing Hank Williams' *I'm So Lonesome I Could Cry.*

"If there was one person I would compare Elvis to in his loneliness," Rick says, "it was Hank Williams. Kindred spirits, men with a lot of pain and a lot of music who died young."

Even at the very end, on those last few tours, Elvis had enough left to dazzle. He would tell his piano player to get up and would sit down himself to perform *Unchained Melody,* pulling his audiences into the time machine of his life as he struck the chords, his eyes closed, lost in himself, his voice richly mellow and still feral with anguish, as he burst forth,"... Oh! My love! My darling! I've hungered for your touch...."

They didn't call him the King for nothing.

The last years at Graceland as described by Vester Presley:

From the latter part of 1975 or the first part of 1976 on, I really didn't see an awful lot of Elvis. He'd come in off of a tour and since he slept during the day, I wasn't around him all that much.

"Oh, I'd see him enough to say, "Hello, how are you doing?", things like that. I didn't want to bother him, though. He was tired quite a bit and he didn't look like he was feeling very well.

He spent a lot of time upstairs, either resting or reading. He read an awful lot.

He seemed to enjoy reading. People from all over the world had sent Elvis books, all different kinds of books. I believe he preferred the religious books and material that had been sent to him.

He talked to my mother, his grandmother, about the different scriptures and what they meant. She doesn't read very much because of the poor condition of her eyes, so he was always reading to her. She enjoyed that an awful lot, and so did he.

CHAPTER 19

FATHER'S DIVORCE

Elvis' reaction to his father's divorce as described by his stepmother.

Elvis Presley was saddened by the breakup of the family and worried about his father's health. When Vernon and Dee forged ahead with divorce plans, he became petrified that Vernon would not be able to withstand the experience of a publicized divorce, with all of the depositions, testimonies by other members of the family, and other unpleasantness. He was somehow sensing that time was running out, and he wanted desperately to get in touch with Dee.

One afternoon at Graceland, exactly two weeks before his death, he had Ricky get in contact with Billy, for Elvis knew that if ever there was a person who could get his mother's ear, it would be her firstborn son. Elvis took the phone as soon as Rick managed to raise his brother.

"Billy," said Elvis, "I want you to do me a favor, OK? This is so important, man. I need to speak to your mother ... I'll give you five thousand dollars if you just get her on the phone for me. That's all I want, man ... just to talk to her."

Jesus, his voice sounds bad, Billy thought; there was an urgency and a desperation in it.

"Hell, Elvis," he said. "I don't want the money. I understand. I'll call her right now."

Billy hung up the phone and called Dee in Nashville. She returned Elvis' call immediately. When he picked up the phone, he was weeping and mumbling his words almost incoherently.

"Elvis, are you sick?" she asked anxiously.

"Naw, I'm OK, Dee," he sighed, "but I'm so worried about Daddy." Then he started to cry again. "This thing... this isn't what I wanted for us... Dee... everything's shot to hell, it seems. The family's spread out every-where... Please, Dee... Don't do this to him... I don't want to see this hap-pen... please." Her heart sank as the premonition spread horribly over her, up her spine, making the flesh crawl. She knew that she was speaking to a drowning man, reaching out and trying to put things straight before he went under. She began to cry, knowing in that instant that it was all going to go up in smoke and that she had to do anything not to hurt him.

"But Elvis," she said softly, trying to make him understand her hurt, "he's in love with her."

"He thinks he is," he said, trying to assuage her.

"If he's confused, Elvis, he's old enough to know better," she said sad-ly. "He's with her, Elvis... she washes his clothes and cooks for him and works in the garden and they go to the country to pick blueberries.... He wants her, Elvis—she's not as demanding as I was. He's comfortable with her, and he doesn't have to be afraid of losin' her."

There was a silence on the phone before he sighed deeply and began to sob, and it broke her heart to hear him crying.

"Nothin' worked out the way I wanted it, Dee." He seemed to be talking to himself. "I'm losin' everything... Cilla... and now Daddy's sick and I'm scared... soon you'll be gone. Nothin' worked out the way I wanted it."

"Tell me, Elvis. Please, what can I do... anything..."

He brightened a little then, and she could hear hope in his voice, as if maybe at least he could put something right after all. "Promise me that you'll keep this thing outta court," he pleaded for his father. "It'll be better for everybody that way, Dee—Daddy, the boys, you—we can settle it all outta court. You'll be taken care of, Dee, and live in the manner that you're accustomed... you know, we all want that. You know how I feel about you and the boys... I'll always want to take care of y'all...."

Dee thought about Vernon and her sons and Lisa and Cilla and how she never wanted to hurt any of them by going into court with Vernon and agonizing over a divorce when she would have to bring up things that might hurt him.

"Don't worry, Elvis," she tried to assure him. "I understand how you feel 'cause I feel that way myself—you know what I mean? We'll find a way to work it out. Don't worry."

Elvis sighed. "Bless you, Dee," he said. "I'll never forget you. You'll always be a part of this family as far as I'm concerned, you know. I've always respected you, Dee. You came in like a lady and you bore it like a lady. I love you, Dee."

"I love you too, Elvis." The words warmed her, but she was still afraid. "Will you promise to come up here and see me when you come back home?" he said happily.

"I'll be there, Elvis."

Shaken, she hung up the phone.

CHAPTER 20

LISA, DIVORCE, AND LAST DAYS:
"ELVIS: WHAT HAPPENED?"

Elvis' last days spent with Lisa and his reactions to the book "Elvis: What Happened?"

Elvis' times spent with Lisa were the most precious and meaningful moments of his last years. Whenever Lisa visited Graceland or Elvis' L.A. home, for a time they would be entirely alone, sitting, talking, playing together, making up for time spent apart. "Elvis used to call her all the time," recalls David. "He'd be just sitting there and up and get the urge to talk to her and get her on the phone, or if he was in Vegas, he just might send me to L.A. to go bring her out for a little visit."

Christmastime took on an even greater significance for Elvis after his divorce because they were all together again at Graceland. "Elvis really felt good around Christmas," says David," " 'cause he would get off on doin' the whole number for Lisa. He'd wait up all night long on Christmas Eve so he could be waitin' downstairs first thing in the morning when she got up and he'd play Santa Claus for her. Those were some of the closest moments between him and his daughter. "

The intimacy between father and daughter increased as time went on, but Elvis still felt in his heart that it wasn't enough. As his health declined in subsequent years, she was the most important person in his life; when his boredom and unhappiness reached rock bottom, she cast the single beacon of brightness into the descending gloom. If there was one thing in the back of his mind that compelled him forward when he was faltering, it was the continuing need to make his daughter proud of him. The knowledge that his daughter would one day have to grow up to confront the contents of *Elvis: What Happened?* with its shrill hawking of his "wrongdoing" was, according to both David and Rick, the most crushing and desolating effect of that book on his life.

It didn't take the Boss long to know what was going on. "As soon as Joe Esposito heard about the book," remembers David, "he called us all into a room and said, 'OK, boys, this is it.'" What followed was a TCB summit meeting to tell Elvis about the book and plan strategy, the kind of meeting that Elvis only held after the most serious events and problems in his life. Ashen-faced, Elvis just stood there in complete disbelief. It had never even occurred to him that they would ever think of doing something like that to him! "In 1977, when he heard about the book," Rick says, considering Elvis' overall state and the effect of the news, "his whole life went like that." (He snaps his fingers.) "That was the final blow—the heaviest thing that could have happened to him. How much can a man take?"

The change in Elvis was apparent; it seemed that somebody had just pulled the plug on him. "He was miserable," says Rick. "He would relate to me and David and Billy Smith and Esposito and say things like, 'Hey man, everything's gonna be cool—this book's not gonna hurt me,' but you could tell that the man was just trying to convince himself. We were trying our best not to let it bum everything out. When he'd really get down, we'd say, 'Come on, Boss, don't worry about it. Let's not let this thing bring you down. Those SOBs can't hurt you with literature like that.' You'd find yourself being very, very careful about your actions and things you said around him. The slightest reference to the book could depress him."

"It hit him so hard," David observes, "because Elvis was always so private about everything he did for his whole damn life. He was so freaked out that they would even consider doing it. That last year when we were back in town and I would spend the night with him, he would talk about that book every night. Every single night, man."

Elvis: What Happened? was released some 15 days prior to Elvis' death.

CHAPTER 21

TENSION, DRUGS, AND DEATH OF BROTHER

The tensions built up. Elvis found himself taking pills to sleep by, pills to pick up from the hangover induced by the sleeping pills, and tranquilizers in between. He made no secret of this habit.

He was friendly with Welsh singer Tom Jones and could hardly believe that Jones could handle similar pressures without calling on the medicine cabinet.

Jones wondered why Elvis couldn't release his tensions through the meditation he advocated. But the habits of youth were ingrained. It was indelibly stamped on his subconscious that his brother and mother would have lived had the proper drugs been available. The tensions never diminished.

I knew something had to be done. The source of the pills was Elvis' great friend and physician, Dr. George Nichopoulos. I absolutely hated what that man had done to my husband under the guise of medicine. My husband was addicted to drugs, our lives were being ruined, and Nichopoulos kept the pills coming as fast as Marty wanted them.

I went to Graceland to see Nichopoulos and told him to stop the drugs. I told him I was going to report them all if anything happened to Marty, I begged and threatened, and Dr. Nichopoulos laughed at me. I'm only sorry now that I was too afraid to carry out the threats.

I considered going to Elvis, the only person who had any influence with Marty, but did not because of his frame of mind. Elvis was also taking pills, and I was sure he would also be angry with Marty because of me and that he would stop seeing Marty. Undoubtedly, this would have been the best thing for Marty, but my real fear was that it would cause an irreparable split between Marty and me. I did not have the courage to force upon Marty a choice between Elvis and me; I was afraid I would lose.

There were thousands of pills, and I mean thousands. I don't know how many Elvis took a day, or if they led to his death, but I do know that he went downhill just as Marty did. The drugs may or may not have been the direct cause of his death, there seems to be some doubt among the medical authorities, but the pills were ruining his life. He was very overweight, bloated, and he slurred his words to such an extent that anyone around him had to know what was going on.

Priscilla told me Elvis' father said to her after the funeral that he didn't know Elvis was on drugs. Her reply to him was that he had to know. We all knew, but we failed to do anything about it.

It was a nightmare life that ended for me when we finally ran out of money, and Marty found the strength to kick the pills. It was a living hell when it was going on and a dying hell when he was trying to quit. There were nights when he was in so much pain, I offered to buy him some of the Placidyls; I couldn't watch him suffer the way he was. Marty was strong enough to say no, and somehow we got through it alive.

At least we did get through it alive, which was a better fate than Elvis', and for that I am grateful. Not being strong enough to help Elvis is a burden of guilt we'll all have to carry for the rest of our lives. Had he been different and had we been different, our lives could have been full of the joy of love and friendship because we did love him and he loved us. From the first awe of meeting through the resentment of loneliness, there was always love. I blame Elvis for starting Marty on the pills just as I blamed him for taking Marty away from me so much. I know Elvis didn't twist his arm, but Elvis didn't know the devotion that Marty and some of the other guys had for him.

Toward the end, he seemed to have become completely confused about who cared for him and who didn't. I think all of the guys loved him in their own way. I know Marty did, and Billy did and Sonny and Richard and Red did. I've seen them and lived too close to them, before and after Elvis' death, to believe anything else.

Their love was genuine and I believe Elvis knew it, at least during the better years. They took expensive gifts from him, we all did, and things would probably have been better had none of us taken anything, but Elvis was a giver. He enjoyed giving and we were none rich enough to refuse, but in the end some of us may have been able to help had we not taken so much. If any of us had been able to say we gave more than we received, perhaps we could have generated enough respect in his mind to, at least, have been able to talk with him about how his life was going.

When questioned about the apparent double standard which existed with Elvis' desire to became involved in the fight against drug abuse and his own use of drugs, Marty Lacker says, "Elvis sincerely felt he was a special person. He could do things which were not right for others to do. I can't explain it, but that's the way he was. It wasn't phony or insincere or anything like that, Elvis simply felt certain things which were right for other people just didn't apply to him. He was also very much opposed to hard drugs like heroin and he didn't even like marijuana.

CHAPTER 22

SON OF A BITCH

Son of a bitch —Marty Lacher relates.

There were other times when Elvis would get mad beyond all reason. He was usually very polite and seldom used bad language or did anything to upset anyone, but when he did become angry about something, he would really blow.

Elvis hated to be called a son of a bitch. One time he told me, "I get a little angry when arguing with people, but if anyone ever called me a son of a bitch, I'd deck him. It makes me think they're calling my mother that name."

Guilt Precedes Behavior.

In philosophy, there is a doctrine that says in a search, truth does not exist. The doctrine is also skeptical, saying that nothing exists; if it did exist, we couldn't know it; and even if we did know it, we couldn't talk about it.

The three things wrong with this concept are the following: It is not absolute, such a person is only saying he is 1) 99% blind, and 2) if he did see it he's 99% stupid, and if he did recognize it 3) he's 99% dumb.

Nihilism and skepticism are both negative and as such, pragmatically speaking, are completely useless as far as psychotherapy is concerned except perhaps to serve as a bad example. The thesis can be proven untrue by whacking the client on the back who maintains such a doctrine, and when he cries out in pain, asking, "If nothing exists, then where did your pain come from?"

Assuming truth exists, then, we return to the philosophical question of whether it is subjective or objective truth. This has been dramatized in a paraphrased dialogue between the two chief protagonists of the opposing theories. Consider Plato's recounting of the argument between Socrates, the absolutist, and Protagoras, who believed in subjective truth.

Protagoras speaks: Truth is relative, it is only a matter of opinion.

Socrates: You mean that truth is mere subjective opinion?

P: Exactly, subjective, what is true for you is true for you, but what is true for me is true for me.

S: Do you really mean that? That my opinion is true by virtue of the fact of it being my opinion?

P: Indeed I do.

S: Then my opinion is: Truth is absolute, not opinion, and you, Mr. Protagoras, are absolutely in error and since this is my opinion, then you must grant that it is true according to your philosophy.

P: You are quite correct, Socrates.

To some, this means that the relativist contradicts his own argument. He admits truth is objective since Socrates says subjectively I believe it is true for me; therefore, it has to be objectively true for that person and therefore that makes it so. Such a conclusion is, however, shortsighted. Truth does not operate in a vacuum but only has meaning if it is related to other things. The real problem which neither Plato, Socrates, or Protagoras addresses is to distinguish between the two types of truth. For each is in reality speaking of two different things, and they are both labeled with one word, "truth."

This is the fallacy of equivocation. The use of a term in more than one sense, while the impression is given that it is being used to express only one in the same meaning throughout an argument, is known as the fallacy of equivocation. A word used in more than one sense should be interpreted as two or more words, and the fallacy results from the incorrect assumption that the word is used throughout a given discussion to convey a single connotation. For example: In the following argument, the word "adjective" is responsible for the fallacy of equivocation: "The U.S. is large. Large is an adjective. Therefore, the U.S. is an adjective." Another example: "I hold a glass in my hand; it is true only because I can see it, hear it, feel it, or perceive it in some way. If I have no knowledge of it because my senses are all cut off, it's no longer true for me, but the existence of the glass goes on apart from my ability to perceive it." Truth I or truth perceived, whether objective or not, is subjective. Truth II or objective truth unperceived only can be objective. Both Truth I and Truth II are important to analysis in that the client's behavior instills subjective truth in the form of feeling, emotion, or stored energy, while objective truth is an independent force or energy which brings about behavior.

Now, the difficulty in the past was that because analysts must out of necessity deal with Truth I or subjective truth as perceived by the client—"That is what behavior is truth for him,"—we erroneously assume that when one commits an act of behavior he knows to be wrong, guilt feelings develop therefrom.

In order to live peaceably and effectively in society there is a need for behavior regulation, but not a need to regulate one's feelings. It is the individual behavior which gets the attention. In criminal law, a prosecutor will do his best to get admitted into evidence the acts of the defendant that show a consciousness of guilt, as it is simply assumed that guilt results from doing the act prohibited by law, which is "known" by the defendant to be wrong. Because of this Truth I situation, we presume that guilt follows the act.

Assuming it is behavior we wish to regulate or control, then we must first determine its origin. The common viewpoint is that voluntary behavior is initiated by will and that man intends the consequence of his acts. The reality may be more like the iceberg whose greatest bulk floats beneath the surface. Behavior is mostly caused by the emotions of which the individual is entirely unaware.

Jung points out that "the more one sees of human fate and the more one examines its secret springs of action, the more one is impressed by the strength of unconscious motives and by the limitation of free choice." From an analyst's point of view, one must admit the subconscious origin of behavior in order to regulate it. If we grant this, then a good many conclusions come forth that are not at first perceived. For example: If we have just admitted that subconscious emotions are the cause of behavior, then what do we do with subconscious guilt? An emotion formerly thought of only in terms of result. The guilt comes from the result of the act. For example: A is angry at B because B stole his parking place. A shoots B, B dies, A feels terribly guilty and, desiring punishment, turns himself in. The conscious interpretation of the facts states B's behavior in stealing the parking place caused A's anger, resulting in A shooting B. A's behavior in shooting B caused guilt feelings, resulting in self-punishment.

Now, the most elementary analyst realizes that the stealing of a parking place in and of itself is insufficient to warrant the behavior of murder. It is because we recognize this that we say, Wait! B's stealing the parking place was only the excuse, which allowed A to express subconscious feelings of anger, which had been stored up from some incident long past. For example, A was beaten savagely many times by his stepfather, who also stole his inheritance. A's smoldering anger was merely triggered by the behavior of B, who looked like his stepfather, etc., which served as an excuse. Therefore, A shot B. Now, here it is easy to see that A's subconscious feeling was the cause of A's behavior and B's stealing the parking place only an excuse. But, the point I am making which may be more difficult to see is that A's guilt feelings also preceded his behavior.

The method which brings this about is as follows: A wishes his stepfather dead. He feels terribly guilty because of his hatred. But these unresolved guilt feelings are subconscious and hence unknown to the client. A becomes very anxious because the guilt feelings are building up within him. A needs a concrete act of behavior to hang the guilt feelings on, in the same manner that he needed B's behavior in stealing the parking place as an excuse to shoot him. Then he could symbolically shoot his stepfather. The progression of emotions of guilt and behavior is as follows: Guilt increases on a subconscious level. The client becomes anxious. The client seeks an action to which guilt can be attached. Then he can explain it to himself. The client commits the act. The client is relieved, because he now has a conscious reason, though the wrong one, for his guilt. He disposes of his subconscious anger and guilt by attaching both to this act and is psychologically relieved.

Hence, to really prevent unwanted behavior—that is, to regulate human behavior significantly—we must bring to the surface the subconscious emotions and attach them to acceptable forms of behavior. Surprisingly enough, to prevent the unwanted act the individual must first be freed of all guilt feelings regarding the act which he subconsciously contemplates. In other words, you must say, "You don't have to feel guilty about feeling such and such a thing," then he doesn't do it. That is the first step in getting him to give up the contemplation of the act. The point is, the formation of guilt is a precedent to behavior not a result of it.

Now keep this in mind as you read about Elvis' reaction to the phrase "son of a bitch."

In an incident described by his bodyguards, a girl is attempting to leave a party Elvis is having and desires one of his bodyguards to move his car so she can leave. Elvis, however, is playing pool with the bodyguard and does not want the game interrupted. "Elvis yells, 'God damn it, God damn it, didn't you hear what I said? Get somebody else to move it.' The girl had endured enough embarrassment and she flared at him in return, "Go to hell, you son of a bitch," and that did it.

He took the pool cue in his fist, Sonny recalls. Then, like he was throwing a spear, he just leaned and threw it right at her across the pool table. She had no time to duck. The sharp end of the pool cue bore right into her body. It hit her just above the nipple of the right breast. She didn't scream. It was more like a sharp little gasp, and she crumpled backwards on the floor. The girl had been severely hurt, her breast had been permanently damaged, but she never did file suit.

According to Sonny West, after the incident, Elvis was trying to justify his actions. No way would he say that he was wrong, according to Sonny. Elvis was to say, "look, Sonny, if she had called me a bastard or told me to go fuck myself, it would have been okay." (But not son of a bitch; anything would have been better than degrading his mother.)

Interpretation of SOB and girl incident and identification with Mario Lanza and death.

His feeling for his mother dominated his music, as it did everything else.

He would bear no affront to her, however slight or indirect.

Long before Larry's arrival, it was recorded that Elvis had flung a cue stick across a table at a girl. The incident was blown up and treated as an insult to womanhood by employees Elvis had fired. They left out a few details, which, while not excusing the burst of temper, explained it.

Elvis was shooting pool by himself, to relax. He was concentrating on his game when a girl he didn't know, invited into his home by the entourage, kept peppering him with questions. He finally told her to leave him alone. She turned on him angrily and cried, "You're a son of a bitch."

At this, his face blanched. She had hit the most sensitive nerve in his body. His eyes blazed.

"You're not talking about me when you say that," he cried. "You're talking about my mother. Nobody talks about my mother like that. I don't care who they are."

She bristled back angrily. And then, in a blind rage, he flung the cue stick across the table.

It struck her breast, say witnesses, and she immediately went into an award-caliber performance of the dying swan. She was taken to another room, sobbing, to regain her composure, and later left, never to come back. The story was revived a dozen years later by Elvis' disgruntled aides.

His idol was Mario Lanza, the great singing star who made *The Great Caruso* and *One Night of Love*. Elvis, in his teens, saw *The Great Caruso* a dozen times in Memphis theaters. He was not only enamored of Lanza's voice but felt a certain kinship with him. Before his rise to fame, the Italian singer had driven a dump truck in Philadelphia; Elvis, of course, drove a truck for the Crown Electric Company in Memphis.

He was also struck by the fact that Enrico Caruso, the golden tenor, had driven a flower wagon as a young man.

"I guess," he grinned, "you have to be a truck driver to be a great singer."

He had a lurking fear of following Lanza's fate, for Lanza had ballooned up to over 300 pounds and then virtually killed himself dieting with drugs. He was tragically dead at 38.

"The fifth or sixth time I saw *The Great Caruso,* Elvis recalled, "I began to see myself singing on that screen."

CHAPTER 23

"GREEN, GREEN GRASS OF HOME"

"Green, green grass of home" as described by Marty Lacher.

Elvis was an impulsive man. There were many times when he would suddenly say, "Let's go to Palm Springs." Sometimes it would be Las Vegas or some other place, and we would simply go away for four or five days. There were often times when I thought he had been thinking of doing something for a long time but wanted us to think it was a spur-of-the moment decision. It almost seemed that he enjoyed keeping people off balance. If he thought someone was getting too sure of himself or his job, he would do something to make the person doubt the security of his place. None of us ever really understood Elvis. He was a complex man, a man of many moods.

We were driving in the scenic cruiser to Memphis from Hollywood, and as we were passing through a small town in Arkansas, we were listening to George Klein broadcasting on the radio from Memphis. Elvis was driving, as he usually did, when George played a new record by Tom Jones called *Green, Green Grass of Home*. It was a beautiful record, and Elvis wanted to hear it again.

He stopped the cruiser at the nearest pay phone and said, "Moon, go on out there and call George, tell him to play that again."

"Elvis," I said, "he can't play them back-to-back. You know that." Most of the top stations do not allow their disc jockeys to play a record more than one time during an hour, and some even have rules which forbid the playing of any record more than once in a three-hour period.

"I don't care," Elvis said. "Tell him I want to hear it again."

"Okay," I answered, then got out and went to the phone and called George.

When he answered the phone, George asked, "Man, where are you guys?"

"We're on our way home. Right now we're in Arkansas. You know that record by Tom Jones?"

"Yeah, *Green, Green Grass of Home*. It's great, why? I'll bet Elvis likes it.

"He likes it so much he wants you to play it again."

"Man, I can't do that," he said.

"George, I know. I told him that, but he still says he wants to hear it again."

"Okay," George said.

"Give me about two minutes to get back in the bus, George."

I went back to the cruiser, and Elvis drove away without even asking the results of the conversation. About that time, George's voice came on the radio, "Here's for all the guys out on Highway 64, coming into Memphis." He played the song again.

Well, for some reason the song brought tears to Elvis' eyes, as well as those of several of the guys. Maybe we were just in that kind of mood or something, but it sure made us feel blue.

Elvis stopped at the next pay phone and said, "Hey, Moon."

"Oh no, man," I said. "He can't do it again." "Tell him I want to hear it again."

"Okay, but I'm pretty sure he's not going to be able to do it."

"Just tell him I want to hear it again," Elvis said. He knew George would do just about anything for him.

I called George again, and when he heard my voice he said, "No man, I just can't do it again." "George, I'm just telling you what the man said." George played it again, and I can tell you he was taking a big chance with his job.

When we arrived at Graceland, all of our wives and girlfriends were there and, with the excitement of the homecoming, I forgot the song and my spirits began to lift. I went to find Elvis to see if he needed anything special before I called it a day.

As I went into the hall, I saw Elvis kneeling on the floor, crying. I mean really sobbing. He was suffering as I had never before seen. One of the other guys was there with him, and alarmed, I said, "Elvis, what's the matter? What's the matter?" I was certain that he was sick or had been hurt.

He looked at me with tears streaming down his face and slowly choked out, "Marty, when I came in the door, I saw my mother."

"What do you mean, Elvis?" I asked.

"I saw her, man. She was standing there. I saw her."

His emotion and suffering got to me, and I began to feel tears in my own eyes. I tried to comfort him. "Elvis, she's always here. As long as you are here, she will be here too."

Finally, he gained control of himself, got up, hugged me, and went to his room.

We didn't see him for about a week. He stayed in his private quarters.

According to May Mann: Elvis, at his mansion, says, "I go to the cemetery once a week to visit her grave. I usually drive out there at night when no one's around. (Elvis is now 31, eight years after his mother's death.) When I am away I have flowers placed there every week. There's something...I never return home after being away that I don't see her opening that front door and running out and putting her arms around me.

Now the dreams I have of her are always such happy dreams. She is always happy. They have been a great comfort to me, for when the dreams do come at rare unexpected times—well, it's like seeing and being with her again.

(At about this time he wrote a song called *That's Someone You Never Forget.* The song has an eerie tone to it and may very well have represented feelings about his mother. It can be heard on his album *Pot Luck.*)

CHAPTER 24

"FASCINATED WITH DEATH"

Some of his friends saw his behavior a little differently, Red West recalls: "There was a very nice guy, a Memphis policeman who ended up as an inspector. His name was Woodward. Well, he took a real fatherly interest in Elvis right from when he just left school. They were very close. Well, 1961, the old guy died. I'm sure Elvis was sad about the whole thing, but do you know what he did? He watched a mortician embalm his friend, this old man Woodward. Can you imagine that? Someone watching someone else cutting into the body of a friend. Elvis could tell us details that would impress a doctor. He knew all the right terms, and he would tell us how a body is bled and blood is taken out and replaced by the embalming fluid. It used to make me sick.

"There were other things too. When he was at funerals, he would act in the most strange ways. I'm not talking about his mother's funeral because he was genuinely shattered. But even way back in 1964, when Dewey Phillips, the disc jockey, died—the guy who got Elvis all the breaks—well, Elvis is at Dewey's funeral, and suddenly he gets a fit of giggles. Just laughs his head off. I've seen him at other times cracking jokes."

Sonny West says: "He would go on these damn trips through graveyards, he would tell us to see if we could scare ourselves. He'd pull up on a dark road to feel the experience of being scared. But worst of all was his trips to funeral homes. He used to return to the funeral home where his mother was laid out, on Union Avenue in Memphis. I don't mean he would go there during the day and look around. I mean he would go there at 3 in the morning and wander around the slabs looking at the embalmed bodies. It scared the shit out of me.

"One night in 1972, Presley, as was his practice, took over the Memphian Theatre to see a movie. Elvis loves horror movies. So this night we see a horror movie, and it must have got his mind working. Anyway, Linda Thompson was there this night. It's about 3 in the morning. We all hop in the car and suddenly Elvis says, 'Let's go down to Union Avenue.' Already I've got it in mind what he wants to do. We pull up outside the funeral home. We went around back, and Elvis is leading the way as calm as if he was going to a movie. Anyway, it's 3 in the morning, the door is wide open and we just walk in, Elvis, Linda and me. I can't believe there is no security guard or something, but we don't see a person.

"Anyway, Elvis just wanders around calm as anything trying doors to some offices. Some are locked, others are opened. I've got my jacket open ready to go for my gun. I'm scared some security guard is going to come along, see us, think it is a robbery or that we're grave robbers or something and start blazing away. I'm nervous as a cat, because we don't see anyone and it is dark and eerie.

"Then I get the shock of my life. We come into this big room with heads sticking from under the sheets. They were bodies, and they were sort of tilted upward, feet first. This was the damn embalming room. I'm horrified. But this was apparently what Elvis was looking for. He is happy he has found the room. The he starts lecturing on how people get embalmed. He is walking around and lifting up the sheets looking at the bodies, and he is telling all the cosmetic things morticians do when people are in accidents. He is showing us the various veins. The jugular veins and things like that. How a body is bled. Then he shows us where the bodies are cut, and because the cuts don't heal, there is only stitches holding the body together. He led us into another room, and he is still lifting up the sheets pointing out various things that have been done to the bodies." 26

"Dave Hebler says: After getting to know the scene with Elvis, I was surprised. It is absolute insanity that would bring a human being to commit *slow* suicide, which I feel he is doing with the drugs. I can't understand how anybody can deliberately set out to do himself in. Here is a guy, one of the greatest in the world. He can do anything he wants. He has the means. He could have been a fantastic physical specimen. It is hard for me to understand how he can deliberately set out to destroy himself. It seems he is bent on death.....

"The thing about him is that Elvis doesn't care. He doesn't give a fuck. I can't find the words to say it strong enough." 27

Says Red West, "In earlier days, Presley lived with a genuine vibrancy. He had a lovely irresponsible love for life that never seemed to be satisfied 28. By now Elvis had gotten out of the pink car stage, the pink car had been for his mother; now he only wanted black or white. 29 (the colors lacking life and looking like a hearse.) Also, if money meant nothing to Presley during the first years as a millionaire, by 1974 it was treated with more contempt than ever. 30 (Remember now that the money had been for his mother and now she was dead.) Elvis in those days demanded that we wear suits and ties. We looked like the Mafia. 31 (This also tends to make them look like corpses, with whom he seems to associate himself.)

"His mother's death was the worst thing that ever happened to Elvis, worse than his divorce, worse than anything else. 32 Elvis' mother appeared as a member of an audience in *Loving You,* a 1957 Paramount picture about a young truck driver who makes it big as a singer. There were so many parallels with his own career, it must have been an easy role for him to play. But for years after his mother's death he wouldn't watch the film because she was in it. 33 According to Red, "He simply worshiped the ground that his mother walked on. To him, she was a mother, a friend, a big sister all rolled into one. I mean, she was his whole life. If he ever talked about his family going anywhere, he would never talk about his family as a whole. It would always be Mom and them went to church, or Mom and them went to the movies. It was like she was the only one in the whole family, and the rest were just along for the ride. It was like that even after she died. He still talked about his mother like she was living."

"Presley does not have the slightest respect for them (guns), although he does know the respect they can produce. Elvis speeds like a madman all the time. (There is no fear if you are 'dead'.) He loses sight of reality, because when he gets out into the real world, our world, he cannot differentiate between the two. 'It was,' says Red West, 'as if he said to himself, 'Dammit, man, if I cannot be like you guys, then I'm gonna be someone else,' and he was."

"You know I would give anything to go back to those simple crazy days. Elvis was such a great guy and we all got along so well. In his later years, he was to regard sleep with the passion he once reserved for his inordinately healthy sex life. Elvis once said, 'When I come here to Graceland, it's not that I'm trying to withdraw from my fans,' he told Becky Yancey, one of his secretaries, 'I guess, if anything, I'm withdrawing into myself.'" (There will never be anyone in the whole world like my mother.)

Dave Hebler, bodyguard, says, "He had a very good and very inquisitive mind. When he'd hear somebody tell a story that interested him, he would absorb it, build on it, and make it into a whole monologue."

"Typical," says Red, "was an incident attached to the song *Softly,* which is one of the songs he would sing onstage. Now, one night backstage, some guy who was feeding Elvis a line said, 'Do you know the story behind that song?' Elvis pricked up his ears and said, 'No, I thought it was a love story.' Anyway, this guy tells him it wasn't a love story. The lyrics, this guy says, were written by a dying man.

"Elvis gets to thinking about this and, in his way, he will often talk to the audience about the song he is going to sing. So he has made up this incredible story. We heard him tell it onstage so many times that we started to get where we believed it. He would get up there and tell them, 'Now this is a story about a man who is dying. He was in the hospital and his wife was with him. She sat with him for three days and three nights. On the third day, she lay down beside him and went to sleep. Just then this man felt himself dying. He didn't want her to see him pass away, so he reached for a pad and a pencil and wrote these words: 'Softly, I will leave you softly, long before you miss me …. etc.'

"Well, I guess the audience ate it up. Anyway, I spoke to a guy who knew the writer of the song and told him this story, and the guy looks at me and says, 'oh bullshit, it's a love story.' But to this day, Elvis will tell that story onstage. His imagination is great."

(Recall that Elvis arrived at his mother's deathbed three days before she died. She died while he was sleeping. He may have felt that his mother died in this fashion to save him from the sorrow of her death.)

Conversation with Red West about a year before death.

Toward his death, Elvis will withdraw more and more into his own private world. A year before his death, he fires his friends and bodyguards. Red West says, "It's been straightened out a long time. It's just a failure to communicate." (This may be a direct quote from a Paul Newman movie of the day, *Cool Hand Luke*. It is about a man who succeeds in getting himself killed. His mother's death is in the film.) Like that song Roy Hamilton did, *Understanding Solves All Problems*. Without communication there can be no understanding.

Red responds, "We didn't have much understanding there…"

Elvis responds, "I don't know whether it was you and I as much as it was coming from somebody else … you know, negative vibes."

Red answers, "I'm not into the psychic thing."

Elvis defends his position: "I'm not either, but I do know we are constantly sending and receiving … all the time…I could pinpoint the negative things, but I couldn't exactly pinpoint what it was. I didn't feel I could communicate with anybody."

The conversation continues, "Well, we were known as the wild bunch," says Red West. Elvis responds, "Yeah, the good old days are still a fact." Red observes, "But the fun left." Elvis corrects Red and says, "The fun ceased to exist. I couldn't pinpoint, I couldn't pin it down..." He is aware that Red, his brother Sonny, and Dave Hebler are preparing a book called *Elvis: What Happened?,* asking many embarrassing and unanswerable questions for Elvis. To this, Elvis says, "I mean it, I don't give a god-damn thing to do with or no publication or none of that shit ... is there anything I can do, any way of getting a job, anything else, let me know. I'm still here, son. After analyzing the blamed thing, I can see it, I can see it clearly. That's why I'm saying, anything I can do at all. Worried about the book? I don't think so, not on my part. You do whatever you have to do. I just want you and Pat to know I'm still here. To know I'm still here."

CHAPTER 25

FASCINATION WITH BIRTH

Dave Hebler was driving Presley, Linda Thompson, and Dick Grob, another bodyguard and Palm Springs policeman, to a movie in the spring of 1975. "We were going to the Memphian for a private showing. Linda mentions that her brother, Sam Johnson, and his wife Louise have just had a baby.

"She is talking about how thrilled she is and suddenly, at 1 in the morning, Elvis decides to go see the baby. We finally got in the back entrance and once inside the hospital, we're causing a riot. Nurses are dropping patients everywhere and running to get his autograph.

"Anyway, it's against hospital rules for strangers to come and look at a baby at 1 in the morning, but Elvis cons the nurse and sure enough, we get to see the baby. Then someone wakes up the mother, Louise, and she comes out. Then her husband is brought to the hospital to join the party. Then Linda's parents showed up. There are the doctors and nurses. We had a convention there.

"Anyway, down the hall there's a bit of activity. Elvis sees some doctors and nurses wheeling this woman along on one of those mobile stretchers. She is yelling in pain. I notice she is in labor, and they are rushing her into the delivery room.

"The next thing I know, Elvis has stopped the emergency charge toward the room and starts talking to the lady. Here she is in labor, but here Elvis comes along and she starts flipping out despite the pain. He lays hands on her stomach, and he starts saying seriously in a sort of mystical way, 'Now there, it won't hurt anymore. It won't hurt anymore. Everything is going to be fine. You're not going to hurt anymore.'

"He's laying on the hands and taking the pain from her. Well, that might sound pretty ridiculous for a woman in labor, but the funny thing was she was saying, 'You're right, the pain is gone, you're right.' (Hypnosis, faith healing, etc. are very similar and do work, especially for the reduction of pain when coming from a prestigious figure.)

"Well, the doctors are doing flips. They want to get this lady into the delivery room, and Elvis is doing his psychic healing. Then he asks the doctor, 'Can I come in the delivery room? I have never seen a baby born. I want to see life.'"

CHAPTER 26

THE LAST CONCERT

Statement of death at last concert.

It was the first time that Elvis would be in front of cameras of any kind in quite some time. The criticism of the tours during the previous year churned in his mind: "His attempts to perpetuate his mystique of sex and power end in weak self-parody," and "Elvis is neither looking or sounding good. He's thirty pounds overweight: he's puffy, white faced, and blinking against the lights" (Variety). What seemed strange as they stood there was that the cameras, friends to Elvis' career for so long, now seemed like cold intruders, even adversaries.

Elvis was tired, troubled, savaged by drugs, and grossly overweight. He looked terrible, and he knew it. For the first time in his life, he had to step out to public scrutiny without the benefit of his good appearance. Knowing that the cameras would unsympathetically reflect all that had happened to him and all that he had become, he felt naked.

Vernon Presley sat out front in the audience, knowing how important and difficult the night would be for his son. He looked frail and wan since his heart attack, and Elvis would announce during the show how nice it was to have Daddy back on tour for the first time since his illness. He would also introduce Ginger Alden as "my new girlfriend," and she would stand to bask in the exhilarating spotlight of national exposure. Everyone else in the TCB entourage was assembled and deployed, knowing that Elvis would have to rise to the occasion, hoping for the best, worrying.

The band broke into the rumbling barrage of drums that led into *Also Sprach Zarathustra* and the introductory strains of *See See Rider* and *That's All Right (Mama)*. Rick again glanced at the Boss: He had that faraway, lost look of a man pondering his life and staring into the abyss of himself, when the images and events of a life all seem to blow through a mind at once. Rick had seen that look before, when Elvis would wax philosophical about something. Still, he wondered what was tumbling through Elvis' mind...probably Gladys... Cilla and Lisa ... Linda ... Daddy being so sick ... the bad articles ... now Red and Sonny were writing that book about him. He knew how tired Elvis was as the Boss licked his parched lips, took a deep breath, and steadied himself.

Elvis frowned sadly and turned to him. "Know what, Rick? I may not look too good for my television special tonight, but I'll look good in my coffin."

And with that, Elvis Presley stepped out to face America for the last time.

CHAPTER 27

ELVIS: WHAT HAPPENED?

The subject of Red and Sonny West and the book *Elvis: What Happened?* is still a touchy one for Billy, Rick, and David. Though all three are outspoken about their feelings, David is still the most bitter. "I don't care what anybody else says," he contends angrily, "I was with him closely all that last year, and that goddamned book did more than anything else to kill him because it crushed his spirit. We all saw the effect it had on him."

"It was a Judas act," Billy says simply. "It was nothing but a cheap shot that just happened to be a book. I want everybody to know that those guys were not angels trying to make Elvis improve his life. They didn't give a flying fuck about him, and that's why they did it in the first place."

"Man," reflects Rick with a philosophical tone in his voice, "the most incredible thing to me was that it was a high school friend that did it to him, a friend of 20 years. Twenty years! They didn't do anybody any good except their bankbooks. I bet Red's sorry he did the book. The man's dead, and that helped kill him."

On July 13, 1976, Red (Bobby) West, Elvis' bodyguard and companion for close to 20 years, and his cousin Sonny, who went to work for Elvis in the early '60s, were fired by Vernon Presley. Vernon cited a financial reason, but as the West boys describe it in their book, they believe the "execution," as they called it, came about as a whim of Elvis Presley's. Red was particularly incensed because after all of their years together, Elvis simply flew out of town and left the dirty work for his daddy, leaving Red out in the cold with no warning, no income, and nothing to do. Sometime after their termination, they contracted to write and publish a book, an "inside" look at Elvis Presley's life which became *Elvis: What Happened?*

Most people have surmised that Elvis must have been disturbed about the book even though there were reports to the contrary, but as with everything else in his life, its effects went much deeper than one might suspect. The knowledge of the book was the most significant final episode in the life of Elvis Presley. It removed the last emotional and psychological barriers between life and his acceptance of death.

Elvis: What Happened? was not so much guilty of deception as it was the trivialization and sensationalism of Elvis' life. Here, then, is the indignity and cruelty of the book. It garishly highlighted the blackness in Elvis' life, the drugs, the self-destruction, his most selfish, irresponsible, and insensitive moments, without allowing him the dignity of understanding or compassion. It pointed out and pumped up his destruction without recognizing the despair that unleashed it. It robbed him, finally, of self-respect because it rendered him inhuman and grotesque. A work of vengeance, it sought to exploit and not understand, to simply "reveal' and not to explain.

Sorting fact from fiction in life and death.

A commentary on *Elvis: What Happened?* by Marty Lacker and the drug-connected death of Elvis:

The sorting of the truth from the fantasy is difficult. There are a lot of stories, and a lot of facts concerning the life and death of Elvis Presley. Reasonable conclusions can be reached when proper patience is exercised and sufficient time is spent reviewing the facts and the opinions. A certain amount of speculation may be in order when that speculation is based on known facts and known behavior patterns. To begin, there is the story as told by Sonny West, Red West and Dave Hebler in their book, *Elvis, What Happened?*

We know that certain facts are true. Sonny, Dave, and Red were close to Elvis and in a position to know what was happening. They had been fired, were in difficult financial positions, and were somewhat bitter. Their story was told to a writer who worked for a weekly newspaper known for its sensationalism. The facts of the story were corroborated by others who were near Elvis, but some insist these facts were exaggerated in the book.

The conclusion which may logically be reached from the above is that the facts of the book are true, but the story is told in a way to make events more dramatic and sensational than they actually were.

Some comments here may be in order. Learning can be painful. It often demands a cleansing of preconceived thoughts, a rejection of long-believed truths, and an opening of the mind to ideas new and different from what has been a closely held part of our lives. Learning can be painful and the price of examples, from which we learn, is often high. No man's life has a greater intrinsic value than that of another, but some, because of wealth, talent, intelligence, or even terror, are better known, and by being better known are more readily visible as examples from which we may all learn.

Learning from the life and death of Elvis Presley was painful for his associates. It may be painful for those millions of fans to whom Elvis was a very special person. But for the sake of his memory and the growth of all of us, an effort should be made to learn and to understand. It is important for those who would follow in Elvis' footsteps to know that he was neither good nor bad because of drugs. Drugs made no difference whatsoever as far as his talent was concerned and only affected his ability to perform when their excessive use began to interfere with his memory and coherency. There was never a time when Elvis was a better artist because of the drugs, and those closest to him tell of his greatest performances being executed when he was free of the drug interference. It would be easy for a young man or woman to believe that Elvis Presley became the great entertainer he was with the help of drugs, but the facts are just the opposite. Elvis became great before he ever heard of narcotics and certainly not because of them.

It is also important to understand that it makes not one bit of difference whether illicit drugs or prescription drugs were being used. To argue that Elvis Presley was any less addicted to drugs because he used Quaaludes for a fix, rather than cocaine or heroin, is the height of absurdity. It would make as much sense to argue that an alcoholic is less an alcoholic because he gets drunk from a high-priced Scotch rather than bathtub gin.

Like it or not, our society is drug-oriented. Cocaine is the new fad and considered to be the rich man's toy. Abuse of prescription drugs is far more prevalent than generally known, and many members of the medical profession find it easier to give a patient what he wants rather than what he should have.

Drugs, including alcohol, are part of our way of life. The United States government reports that 7 percent of the population has an alcohol abuse problem. The cost to society is estimated to be $43 billion a year for the problems caused by the 10 million or so who abuse alcohol. The figures are staggering, both financially and in the number of people whose lives are affected. When we add to this information the number of people who have prescription drug problems and those who have illicit drug problems, the numbers become almost incomprehensible. But it is a very real part of our everyday life and a situation we as a society must someday resolve.

Most importantly, we must understand that Elvis Presley was not the culprit, he was the victim. To discuss the drugs, to try to learn how they affected Elvis Presley's life and to try to understand what they can do to any of us does not imply that Elvis was any less great because of their use. He was an uncommonly talented entertainer who won the love and respect of millions of people around the world. His fans should understand that his ability to remain at the summit of popularity even after having fallen prey to the all-too-common disease of drug abuse speaks highly for his skill as a performer.

The conclusion must be that an overdose of drugs was not the immediate cause of Elvis' death. Had Elvis taken an overdose and fallen dead as a result of so doing, the drugs would have been easily found during the autopsy. There is no question, however, among medical authorities that the use of drugs to the extent that Marty Lacker, for example, used them for a 10-year period will eventually lead to severe bodily damage and death. The amount of time, the quantity of drugs, their interaction, and the general physical condition of the individual involved are factors which determine the period over which the drug abuse may be continued.

Drugs did contribute to Elvis Presley's death, either by affecting his heart, if reports attributed to Baptist Memorial Hospital are believed, or, at the very least, by keeping him from being sufficiently concerned about his diet and general health.

CHAPTER 28

ELVIS DIES

Interest and attitude close to death. Elvis' death described by Larry Geller:

Two months before he died, Elvis showed a deep and abiding interest in the Crucifixion and the Resurrection.

He had a feeling of empathy with the cross-bound Christ. "He was doing it for all of us, Larry. Don't you feel that? He must have known there would be people like us, who could reach out and sustain themselves out of His experience, scorned, humiliated, and tormented as He was, and yet forgiving."

He was interested in the artifacts bearing on Christ's death. The sacred pieces and fragments of wood that some said were relics of the cross, the jug that a thirsting Jesus was offered on the way to the cross, the robe that covered his agonized frame on the cross, and the shroud He lay in before He ascended.

Elvis was given now to looking abstracted. His eyes often seemed distant and his manner preoccupied. He no longer spoke of marriage, and he found it hard to enthuse about anything for very long.

He read everything on the Resurrection, in the Bible and other sources. And he remarked how difficult it had been for Christ to convince even his Apostles that he had risen. He was used to skeptics himself, and so gloried in the story of Doubting Thomas, the apostle who denied the resurrected Christ until he touched him.

Elvis loved Jesus' mild rebuke:

Thomas, because thou hast seen me, thou hast believed; blessed are they that have not seen, and yet have believed."

And yet Elvis understood, for he, too, had not believed.

He was asked by a doubter: "Where am I going?"

He smiled, and rejoined:

"If you don't know where you're going, you're not going there." At times, he seemed more interested in the Resurrection than the Crucifixion.

"Larry," he said, "do you remember that book on the Holy Shroud? Can you get me another copy?" This was the shroud legend that the crucified Jesus had been wrapped in just before the Resurrection.

Larry looked at him curiously. He had been struck by Elvis' recent allusions to death, not in any mournful sense, but casually and contemplatively.

"Why this book?" he asked.

"There's something about Jesus' death I want to look into; something I think I should know."

The tour ended, and Larry joined Elvis at Graceland for a brief hiatus before returning to Los Angeles. As he took his leave, Elvis sat up in bed and gave him a bear hug. "Now, Lawrence," he said, "don't forget the book." Elvis did not let Larry forget. Two weeks later, he put in a call to remind Larry. After rummaging around for a while, Larry picked up a paperback, *Scientific Search for the Face of Jesus*. It carried a vivid description of the Holy Shroud, in which Jesus supposedly lay in the Holy Sepulchre before He rose to His heavenly home.

As Larry went through the book, noting the faceless outline of Christ on the cover, he again wondered about Elvis' preoccupation with Jesus' death, and his own demise. He remembered other conversations. In Providence, Rhode Island, Elvis had turned to singer Kathy Westmoreland: "I look fat now, and I'll look terrible for my TV special coming up. But I'll tell you this, I'll look good in my casket."

The remark sent a chill through Kathy. She mentioned it later to Larry, looking for reassurance.

He shook his head, glumly. "He may have only been talking, but he told me he thought he had cancer."

Elvis had also told Kathy Westmoreland: "Just as the Kahuna in Hawaii know, so will I know when I am going to die. They don't tell anybody. They just go off by themselves. It will be about the same date my mother died."

Two days before he died, his stepbrother David Stanley said casually: "Good night, Elvis, I'll be seeing you."

Elvis looked up from his bed with a trace of a smile. "No, you won't, David. You won't be seeing me here anymore."

David stopped in his tracks. "What do you mean, Elvis?"

Elvis' smile widened. He appeared to enjoy the younger man's confusion.

He held up a finger for emphasis. It was his last lesson for the 22-year-old he loved as a son.

"It won't be here, David, but in another time and space."

Elvis was engrossed more and more in Christ's salvation now and the life hereafter. He speculated, half-seriously, on reincarnation and what he might come back as, should he return in a new form.

"I'd like to be a doctor," he said whimsically. "I'd be my own best patient."

In the midst of all this theorizing, he had ballooned to over 200 pounds. He was determined to visualize himself thin and diet at the same time. He was meditating for longer periods now, and he seemed fascinated with the blue lights that appeared on the screen of his mind.

"I keep seeing these blue lights," he told Larry, and then he laughed. "I don't know how much it has to do with the story Daddy told us. But it was always my favorite color. It stands for truth, and for Jesus as well."

He would concentrate on the third eye, the pineal gland in the center of his forehead, and he reported visualizations such as he had not had before. They were almost astral projections. He felt as if he were floating through the clouds. He felt a tremendous peace and saw the hazy outline of a face, sensing it was Christ, while not quite determining the features. "I could almost reach out and touch him. It was like that day over Flagstaff, but immensely more personal."

He could get into animated discussions about death. By this time, the more artful girls knew how to capture his interest. "Elvis," said an aspiring actress, "my mother died last year, and since then I've really been confused about death. It made me wonder about life, and why we're here at all. It made me realize, as young as I am, that I will die one day. I always knew it, of course, but it was in the back of my head, where I didn't have to deal with it."

She paused. "Are you afraid to die, Elvis?"

"No, I am not afraid of death. If I were to die tonight, that would be all right. That doesn't mean I want to die. I love life. But I feel that death and life are parts of one and the same thing. And death is as natural to life as night is to day."

He took the girl's hand. "I know how you feel. Remember when I lost my mother, it tore me up. But I keep thinking of her, as if she is still here. And my twin brother as well. I used to talk to him when I was a small boy. It was comforting." He laughed. "I didn't tell anybody, they would only think there was something wrong with me. But what difference does it make what people think, it's what you think that counts."

He could see the girl's doubts were not resolved.

"Look," he said, "If this life was the whole thing, and nothing was awaiting us on the other side, I could understand how you feel. The thought of extinction would frighten me, too. But I know the soul is immortal."

"*How* do you know?" she asked.

Elvis grinned. "You thought you had me, well, you do, in a way. It's more of an understanding I've come to through reading, meditating, listening to others, and experiencing. You have to experience."

He wagged a finger. "I'm not trying to convince you. I'm only sharing my philosophy with you. To me, the soul, the inner person, the spirit, is involved in a particular body for as long as that body lives. The soul lives on, to profit by certain lessons we need for our growth, and ultimately to recognize its oneness with God."

He gave her a dazzling smile. "I'm convinced of all that, as sure as my name is Wayne Newton..." He saw the flash of perplexity in the girl's eyes. "No, no, I'm only kidding." He patted her hand. "You asked me a question, I tried to give you an answer. For those that believe, no explanation is necessary. For those that don't, no explanation is possible."

She looked at him gratefully. "Somehow, I feel you speak the truth. But I've had no experience, I've seen no vision, as you have."

"You will; keep searching."

Elvis held out a book he had been carrying. "Here's a very special book. Read it, and follow its advice. It will help you in more ways than you know."

It was a copy of *The Impersonal Life*. He had given away hundreds of them.

Larry arrived in Memphis on August 15, with his usual cargo of books. He checked into a motel down the road from Graceland and phoned Elvis. "Well, son," said Elvis, "did you bring the books?" Larry said, "Wait until you feast your eyes on what I've brought you."

"Okay," said Elvis, "I'll rest up a little, and I'll catch you tomorrow."

They rang off. Larry was reassured by Elvis' apparent buoyancy and struck by the light, boyish quality of his voice. All the hoarseness was gone. He seemed as lighthearted as a child.

Larry read for a while, climbed into bed, and was about to turn off the light when the phone rang. It was Elvis' aide, Al Strada.

"Guess what," he said. "Elvis wants the books now. He says he can't fall asleep."

Larry had marked one passage in Frank Adams' *The Face of Jesus* that he knew Elvis would be especially interested in:

"The idea of a human body being in apport (spiritually induced movement), with no visible agency is not necessarily a unique thing. It is not a question of the sole example occurring in the tomb of Joseph of Arimathea (the Sepulchre) nineteen hundred and thirty-eight years ago (sic). No there have been other cases noted in Psychical research as well as recorded in church history. So the movement out of the Shroud into the area outside of it is not an impossible thing in our still limited knowledge of the laws of physics, and the behavior of atoms."

Al Strada brought back the books, and a restless Elvis skimmed through them. He was preoccupied with his new tour, ready to take off the next day for Portland, Maine. And he was up in the air with Ginger. He was still urging her to go, but he had a replacement picked out, a local Memphis belle.

He also saw a Memphis dentist, Dr. Lester Hoffman, for minor dental work that last night, and tried to book the film *MacArthur* at the Memphian, but no projectionist was available. He came back to Graceland about 2 a.m. to find that Larry had just left. He played racquetball with his cousin, Billy Smith, and Billy's wife, Jo. As he left the racquetball court, a little winded, he stopped at the wishing well next to the Meditation Garden, and said: "This is the most beautiful place in the world to me, more than anyplace I've ever been."

There was a soft smile on his lips and an almost ethereal look on his face. And then, for no apparent reason, he turned to Billy and said: "Don't let your grief keep me earthbound. Let me go where I have to go."

Billy had listened to Elvis over the years. He understood.

Elvis and Ginger went upstairs at 6:30 a.m. He was still up at 9 a.m. He said to Ginger, "Honey, I'm going to the bathroom, I'll be right back." He took with him *The Face of Jesus.*

Ginger fell off to sleep. She woke up twice and saw no Elvis. She didn't investigate until 1 p.m. She went into the bathroom and saw Elvis lying on the floor. He was in the fetal position, the book clutched to his breast.

Larry had awakened at 11:30 a.m. He felt completely drained. In a dream, he had seen Elvis, trying to tell him something, but he couldn't quite make out what he was saying. He got up, finally, strangely glum. He dressed and drove to Graceland, noticing, as he approached, three helicopters circling the property.

There was an unusual number of people and some television cameras and sound equipment. People were pressing against the gate. He could sense the suppressed emotion and felt the first rustlings of alarm. Elvis' uncle, Vester Presley, opened the gate.

One look at Larry, and he could see that he didn't know. "Elvis is dead," he said in a broken voice. "He died an hour ago."

Larry sat petrified for several moments, unable to move. And then felt a frantic urge to get into the house and be near Elvis. He spotted Vernon in the den, sitting lifelessly in a chair. As he saw Larry, Vernon cried out, "He's gone, Larry, he's gone. My boy is gone. What am I going to do?"

Larry came close to him and hugged him. He couldn't say anything, and neither could Vernon right then. What was there to say?

Little Lisa Marie, who had been vacationing with her father, was walking from one room to another, sobbing.

"My daddy is dead, my daddy is dead."

She showed remarkable composure for a child. She took hold of herself and quietly walked into the den, where Larry and a few friends were glumly sitting, and said, "I just can't believe it. Elvis Presley is dead."

Elvis' aged grandmother, Minnie Mae, now 88, collapsed and had to be carried to her bedroom. She sobbed over and over, "Oh God, oh God, he was the prettiest thing I ever did see."

Larry couldn't help but remember what Elvis had said at that healing service long before. It kept ringing in his ears: "She's all right. She'll outlive me."

Elvis had died from what the doctors called cardiac arrhythmia, an irregularity in the heartbeat, aggravated perhaps by stress and exertion, leading to a cardiac arrest. He had been panting on the racquetball court just a few hours before his death.

The autopsy revealed what Elvis had already suspected, because of the almost unbearable pain he felt at times, causing him to use Percodan, codeine, Demerol, and other painkillers.

"I must have cancer," he had confided more than once. "I feel so dragged down, in constant pain."

PART VI
ELVIS' PHILOSOPHIES

CHAPTER 29

ELVIS' DEATH RELATED BY DEE PRESLEY AND HER THREE SONS

The bright lights of Memphis twinkled in the distance and the Mississippi snaked sluggishly off into nothingness as the roller coaster slowly climbed to a dazzling height with a jerking motion. Preparing himself for the adventure, Rick turned to wink at Elvis, who sat in the car behind him, ailing, with his am around Lisa.

Lisa knew something was up because Rick and Elvis always acted like a couple of idiots to make her laugh when they took her out to Libertyland. Rick stood and perched himself on the side of his car at the split second when the train paused before it dipped. He wailed like a banshee into the night and leapt through the air to clutch onto the rafters and side railing, where he hung like a monkey to enjoy Lisa gasping and Elvis roaring with laughter. He stood there chuckling as the train disappeared down the tracks, shaking the rafters and trailing away in Lisa's long and delighted scream. When the train came around again, Rick popped back into his car and Lisa looked reproachfully at him and said, "Ricky, don't do that!" before they plunged again. Then they got on the Dodge 'Em bumper cars and rode for what seemed liked hours before dawn, when they got back in the car to head home.

Lisa was enjoying her several weeks visiting her daddy and granddaddy at Graceland before returning to Los Angeles to start school. The weather in Memphis that August had been tropical in humidity, blistering under a Southern sun that hung day after day in the sky to scorch the city, turning the poorer sections into an inferno and making it so hot that you couldn't even go outside without sweating clear through your shirt in a matter of minutes.

Elvis had returned from his last tour to spend the final few weeks of Lisa's summer vacation at Graceland. He was gearing up for an 11-day tour slated to begin on the 16th, when he would fly off to do a show in Portland, Oregon, and finish with two successive shows back in Memphis at the Mid-South Coliseum on the 27th and 28th. As usual, he avoided the heat, preferring the air-conditioned and dehumidified atmosphere of his bedroom during the day and the cool of the night, when he would take Lisa out to Libertyland for excursions on Casey's Cannonball and the Little Dipper.

The usual contingent was there at Graceland getting ready for the tour: Charlie, Ricky, David, Dick, Billy Smith, with the other principals expected to arrive in town by the 16th for the tour. Ginger Alden was spending her nights with Elvis at Graceland, and David and Rick were on duty as usual, alternating their nights and days on call for the Boss. Joe Esposito, who usually arrived in town a day or two before the tour to put things in order, was in town by the 15th. Things were progressing. Taking care of business as usual.

The Boss got up late the afternoon of the 15th and David then came by to talk to Elvis about his impending divorce. He was depressed about Angie, and Elvis counseled him to remain strong and keep on pushing despite his vanishing hopes for a reconciliation. David left and tried to psych himself up for the tour. At nightfall, Elvis took Ginger out for a ride in his Stutz and then returned to relax and put some of his affairs in order before the tour.

Anyone passing the mansion on the night of the 15th or the early morning hours of the 16th would have seen the light burning brightly on the second floor where Elvis stayed. Rick was on duty, and he was busy getting Elvis's trunks ready before David was scheduled to come on duty at noon. Rick hadn't had a chance to get his own clothes washed, folded, and packed for the tour, so he was planning to double back to his apartment when David arrived. He was no longer seeing Jill, but they were still good friends and she would give him a hand.

Sometime around 2:00 a.m., Elvis wanted to play racquetball. Though terribly out of shape, he had been doing a little swimming and racquetball to limber up for the tour and that way avoid muscle pulls onstage when he moved. The court, which Elvis had built when he became a racquetball enthusiast, is located at the right side of the house, in the left part of the backyard, and Elvis, Ricky, Ginger, Billy Smith, and his wife, Josie, accompanied him down there. In sneakers, shorts, and sweatshirts, Elvis, Rick, and Billy smacked the ball against the wall for some two hours. "Elvis didn't get out there and bust it," Rick remembers, "but he played. It didn't seem that he was overexerting himself or anything like that." Rick stayed with Elvis until 5 or 6 that morning, when Elvis handed him a prescription for Dilaudid. Rick went out and had it filled quickly. The drug was in capsule form and Rick noted that the dosage was no more than usual, certainly not enough to cause any undue concern on his part. "It wasn't any amount that could have even came close to killing him," he says flatly, "but if he had been straight when he had the heart problem, who knows, man, he might have survived."

Rick and Elvis spent some time alone after Billy Smith left and Ginger was out of the room. Elvis was in the mood to pray. Rick was one of the few people that Elvis showed his spiritual side to, and when the mood struck him, they often prayed together. That year, with his knowledge and anxieties about Red and Sonny's book, they prayed more often than ever before. Around 6 o'clock they sat on Elvis' bed, clasped their hands together, and closed their eyes.

"Lord," Elvis prayed aloud, "help me to have insight and forgive me for my sins. Let the people who read that book have compassion and understanding about the things I've done. Dear God, please help me to get back when I feel down like this, and to always strive for good in the world. In the name of Jesus Christ. Amen." Rick nodded his amen to Elvis.

"Ricky, tell David when be comes on tomorrow not to disturb me under any circumstances," the Boss said. "I don't want to get up until about 4. Need plenty of rest for the tour."

"Okay," Rick said, "I'll start getting the rest of your stuff down and I'll see you later."

"Good night, Rick.

"Sleep well, Elvis," he said, closing the door quietly.

The morning air was still as the sun began to poke its head over that part of the world, sending low, mellow rays over Graceland and casting the estate in summer dawn tones. The horizon was tinted a beautiful orange-red; birds chirped peacefully as Elvis slept and nothing disturbed the tranquility of the morning, save a random car or two passing the mansion on Elvis Presley Boulevard.

Inside the mansion, silence also reigned. Elvis and Ginger were asleep in his bedroom, and Lisa slept in her bedroom upstairs. Aunt Delta was asleep downstairs in her bedroom; so was Minnie Mae Presley. Vernon and Sandy Miller slumbered in the house on Dolan where Dee Presley had raised her boys.

The others on the grounds also slept soundly, Charlie Hodge in the furnished apartment above the garage and Billy Smith with his family in their trailer quarters. Joe Esposito was in his room at the Howard Johnson's Motor Lodge in Whitehaven. The only people awake were Pauline Nicholson, Elvis' trusted housekeeper; Harold Lloyd, who manned the front gate; and Rick, who busied himself with various chores and waited for his brother David. He would remember to pass on the message about Elvis wanting to sleep for as long as possible.

Elvis woke up sometime around 9 o'clock. It was not unusual for him to rise after only several hours of sleep (even with the sleeping medication) and sometimes take more medication to get back to bed; other times, he felt like staying up and reading or watching television. These were the moments when the TCB boys would have to be most on their toes in case Elvis needed them or something was to go wrong. If a woman was sleeping with him, she was always instructed to call if anything unusual happened, unless it was Linda Thompson, who was always on top of the situation. Ginger had learned the score, but that morning, after Elvis told her that he was going to his bathroom, she dropped back to sleep. Considering her scant three hours of sleep and that she was probably not fully awake in the darkness created by Elvis' specially lined dark curtains, it isn't hard to understand why.

Located off his bedroom on the second floor was Elvis' outsized and luxurious bathroom. With its walls knocked out to create space, Elvis had transformed it into a combination bathroom-office-study-lounge. One wall is mirrored and fringed with those large, spare light bulbs that one usually associates with the dressing room of a star. Under the mirror is a large Formica tabletop with a sunken purple sink, upon which were strewn all of Elvis' toilet articles. The shower, a circular one with its walls done in a brown, black, and white tile design, is situated right next to the counter. The room is carpeted in plush purple; books, comfortable easy chairs, a television, and other items of leisure were placed casually about. The Boss's bathroom was the most private room in the house and the most private place in his life. Nobody ever went in without knocking. It was logical that the most private sanctuary in a life so fraught with publicity would have to be the bathroom, so Elvis made it into the place where he could be alone with his thoughts and most intimate with himself. The distance from the bathroom door (a heavy wooden one) to the bed where Ginger slept is approximately 30 feet.

Very few people know exactly what happened next, and that's probably the way Elvis would have wanted it. It is known that he sat on a chair and read for a while, and David would later recall that it was *Shroud of Turin* by Ian Wilson, a book about Jesus and the evolution of Christian theology that Larry Geller had given Elvis as a present. It is also known that sometime between 10 and 2:30 that afternoon, Elvis had a heart attack. The preliminary findings by Dr. Jerry Francisco, the Shelby County coroner, would rule that cardiac arrhythmia and hardening of the arteries were the "natural" causes of death. Elvis may or may not have taken more of his sleeping medication; he may or may not have taken a dangerous amount of that medication if he did take more. If he had taken more and then had his coronary difficulty, the narcotics, as Rick has suggested, may very well have impaired his ability to react and help himself. If he experienced a serious heart failure with acute chest pain such as that felt during a massive heart attack, he couldn't have lasted for more than three to five minutes, in which case the narcotics would have lessened the pain considerably.

Whatever it was, sometime, some way, before 2:30 in the afternoon of August 16, 1977, Elvis Aaron Presley, wearing a pair of blue cotton pajamas, alone in his bathroom, dropped his book, kneeled over onto his face, gasped desperately for the vital breath that the sudden lack of oxygen shouted for, and was unable to find it. In an instant as long as eternity, he left his trouble behind, found his final meaning, and took it to the last limit. His body was prostrate on the floor before his Maker, but his soul—as relatives, friends and the millions of people who adored him believe—immortalized, rocked gently once again in the loving arms of the mother who rocked and sang him to sleep into the quietude of the Mississippi night.

The world outside the door of the bathroom had remained oblivious to the sublimely private moment and drama of his death.

Drugs and death related by Marty Lacker.

The autopsy of Elvis Presley required almost two months. It contains the reports of laboratory specialists and pathologists from California and several other places, as well as from those in Memphis. It is probably as complete as any autopsy has ever been. There are conflicting opinions concerning the results.

Dr. Jerry T. Francisco, Shelby County medical examiner, announced that

Elvis had died of cardiac arrhythmia due to unknown causes. He also said there was no evidence of drug abuse. Dr. Francisco is reported to have said his diagnosis is often used by medical examiners who arrive at their findings through inference; that is, by interpreting what is found during an autopsy when no specific cause of death is apparent.

Dr. Eric Muirhead, chief of pathology at Baptist Hospital and an internationally recognized authority on hypertension, has said that he does not consider heart disease as a possible cause of death.

The autopsy report of Baptist Hospital lists Elvis' death as a drug-related death known commonly as polypharmacy. This has to do with the action of more than one drug where the combined effect is greater than if each were used alone. Some of the laboratories used by the various authorities reported finding 10 different drugs, while others found eight, and Dr. Francisco has said only four were significant and these were not present in sufficient levels to cause death.

All of the authorities had access to the same reports. The kindest thing to say is that someone is mistaken.

I am not a medical doctor, nor was I at Graceland when Elvis died, or present at the autopsy. But I do know that Elvis had a drug problem! That's a direct and honest statement by someone who was as close to him for over 20 years as any human being in this world. More important, it is a statement by someone who shared the same drug problem with him. There are those who have blown the drug use out of all proportion, and there are those who would prefer that it not be mentioned. Both are wrong. The truth is no less the truth because it goes unspoken, as the truth ceases to be the truth when it becomes distorted.

Elvis contributed much to the world, as much, I believe, as almost any man who has ever lived. He has now the opportunity to make one final contribution to the millions of fans to whom he brought so much joy. He can share the results of drug abuse.

Elvis had a drug problem. I had a drug problem. Let me define the words "drug problem," before any of his critics begin to say, "I told you so." Aspirin is a drug and if someone takes too many, he then has a drug problem. This is true of alcohol, tranquilizers, diet pills, and the host of other things which the American people administer to themselves every day, with and without, the blessings of the medical profession. The more commonly accepted definition of the words "drug problem" is someone using marijuana, LSD, heroin, or something of that nature.

I can categorically state that Elvis did not have a drug problem if we use the second definition. He did not use what are known as hard drugs. He did, however, have a drug problem, and it began with the diet pills. The diet pills, which were prescribed, allowed him to stay up and work for long hours. These pills have the side effect of being stimulants; they make those who take them feel good. They turn people on to the excitement of the world around them, sometimes real, but more often not. They're easy to get, easy to take, and unfortunately, easy to continue taking.

Most of us began taking the pills because we kept the same hours as Elvis and some of us also had weight problems. We used the pills throughout the movie years.

The diet pills can make the user feel great one minute and depressed and miserable the next. There were times when we would go two or three days without sleeping and be irritable as hell.

One type of pill leads to another.

To counteract the diet pills, we began taking sleeping pills, tranquilizers, or sedatives in order to sleep. All the pills were easy to obtain. They came in every color, shape, size, and variety. They made us feel good during the day, they made us feel rested when we were tired, they gave us courage to do what we were afraid to do, and they made us sleep when we went to bed. They caused me to lie in bed and wonder why the television set was turned on its side, but they kept me from thinking it was my head, and they made me not care enough to worry about it very long. Where two first did the job, four soon became necessary and before long, it took eight to bring back that old feeling. The pills led us to believe they were doing us no harm, and we felt so good we knew we could quit when, if ever, it became necessary.

Fortunately, for some of us, it became necessary and we were able to quit. Unfortunately, none of us was strong enough to help Elvis. Perhaps he simply didn't have a reason to quit, or perhaps he was going to, or perhaps he never really cared. He was a strange and unusual man of strong feelings and strong desires, and that very strength may have kept him from doing other than he did. I don't know.

Drugs take you nowhere and leave YOU there.

But there was a lot more to the 42 years, seven months and eight days of the life of Elvis Presley than the abuse of prescription drugs. There were years of understanding, generosity, and friendship. There was a legend left for millions of fans who loved and respected him, and if any one of them can accept this moment of failure in a lifetime of success, and understand what can come from the abuse of any drug, then perhaps even that was of some value.

There has been so much said and written over the years about Elvis, his habits, his family, and his friends that it must be difficult for anyone to separate the wheat from the chaff. It was reported that Elvis and his mother were both 42 years old when they died and because Elvis had always openly praised his mother, something mysterious was made from the age. The fact is Elvis' mother was 46 years old when she died. One noted columnist wrote that Elvis had said he would never live as long as his mother had. In all the years I knew Elvis, I never heard him say anything even remotely similar to that. It has been written that Elvis had a death wish, but in fact he often told us about how he wanted to live forever. He would say we were all going to live to be old and gray. What he did have was an immense thirst for a knowledge of life, the meaning of it, and how it began. He constantly read about religious and the supernatural. Elvis was curious about reincarnation and life after death. He had a great faith in God upon which he built his life, but he was in no hurry to find out what death was like.

CHAPTER 30

ELVIS MEETS LARRY GELLER
HIS SPIRITUAL ADVISOR

Larry Geller described by Dee Presley and Elvis' two stepbrothers.

Since the Boss's moviemaking days, Larry Geller had been Elvis' hair-stylist and kindred spirit in the pursuit of knowledge. Larry was Elvis' connection to the California culture and the world of esoterica, bringing him interesting books to read about meditation, psychology, philosophy, Eastern religion, parapsychology, and all of the interests that Elvis so ardently chased during the last decade or so of his life. The two of them would sit for long periods of time, talking. A handsome man with brown hair and piercing eyes, Larry was another of Elvis' closest personal friends.

Elvis meets Larry Geller, as related by Larry Geller.

"I've heard good things about you," he said. He brushed his hand through his finely spun dark hair, in a characteristic gesture, and threw his head back. He was more down to earth than Larry had expected, treating him with the same casualness he would have shown a studio head or a plumber.

He took Larry across the hall to a large bathroom with marble counters and shelves, and porcelain fittings on the basin and shower. A full-length mirror comprised most of one wall.

Wrapping the star in a gray cape and dunking his head under the faucet, Larry was struck by the baby fine hair and the tiniest outgrowth of light, sandy hair. He knew then that Elvis dyed his hair black.

As Larry picked up his scissors, Elvis explained that he only wanted his hair trimmed. He had to be at Paramount the next day for publicity shots for the movie *Roustabout,* which he was just finishing, and the still shots had to match the movie.

As Larry cut his hair, they talked. Wisps of hair fell from the cape to the floor.

Jay Sebring came over and took his hand.

"Good luck," said Jay in his pleasant voice. "Remember that Sebring look."

Larry thanked Jay perfunctorily, little knowing it was to be his last day in Sebring's shop. He was not that psychic, nor sufficiently psychic to know that five years later, on his, Larry's, August 8 birthday, Jay Sebring would fall victim, with Sharon Tate and two others, to Charles Manson and his band of killers.

He pulled up to Elvis' mansion in the exclusive Bel Air section of Los Angeles just before 4. He could spot the place by the clusters of excited tourists snapping pictures outside the gate.

They were nearly all women, of all ages. Elvis affected them all similarly. He was part of their lost dreams and fondest hopes.

The wrought-iron gate opened, and Larry walked into the compound beyond, looking back just once to catch the awe in the sea of female faces. Allan Fortas greeted him at the door. He shook his hand, saying, "You must be Larry."

He nodded, and looked past Fortas, into the dining room. He could see Elvis at a table with four or five other young men who were part of his entourage, the so-called Memphis Mafia, who did his bidding and were his link to his hometown roots.

Larry was immediately struck by Elvis' youth and vitality. He spoke volubly, his hands flying out to make a point, laughing heartily as the others joined in. He was wearing a sea captain's peaked cap, styled after the cap worn by Marlon Brando in *The Wild One,* in which Brando played the leader of a motorcycle gang.

Elvis broke off his conversation to greet the newcomer with a smile and a wave.

"Hey, man, I'm finishing up. I'll be right with you."

Fortas took Larry through the spacious living room, past a fireplace that swept to the ceiling, into a large den. Fortas smiled and backed off, saying Elvis would be along in a few minutes. He spoke in a soft drawl, the first Jew that Larry had ever heard speak in a Southern accent.

"Never mind cleaning up," Elvis said, looking at the floor, "a maid will take care of it."

"I'd just as soon," Larry said. "I like to do my own cleaning up." Elvis shook his head.

"We all have responsibilities," Larry continued. "We shouldn't shirk them."

Elvis turned sharply. "Where did that come from?"

"It's part of my belief."

Elvis frowned. "What do a few scraps of hair have to do with beliefs?"

At the risk of seeming pretentious, Larry replied: "In yoga, the great masters say the means and the ends are the same. It's the way you run your life that counts. Picking up after yourself is a way of life."

He could sense Elvis' growing interest.

"You're a strange cat for a barber."

"Barbering," Larry replied, " is what I do for a living. I am a human being before I am anything else."

Elvis started to laugh. "I thought I was getting a barber, and look what I got."

"Tell me, he said, "about this interest of yours, what you run your life with."

He chuckled again, good-naturedly, but his eyes held Larry's in a tight grip.

"A few years ago," said Larry, "I had a metaphysical experience. I won't tell you the details right now, but it drew me to God, and to Jesus. It gave me a feeling of exaltation and purpose.

"Purpose," Elvis said, practically jumping out of his chair. "That's what I lack in my life. Purpose." He waved his arms and began pacing up and down the bathroom, an unforgettable figure, his hair sopping wet and the gray cape trailing after him.

"Purpose? Tell me the purpose of life. I don't know. You tell me."

Larry gave him a slow smile. "We're here," he said, "to find out why we're here. That's our purpose. And when we find out, and go about fulfilling it, then we know our mission."

"How old are you?" Elvis asked, giving Larry an appraising glance.

"Twenty-four."

"Four years younger than me, and you got all the answers. That's pretty good."

"I don't have them all," said Larry. "But I do have the questions. The Masters have the answers."

Elvis shook his head in mock bewilderment.

"God, man, you go from one puzzle to another, like gangbusters. Now who the hell are the Masters?"

"There's no secret about it," Larry shrugged. "Jesus, for one. Mohammed, Moses, and Zoroaster, a Persian mystic. Buddha, and the Chinese, Lao-tzu."

Elvis persisted. "And what made them Masters?"

It was getting a little heavy, but Larry persevered.

"They were chosen instruments of the Lord, each in his own way." He went over in his mind what he had gleaned from the many books he'd read on the metaphysical. "Some had visions. Others heard voices."

Elvis stood up like he'd been hit by a bolt of lightning.

"Voices!" he cried. "That is really something." He thought for a moment longer. "I think I can trust you." But he still hesitated, looking at Larry uncertainly.

"What would you say if I told you I had heard voices?"

"I have no reason to doubt it."

"Good," said Elvis. "I couldn't tell anybody else around here. They'd have me locked up." He looked at Larry solemnly. "Now what do you honestly think of it?"

"I wouldn't know, unless I knew more about it. But," his face lit up, "I have a book I can show you. It could tell you more than I could about it."

"What can a book do?" said Elvis doubtfully.

"Help you find out about yourself."

Elvis carefully ran his eyes over Larry.

"I'm going to let you in on something," he said. "I've had some idea of my purpose, too. I've always felt there was a guiding hand directing the events in my life. My overnight success didn't just happen. There's a reason for it. I want to find out that reason."

Larry looked at him sympathetically, seeing his own striving in Elvis' groping.

"You know, I heard voices when I was a boy," Larry said.

Elvis' head came up. "What did they say?"

"They kept telling me to do the right thing."

Elvis laughed. "They weren't very helpful, were they? How do you know what's right?" He seemed on the verge of a further disclosure. "It has something to do with my twin brother. He died when I was born, but..."

He broke off suddenly and went back to what they had been talking about earlier.

"I'd like to see that book you mentioned," he said.

"I'll bring it," said Larry. "It will show you the two basic paths of life. One of spiritual development and the other the materialistic, people grubbing to get ahead, each trying to climb over the other."

Elvis' head bobbed vigorously.

"Man," he said, "I know what you're talking about. I've had this phony Hollywood life, guys you don't even know, with fat cigars in their mouths, putting their arms around you and calling you 'baby'. The chicks shining up to you for what they can get. I get the feeling I'm living in a used-car lot. And I'm what's being used. I could never go out to a movie, or to dinner, without feeling like a walking floor show. The only communication I have is with my guys from Memphis, and all they care about is girls. That's their purpose."

He laughed a little hollowly. "Not that there's anything wrong with girls, but there's got to be more to life. There's got to be some serious purpose, something I was cut out to do."

"You've made millions happy with your music and your motion pictures," said Larry.

"I need to do something about myself," Elvis cried. "Nobody knows how empty I feel."

He shook the water out of his hair and frowned. "I don't know why I should be talking so frankly to you."

Elvis gave him a self-deprecating look. "I had to be successful before I realized that what I was struggling for wasn't what I thought. And I'm worse off now than I was before, because I always had the idea that everything was going to be great when I made it."

"I could never get into the 'Hollywood scene'. When I first came out, I went to a few showbiz parties. Man, I couldn't believe it, grown men calling you 'sweetheart'. Everyone acted like they were my best friend. They were just laying it on. They didn't really know me, they were reacting to my name and all that stuff. I heard about people like that before I ever got to Hollywood—the 'beautiful' people."

There was something about the young stranger that encouraged Elvis to unburden himself as he hadn't done since his mother died. "You're a good listener," said Elvis.

Larry smiled. "You get that way cutting hair."

Elvis was silent for a moment. His mind wandered back over the years.

"My mom, bless her heart, was simple woman, but she was very wise. She told me when my career first started to take off, 'Elvis, when you're on top everyone will love you, but if you slip, just watch your friends disappear. Never forget where you came from."

His face suddenly lit up. "Do you know what my mom's middle name was?"

Larry shook his head.

"It was Love." He sighed. "My parents sacrificed so much for me. I'll never forget that. That must be true spirituality. Isn't that what made Jesus so great, giving himself for others?"

He wanted to talk, and Larry let him.

"You don't know how lonely it is to be a star," he said. "I don't really have anybody, not since Mom passed away. I love my daddy, but he doesn't understand what I need."

He brushed a hand across his eyes, and Larry pretended not to notice. "Sometimes late at night, before I go to sleep, I close my eyes and I see my mother looking at me. Her eyes are soft and loving. It's a pleasant, peaceful experience. I go to bed hoping I will see her. It's as real as anything that ever happened to me."

Elvis' eyes took on a faraway look. "It was like she wanted me with her." A gentle smile transformed his features.

"It was thinking of my mom," he said, "that protected me from 'going Hollywood.' I just knew I should stay clear of that scene. I remember when I first met Debra Paget. She was in my first movie, *Love Me Tender*. I never met anyone as beautiful before. I went nuts over her. I even sent her flowers. But she wouldn't give me the time of day. In fact, she even laughed at me, making fun of my Southern accent. It destroyed my ego.

"I went out with Natalie Wood for a while. She is pretty down to earth. She wasn't the typical Hollywood type girl. Neither is Tuesday Weld, and a few others I dated. But when I finish a movie now, we head back to Memphis until the next movie. Staying in Hollywood can warp your values. Going home helps keep things in perspective. Somehow, I didn't change that much. I've lost most of my Southern accent, but luckily, that's all."

Larry looked at this man who had everything. With his perfect profile, he was as handsome as anybody could be. He had tasted fame and fortune at 21. He could live anywhere, go anywhere, do anything, and he was miserably unhappy. It was clear to Larry that his unhappiness lay in an unrealized potential. Larry took a deep breath, wondering if it was his own purpose to turn Elvis on to the spiritual.

"Everybody is lonely without God," he said.

Elvis gave the young man a challenging look.

"What do you know about God?"

"I know He's there," replied Larry, with the conviction of the self-made evangelist. "And Jesus is His messenger."

Elvis' eyes ran over Larry's dark, leonine face, with its aquiline nose and its gently brooding air.

"You're Jewish, aren't you?" he said, with a puzzled look.

"And so was Jesus," Larry replied. "The Apostles were Jews as well. They had no trouble accepting Him. I have none."

At 13, recently confirmed (bar-mitzvahed), Larry had walked into a theater and been enthralled by the old silent movie *King of Kings*.

Jesus, he recalled, seemed like the only sane figure in an insane world.

Larry's interest grew. He read of the 12 lost years of Jesus, years some said were spent in India. He studied the Eastern philosophies as well, and the spreading cult of Paramahansa Yogananda, the founder of the Yogic Self-Realization Fellowship Centers.

Elvis talked about voices he hears, and Larry Geller gave his opinion.

He took a slim, cloth-covered book out of his hairdresser's case and handed it to Elvis. "Here's the book I promised you," he said.

It was *The Impersonal Life,* by Joseph Benner, a Western mystic who wrote inspirationally about the divine consciousness in man.

Elvis thumbed through its pages curiously, then stopped. He was struck by a paragraph which Larry had underlined.

Elvis read the passage through slowly, and then he read it aloud, as if he were trying in this way to impress it on his consciousness.

"The time has now arrived for you to comprehend somewhat of this. Enough has been revealed to prepare you for the recognition of my voice speaking within."

He gave Larry a slow look. "Whose voice is that?"

"It is God's voice in you. Your own voice, inspired by the divine consciousness within you."

Elvis looked puzzled for a moment. He turned to another page and read on:

I speak with many voices—with the voice of all human emotions, passions, and desires. I speak with Nature's voice, with the voice of experience, even with the voice of human knowledge."

Elvis stood up and walked around the dressing room, wagging his head. "It's amazing," he said.

"It was my brother's voice that came to me. It was like a guiding light, I could have been no more than 4 or 5 years old, when I started hearing his voice plainly.

"I didn't know where it was coming from. But he very clearly told me what he wanted me to do." He paused for a moment. "He wanted me to care for other people, to put myself in their place, to see their point of view. To love them. It was like the voice of conscience."

Again Elvis read to himself, then read aloud.

"I will cause even you who thus seek to serve me to do many wondrous things towards the quickening and awakening of your brothers to a like acknowledgment of Me. I will cause even you to influence and affect the lives of many of those whom you contact, inspiring and uplifting them to higher ideals, changing their way of thinking and their attitude towards their fellows and therefore towards Me."

Elvis looked over to Larry, saying almost wistfully, "Is that what I'm being told?"

Larry smiled.

Life after death as Marty Lacker describes Elvis' interest in this area.

Life after death was one of Elvis' beliefs, and he often talked about it. He believed he had been put on this earth for a special reason, but he didn't know what the reason was, or as least he never expressed it. But he talked about everything else. He talked and talked and talked. Geller tells Elvis "resurrection" applies to men as well. "I've always believed in God. But my own church turned me off because of their taboos. They said movies were the work of the devil. But after I saw that Abbott and Costello movie, with Daddy, I knew something had to be wrong. There was no evil in that movie. It was a big laugh. It made you feel good. I didn't like the church using fear to keep everyone in line."

"Yes," agreed Larry, "they make people afraid of dying."

Elvis looked up in some surprise. "Aren't you afraid of dying?"

"There's more to death than dying."

"Hey, man," said Elvis, pulling back his head. "Explain yourself."

Larry opened the Bible he had just given Elvis. He found the chapter in Corinthians:

"For he must reign, till he hath put all enemies under his feet. The last enemy that shall be destroyed is death." Elvis shook his head.

"The Bible means different things to different people. Christ's rising doesn't necessarily have anything to do with us."

"Oh, yes it does," said Larry. "For the Bible points out that if Jesus was resurrected, then all men are."

Elvis look at Larry doubtfully. "I'll have to give that a little more thought. I've had so much hellfire burned into me that I'm gun-shy."

CHAPTER 31

ELVIS PURSUES HIS SEARCH FOR RESURRECTION ACTIVELY

Elvis lingered long over Yogananda's *Autobiography of a Yogi*. What he liked about Yogananda was that although he was a Hindu, he did not disavow any other faith, including Christianity and Judaism. Indeed, one of the stated aims of his Self-Realization Fellowship Center was: "To prove out the practical truth in the immortal teachings of Jesus Christ."

Other Self-Realization goals caught his eye: "To liberate man from his three-fold suffering from physical disease, mental inharmonies, and spiritual ignorance.

"To demonstrate the superiority of mind over body, of soul over mind.

"To overcome evil by good, sorrow by joy, cruelty by kindness, ignorance by wisdom.

"To spread a spirit of brotherhood among all peoples."

Christ had said as much, and more, in the simple phrase: "Love one an-other." But there was no conflict between the two creeds, as Elvis saw; both stood for the universality of man, each supplemented the other. Christ seemed more compelling, perhaps, because he was a living embodiment of what God wanted for man. But Yogananda, living on in his Self-Realization centers, still offered much to a person like Elvis, whose quest for the intangible had constant need for tangible reassurance.

And so one day, during a lunch break in filming *Harum Scarum,* Elvis put down his book by Yogananda and approached Larry with the formality he often affected when he was particularly serious.

"Lawrence, I think I'm ready to be initiated into Kriya Yogi. Will you teach me?"

Larry was horrified. This was almost blasphemy. He patiently explained that the initiate must go through successive stages of meditation to reach this ultimate, self-purifying level of yoga.

"You wouldn't want me to break my sacred vows?"

A devilish gleam came into Elvis' eyes.

"The hell I wouldn't." Seeing the shock on Larry's face, he laughed reassuringly. "I'm only kidding. Well, half-kidding. I really want to know what yoga is all about, spiritually and mentally. Can I talk to anybody about it?"

Larry put through a call to Sri Daya Mata, the worldwide head of the Self-Realization centers, who was originally Fay Wright, from Salt Lake City. She immediately agreed to see Elvis.

Like others in the spiritual world, she sensed a serious purpose behind Elvis' restless quest.

Elvis was overjoyed by her response and thought it time to expose his entourage to a spiritual environment.

At least," he told Larry, "they can enjoy the scenery."

This was to be as close as Elvis ever got to a monastery. He visited one.

He showed up at the monastic center, the ashram atop Mount Washington, in Los Angeles, the follow evening, accompanied by Larry and some of the entourage.

"It's time they know something besides Hollywood and Memphis," he said with a smile.

Sri Daya Mata was a handsome woman with a clear brow and a warm smile. She made them all welcome. There was a brief tour of the establishment, enough to impress Elvis with its pervasive serenity.

"I feel good here," he announced. "There are good vibrations."

"I hope so," smiled Daya Mata.

Elvis observed a few of the order's monks, and sisters, strolling in the halls. They appeared tranquil and at peace, contrasting sharply with the noise and turmoil of the concrete jungle they had just left.

Sister Daya Mata invited Elvis into her sitting room on the third floor. The entourage members remained below and browsed through the library, occasionally poking their noses into a book.

Daya Mata took in Elvis with one sweeping glance. As she sat there, she could sense his reaching out and hoped that she could pronounce a few magic words that would resolve the questions spinning about in his head.

"I understand," she said, "that you have applied for the rite of Kriya Yoga." Elvis nodded silently.

She was intrigued by his interest, knowing that Americans were primarily interested in the physical Hatha Yoga.

"What is there about the Kriya Yoga you find compelling?" she asked.

"I read," he said, "that one who practices this technique is gradually freed from the laws of karma, no longer subject to the condition of cause and effect."

She smiled at his ingenuousness. "It is not that simple," she said. "You are speaking of a very high state, attained by some selected masters. It is not everybody who is ready for this training, any more than anybody can be a Greek or Latin scholar by merely saying they want to be one."

In Kriya Yoga, Elvis had read, a psycho-physiological purifying process takes place by which the blood is recharged with oxygen. This extra oxygen is then transmitted into the life stream to renew the vital centers and stop the decay of cells. Some masters in this technique, he had read, could materialize and dematerialize their bodies at will. Jesus was one, Elijah another.

He wondered if he could do as much.

Her smile broadened. He was looking for more than Larry could do, and more than Daya Mata could give.

She shook her head, but her eyes had a warm glow for the small boy she saw in him.

"It doesn't work that way," she said, "not for anybody. It doesn't matter who you are or how many millions you have. You must be gradually prepared for the Kriya Yoga, if it is to have any value. Each person must earn the right. If it is handed out easily, with no effort involved, it loses its meaning."

"How do I earn that right?" he asked.

"There are lessons, and you must study." She reached around and gave him two books with the lessons from Yogananda in them. "The important thing," she said, "is to take time out each day to meditate on God, and to love. When you love others, you love yourself. It is important to love one's self. Otherwise, how can others love you?"

What he wanted did not come unbidden.

"If you want something you must put out the energy for it," she said.

Elvis mulled this over for a while. He was quick to realize that Sri Daya Mata was showing him special consideration by just sitting there, talking so openly to a novice. He had no credentials but his experience on the mountain, and he mentioned it now, wanting her to sense his own feeling of being especially chosen, without presuming to claim it for himself. She nodded wisely. "God was letting you feel His Presence in His way. What you do with this realization is up to you."

They sat around and chatted leisurely for a while. Then suddenly, she seemed to peer over Elvis' shoulder. "Elvis," she said, "your mother is happy for your success, and she watches over you. She is a very deep and spiritual person."

Elvis started in spite of himself. For when he first laid eyes on Daya Mata, he had felt his mother's presence, and throughout the conversation had the feeling that she was pleased at his being there.

Daya Mata picked out some books and gave them to him. "Be patient, work slowly. Do not try to absorb all the material at once. Take your time, there's no rush, except for one thing." She intoned from Yogananda: "Everything else can wait, but our search for God cannot wait."

Elvis smiled. "Isn't that what Jesus meant when he said, 'Seek ye first the Kingdom of Heaven, and things will be added onto you?"

Daya Mata gave him an acknowledging smile. "Exactly, Elvis; it's the same fundamental."

There was something about Elvis that drew people to him, the religious and the irreligious. As he left, with an invitation to return anytime he liked, several monks lined up at the door to wish him well. One of the sisters of the order presented him with a basket of organic peaches, grown on the property. He was visibly touched.

"It is so heartwarming," she said, "to see someone so famous take the time and interest to visit with us."

Elvis squeezed her hand. "This is my first visit, Sister, but not my last."

And it wasn't. He came there often, and like others who knew Daya Mata called her Ma—short for Daya Mata, and for Mother. He spent many evenings with her, and like others who got to know him, she grew to love him for his essential goodness. She saw that he was more spiritual than he knew. He studied the books that she had given him, learned to meditate more deeply, but found after a while that no great change was taking place in him. He was no closer to Kriya Yoga than before. He was not a Holy Man.

"You were right, Larry," he said one day, " and so was Daya Mata. I was not cut out to be a Kriya Yogi. I have to be myself, a poor ol' Southern boy from Mississippi."

He would have liked to have emulated Yogananda but was bound by a different destiny. He was sure Yogananda must have practiced Kriya Yoga. But it was even after death that fascinated Elvis most. If this were true and it was confirmed by the Forest Lawn Memorial Park in Los Angeles, it suggested the continuing effect of the higher consciousness after death. Elvis and Larry had many discussions about this unique phenomenon.

"In order for this to happen," said Elvis, "Yogananda's spirit clearly had to survive. How else could there be any influence?"

Yogananda had died on March 7, 1952, entering what the Hindus call maha samadhi, a yogi's final conscious exit from the body. His body lay in an uncovered casket, uncorrupted by the normal decaying processes.

"The absence of any visual signs of decay in the dead body of Parahahansa Yogananda," noted mortuary director Harry T. Rowe, "offers the most extraordinary case in our history. No physical disintegration was visible in his body even 20 days after death ... No odor of decay emanated from his body at any time. The physical appearance of Yogananda on March 27, just before the bronze cover of the casket was put into position, was the same as it had been on March 7. He looked on March 27 as fresh and unravaged by decay as he had looked on the night of his death."

To Elvis, this was a revelation that God was not dead, as so many young rebels were dogmatizing in the 1960s. "The day of miracles is not finished," he said. "Yogananda drew on his God-power, his knowledge of universal law, to keep his body together, just like those old men in the Bible, Methuselah, Jared, and Enoch, lived hundreds of years because they were able to keep their cells from decaying even while they lived. They had to be in tune with the Creator."

There were additional excursions to a second Self Realization center in Pacific Palisades, a picturesque 14-acre chapel ground in the foothills, manicured meticulously by the monks and having a lake with white swans, so tame that they playfully pecked the people who fed them. Here it was that Yogananda wrote most of his book, and where Elvis loved to meditate during the week, when he would not distract the weekend worshipers.

Elvis soon became friendly with Brother Adolph, an octogenarian monk who had been an intimate of Yogananda, and a wise and good man, notable for his parables, which shed light and comfort on those who brought their problems to him.

On that first visit to the lake shrine, Elvis was walking toward the chapel, admiring the carefully landscaped grounds, when some visitors passed him on the path and looked up in recognition. They nodded a silent hello and smiled, and kept on walking.

Elvis was impressed by this respect for his privacy. "Perfect," he told Larry. "This is exactly the way I expected it."

Brother Adolph was in the chapel, talking to Brother Roget, one of the younger monks, when Elvis entered with Larry. Brother Adolph was pleased to see him and took his hand.

"People in your position," he said, "seldom take the time to search for God. Wealth and fame can easily keep one bound to the external world and prevent him from discovering his true course. But from what Larry has told me, you already realize that God and immortality are not empty myths."

A year before his death, Elvis had a dream about Daya Mata.

"Her body was much larger than reality, and she was wearing an orange robe. Her face was shining, and she was smiling at me."

Larry was intrigued. "Did she say anything?"

"She just looked at me, as if she was telling me not to worry, that there was nothing to be afraid of."

And so there wasn't. For, as he was beginning to learn: "The only people who are afraid of death are the people who are afraid of life."

Elvis seeks to increase his belief in reincarnation.

Through the Upanishads, the sacred book of the Hindus, Elvis was strongly influenced toward a belief in reincarnation. "The knowing self is not born; it does not die; it has not sprung from anything, nothing has sprung from it. Birthless, it is eternal, everlasting and ancient. It is not killed when the body is killed; the self, smaller than the small, greater than the great, is hidden in the hearts of all living creatures."

He studied the Book of the Creation with great intensity, seeking an answer to the riddle of his own being. He grew excited when he read in Genesis 1:26:

"And God said, Let us make man in our image, after our likeness."

He couldn't wait to point out the passage to Larry.

"Who is 'us'?" he demanded. "Everywhere else God speaks of Himself as 'I'."

He had meditated on it. "He could have been including Jesus," he said, "his only begotten son."

Larry was thrilled. The pupil appeared to have outstripped the mentor.

"And Christ was perfection," added Larry. "And that may be the image that we strive for."

CHAPTER 32

"HOW GREAT THOU ART"
– A PROBABLE SYMPTOM INTENSIFYING EVENT

Elvis' resurrection as described by Larry Geller.

"What am I doing wrong?" he blurted out. "Why don't I become more spiritual, instead of just talking about it? What is wrong with me?"

"There is nothing wrong with you," returned Larry. "You've been jamming too much material into your head too quickly. Your whole experience so far has been cerebral. You're not a computer, you cannot program yourself with data and automatically produce a higher awareness."

"Then why am I reading all this stuff?" He nodded to his books. "And why are you feeding it to me?"

Larry saw no point in coddling his pupil.

"You want it all at once," he said, "like you want everything. It doesn't work that way. It didn't work that way for me, and it won't for you. You are no different before God than anybody else. He doesn't care about your millions of fans or the money you make. You must plant the seeds, and that is what we have been doing. You must not only read, but understand as well. And, as I told you, this usually doesn't happen without a religious experience."

"And where is this experience coming from?"

"From within yourself."

Elvis was more confused than ever. "What should I do to get this experience?"

Larry thought of an old Zen story. "Would you like to hear a story about an old Master? It might be illuminating."

Elvis nodded perfunctorily.

And so Larry began.

"The Japanese master Nan-in gave audience to one of his pupils who had been with him for many years. The pupil lamented to his Master: 'I do my daily meditations. I follow all the rules. I obey your instructions. Why does enlightenment elude me? Why am I in darkness after all the hard work and sacrifice?'

"Nan-in brought out the tea kettle. He filled his pupil's cup, and kept pouring. The pupil watched the tea flowing over until he could no longer restrain himself.

'It is already full,' he said, 'no more tea will go in.'

"Nan-in smiled. 'Exactly. And like the cup, you are running over and nothing more can come in. How can I show you Zen unless you first empty your cup.'"

Larry elaborated. "Get rid of your ego, Elvis, and make room for God.

You are restless as well because you are searching for a mate, a soul mate at your spiritual level. Maybe it's Priscilla. I don't know. But you've got to clean house, if you want God to come in."

Elvis didn't say anything for a while. He gazed down at the floor, reflecting. Then he stood up and grinned. "Well, I guess I needed that. Let's hit it."

The next few hours driving through New Mexico and Arizona were relatively quiet. Larry could see Elvis mulling over the conversation and trying to come to grips with it.

And then it happened. Just before twilight, as they were climbing the mountains south of Flagstaff, Arizona. Larry was in the front with Elvis, while Jerry Schilling, Billy Smith, and Red West were in the back, chatting. Drawn perhaps by the same impulse, Elvis and Larry looked up into a glowing sky that was a strange iridescent blue. As their gaze wandered off to the horizon, they saw a lone cloud. And then their eyes stopped and they sat almost transfixed. The cloud was in the shape of a man's head. And inside the outline of this cloud they saw clearly the definite image of a face. It was a face they had seen many times before. There was no question whose face it was. The features were all there, set off by dark ridges in the fleecy white background. There were even the familiar mustache and beetle brows.

It was the face of Joseph Stalin.

Elvis cried out in excitement, "Do you see what I see? That's Stalin's face up there."

Larry was equally excited. "It's exactly like him," he said. "What's he doing up there?'

The features began fading, until Larry saw them become completely dissolved. He turned to Elvis and saw him still staring. A radiant expression had come over his face. His eyes glowed with a soulful quality. And then, suddenly, he shook his head as if bringing himself out of a trance.

With one twist of the wheel, he brought the bus over to the side of the road.

"Follow me," he said to Larry in a hoarse voice. He jumped out first, and rubbed his hand over his eyes. Larry had never seen him like this before. He looked like he was about to burst with excitement. He grabbed Larry and hugged him, crying:

"My prayers have been answered. I have seen the Christ and the Antichrist, and I know what I have to do."

There on the lonely road, as the entourage looked on uneasily, the tears streamed down his face. "I have felt the presence of God," he announced.

'It's happened," he shouted. "It's God, it's love, it exploded inside me. I've finally seen what you were trying to tell me. And you were right, there's no way to convey it. It's beyond words, beyond mental concepts, it's the very essence of life." Emotionally, he flung his arms around Larry again. "Thank you, I love you, what can I say. I feel like Paul on the road to Damascus. I am reborn." Elvis was now laughing and crying simultaneously. One of the entourage, thinking he might have snapped, approached cautiously. "What's wrong, Elvis? Are you all right?"

Elvis was fighting to maintain his composure. "I'm okay," he said. "I'm okay."

Only Elvis saw the vision of the Christ.

He was too agitated to drive. Red West took the wheel. Larry and Elvis sat together in the back, neither speaking for a while. As they plodded up the mountain, Larry thought about his own experience. It had taken place five years before on the other side of the same mountain. He felt it was time now to tell Elvis of his own experience.

He was 21 then, climbing the Flagstaff slopes toward the Grand Canyon. Suddenly, he heard a voice. It seemed to come from a great distance. "Look back and know the truth," it said. His mind flashed back to his childhood, and he remembered his bewildered feelings when he had been told by his Temple and his parents that Jesus was not a divinity but only a wise man, a prophet. But even as he was thinking back on this, the words flooded back inexorably.

"You know the truth."

He now described his own transformation to Elvis.

"In the twinkling of an eye, I was reborn. I had the sense of floating in the midst of infinity. The voice kept saying, 'Jesus, Jesus Christ.' The earth had become another realty. Paradise and Christ was my center. My guilt vanished, I knew I belonged to Christ. We were merged in God."

Elvis was silent for a long moment, then shook his head in wonderment.

"How amazing," he said, "that we had our experience on the same mountain."

Saul, who was to become Paul, was blinded by a light from Heaven on the road to Damascus. Elvis was struck by what he considered an omen. He was still reflecting on the vision in the sky when he had still another omen to consider. The bus caught fire.

As clouds of smoke billowed from the vehicle, Red West hastily pulled over. The fire had started in the wheel system and spread to the undercarriage. Elvis and the others attacked the flames with a fire extinguisher, and handfuls of dirt, and soon had it under control. But the vehicle was heavily damaged and barely limped the three miles into Needles, California.

As they hit Needles, Elvis looked at Larry quizzically.

"You know," he said, "cars have always been a symbol in my life, of movement and progress, and now just after I saw that vision, the bus burns, and I have to get a new one. Coming on top of that vision, could it be a sign that I'm turning in my old life for a new one?"

"You can make whatever you want of it," said Larry.

"I can't go on the way I have," he said. "Now that I have seen Christ, I know the truth. I know now there is a God. How can I continue to make these silly teenybopper movies that have no truth or substance?" His voice took on a contemptuous note. "What the hell purpose is there to things like *Girls, Girls, Girls, Tickle Me,* and *Girl Happy*? They're all the same dumb movie. All they do is change my name in it and throw in a few new sets. I have to do something meaningful, something God will take notice of."

His eyes lit up. He appeared almost ecstatic. "I have come to a decision. I have decided to join a monastery and serve God."

Larry was appalled. He had never expected anything like this. He couldn't imagine Elvis in a monastery, wearing a monk's robe, praying, and perhaps doing a little gardening and wall mending. It was staggering. The greatest entertainer in the world, the idol of millions, going into total retreat. And what would it accomplish? All this stirred around in Larry's head. At the same time, he saw all the recriminations coming home to rest on his shoulders.

Elvis' voice, raised in excitement at times, had obviously carried to the outer room. From the rustling outside the door, Larry was sure that Elvis' camp followers had their ears glued to the door. He didn't blame them. If Elvis went into a monastery, ending the most profitable career in the history of entertainment, what would happen to them?

Larry tried reason.

"And what do you consider meaningful, burying yourself away in a mausoleum?"

"God will tell me," said Elvis. "Why else did He show me the face of His Son?"

Larry was in a cold sweat. It didn't take much imagination to see how this latest stroke of news would be received by Colonel Parker and the others. Everything had been going smoothly until Larry turned up with his books and talk. Elvis had been making his three films a year, for a million dollars a picture and half the profits, one hit record after another, and now all this would be lost for a whim of the moment. He looked at Elvis, took in the sensuous face and eyes, the lithe, muscular body, the animated motions. Obviously, Elvis wasn't cut out for the monastery. At that moment, Larry knew he had to talk Elvis out of it, or else, he thought grimly, wind up in a monastery himself. He could see himself the object of total scorn. He made a silent prayer that God would make him convincing.

"Elvis," he began, "it isn't as simple as you think. Your prayers were answered on that mountain. You were shown something, and that something is not the road to oblivion. Twelve hours earlier you were complaining about not having an experience, and then it happened. This was God's way of revealing to you His existence. And that is all people are trying to find God? You've already found Him. And He's found you. You're way ahead."

Elvis allowed this to kick around for a while.

"But what about these damn films?" I'm not serving God with them, not even a little bit."

"Elvis," countered Larry, "your voice is the gift of God. He has given you a special ministry. You and your music represent life and hope to millions of people. Would you deprive them of it?"

"Well," Elvis rejoined, "what about the Bible saying that it is harder for a rich man to enter the kingdom of Heaven than for a camel to pass through the eye of a needle?"

"That applies to the man rich in material things and poor in spiritual ones. You are already very generous and are not attached to worldly possessions. That's not your problem."

Elvis still had not heard enough to resolve his doubts.

"I would deprive nobody of anything, but I have to live my own life."

Larry felt the matter would be properly resolved once Elvis had settled down and thought it over. He couldn't see Elvis enduring any retreat for more than a few days, without his entourage, and the excitement of his frenetic lifestyle. He met Elvis head-on.

"Jesus said that man should be in the world, but not of it."

Elvis looked baffled for a moment, and then his brow cleared. "Look," he said, "you're my guru, you tell me what I should do." His irrepressible humor asserted itself. "After all, you got me into this. You have to get me out."

Larry had a brainstorm. "What about Priscilla?" he said. "What are you going to tell her? I suppose you and Priscilla can communicate by thought-wave while you serve God in some mountain retreat secluded from the world. And how about the girls that wait on the doorstep every night? What will you tell them? You know, monasteries aren't strong on girls.

"And your millions of fans, whom you say you love. What will you tell them? And your entourage, the guys you say you are for. What about them?"

Their eyes met, and it was still evident that Elvis was unconvinced.

Larry felt time was on his side. He had given Elvis something to think about. "You are drained from your trip," he said. 'Sleep on it, and let your inner consciousness meditate on the answer. It will be there when you awaken in the morning."

Larry picked up a copy of *The Impersonal Life* and read aloud: "For I am your real teacher, the only real one you will ever know, and the only master; I, your divine self."

Larry looked up. "There," he said, "is your guru."

The next morning, Elvis looked at Larry calmly as he walked into the den.

"I'm glad you're on time," he said crisply. "We have to get to the studio. It's the first day's shooting of *Harum Scarum*."

Larry waited.

Elvis smiled faintly. "You were right," he said, "I see it now. I can do more where I am." And then with a flash of his old whimsy, "You still have your job, Larry. You have nothing to worry about.

"Oh, by the way," Elvis added, with a sheepish look, "I'm having Priscilla fly in tomorrow."

Not long after, Elvis started planning his first spiritual album. He took months to go over his selections, and decided finally that his tribute to the Lord could best be expressed by the gospel song *How Great Thou Art*, which was to become the title of the album as well. The other songs had a similar quality: *Without Him, Somebody Bigger Than You and I, Where No One Stands Alone*, and *If The Lord wasn't Walking By My Side*.

After immersing himself in black gospel music so deeply, Elvis told Larry, "Colored musicians have more soul in their little finger than whites have in their whole bodies."

He had spent many hours on Memphis' famed Beale Street as a boy, singing along with black performers, and listening as well. He also sang at churches and revival meetings, learning his own brand of soul music.

He chose Nashville, the home of country and western music, to record his gospel album. He wanted people to know he was a Southerner, paying a Southerner's tribute to the Lord.

He confided that this was the most momentous performance of his career. He went over every detail of the production himself and personally handled the arranging of several songs. The actual recording was supervised by RCA's Felton Jarvis, handpicked by Elvis.

But, above all, he wanted God's help. Before going to the studio, Elvis decided to meditate on the success of the album, in his suite at the Albert Pike Motel.

"This album, I am convinced," he told Larry, "is ordained by God Himself. This is not like any other recording I have done. This is the message of the Creator to His children. And for it to be successful, I must completely empty myself of negativity and ego."

He sat down, and his eyes held Larry's for a long moment.

"I'll tell you what we're going to do. We're going to close our eyes and go into meditation. And I am not going to move out of this chair until I am guided by the still, small voice from within. This album shall be a manifestation of my growth, reflecting everything that we have been studying together."

They turned the lights off, then closed their eyes and meditated for 30 minutes. Not a word was spoken. Elvis silently prayed to God, asking that He guide him in this, his first spiritual venture, to make the tribute worthy of Him who inspired it.

At the same precise moment, the two opened their eyes. Elvis turned the light on, and Larry could see the glow in his eyes.

Elvis had flashed back to himself as a child. He was 2 years old and sitting with his parents in the church in Tupelo. The congregation was singing hymns.

"As young as I was," Elvis recalled, "I felt a sudden urge to scramble up to the pulpit and sing before that congregation. And I ran up there before anybody could stop me. And I sang the best I knew how. Something within me knew even then that I was destined to be a singer. All I ever wanted to do was sing for people and make them happy."

He shook himself, as if bringing himself back to the present.

"So be it," he said. "I am ready."

Elvis was never in better form. Larry wandered from the control room, manned by the engineers, to the studio where Elvis stood and delivered his songs. At the conclusion of *How Great Thou Art,* Larry turned and saw the tears streaming down the faces of the hardened engineers. They took Elvis' hand and embraced him.

"It was a great experience, Elvis," they said. "We can't thank you enough."

How Great Thou Art was to be the forerunner of many spiritual albums. But it remained his most popular, giving hope to the forlorn and changing the lives of many.

After the session, Elvis gave Larry a secret smile. "We did it, Larry," he said, "but we know who was behind us. Don't we?"

The effects of "How Great Thou Art."

The girl looked around the lobby. "Can we sit down somewhere?"

Larry took her into the coffee shop. And over a cup of coffee, she talked about Elvis—and herself. She was an epileptic. During a spasm, she had fallen down a flight of stairs and injured her lower back severely. She had been in constant pain. She took pain pills, but they didn't help. One night she could stand it no longer. She took a bottle of sleeping pills, emptied it on a table, and wrote a note to her family. She was looking around, wondering what she may have overlooked, when she became conscious of the radio playing. She moved over to turn it off. And then a melodious voice came forth, strongly, yet sweetly, rising and falling, with a message of home and love not only for herself but for others as well. It was the album Elvis had recorded years before in Nashville. The song was *How Great Thou Art.* The words flooded her mind and heart:

Oh, Lord my God
When I'm in awesome wonder...
When I consider all Thy world Thy hand have made...
I can see the stars, I hear the rolling thunder,
Thy power through the universe display.

When Christ shall come to take me home,
What joy shall fill my heart.
Then I shall bow in humble adoration and proclaim my God,
How great Thou art.

Before the song was finished, she burst out crying and sank to her knees for the first time since she was a child, and prayed to the God she felt had abandoned her. There were tears in her eyes now as she recalled the scene.

"It was the way he sang it," she said. "All the love of God seemed to come through him. I felt that I could reach out and touch God. He was close to me, pervading the room. I was overwhelmed by His majesty. I felt the courage flow back through my body, and with it the will to live. How could I fail Him when God was there with me, to guide me over each hurdle?

Larry thrilled as he listened. All the teachings, all the long discussions, appeared to have crystallized into that glorious moment of redemption.

"There and then," the girl said, "I vowed to dedicate my life to Elvis, to help and protect him, if I could. For there was no doubt in my mind that God had chosen that moment to send him to help me. I had to live for him and for God."

Larry was touched. He told the girl how Elvis had thought himself a channel of the Lord when he recorded the album.

Her eyes lit up. "Please, Larry, tell Elvis what he did for me. I owe him that. That's all I want. I don't want to bother him. He has enough people doing that."

Larry was a little surprised by Elvis' reaction. He didn't smile or seem elated. His face became solemn instead. He stood out on the hotel balcony, wearing his blue bathrobe with its hood up, contemplating the night quietly. "God," he said finally, "works in His own ways. That's about all we can be sure of. I thank Him for the life that was saved, and thank Him for being used that way."

PART VI

CONTINUED

CHAPTER 33

FAITH HEALER

Elvis, reincarnated, adapts the role of a faith healer, for others, not himself.

Elvis had gone without the foods children crave—candies, soda pop, cookies, ice cream, hamburgers, hot dogs, sugar, and salt. Consequently, he thought nothing of devouring at one sitting four or five jumbo hamburgers, with a serving of French fries for four, plus a gallon of ice cream, washed down with Gatorade. For breakfast, he would consume 25 strips of bacon, burnt to a frazzle, and two large pizzas, with pepperoni, cheese, and whatever other topping was available. And then he went to sleep.

He loved spicy food. He thought nothing of 15 beef or chicken tacos at a time. He poured salt and pepper on his food before tasting it. The first time Larry had breakfast with him, Elvis was talking and dashing pepper on his eggs at the same time. Larry thought he was being absent-minded.

"Elvis," he cried, "your eggs are black."

"I know," said Elvis, continuing to pour the pepper.

At times, he tried to control his intake. He would fast for two days, then eat a couple of cream pies.

He believed in the power of the mind to heal and his power to perform such healings. He was convinced after reading Alice Bailey's book *Esoteric Healing* that the energy exchange through the laying on of hands was a factor in correcting illness.

"It's too bad," he said, "that people are afraid to touch each other. Most people feel it's a mark of homosexuality when two men embrace. But it's important for people to touch. It shows the other person you care." He had underlined a passage in the Bailey book and now showed it to Larry:

"The healer must seek to link his own soul, his heart, his brain, and his hands. Thus can he pour the vital healing force upon the patient."

He toyed with the idea of healing others, but it never occurred to him that he could heal himself in the same way. He had read in the Bible that Christ had said that others could heal like He did, and even more, with the help of the Father. Typically, Elvis wished to give it a try. He had a built-in subject right there at Graceland with him. His aging grandmother, Minnie Presley, who lived with him, had been feeling poorly and was confined to her room. She complained periodically of asthmatic attacks and dizziness. Elvis, always solicitous of his beloved grandma, now approached her bedside in the role of healer.

"How are you today, Grandma?" he asked, in a voice of concern.

"Just one of my spells, Elvis," she said, "don't worry about me."

Grandma was about to be healed, whether she liked it or not. "Larry," said Elvis, "Grandma is sick. Can we heal her?"

"If she's receptive,' said Larry. "Just knowing that somebody cares that much has a beneficial effect. It's a tangible evidence of loving, and that's the best medicine of all."

They meditated for a while, and then after dinner, Elvis knocked on her bedroom door and they walked in. The room, with its pink and blue floral arrangements, looked like a Hollywood version of Heaven. Grandma was lying in bed, the lights dim. She was resting. Elvis approached her with a smile.

"Grandma, how are you feeling, honey?"

She said weakly, "Not so good, Elvis. I don't know if I'm going to make it. "

Elvis patted her hand. "Of course you will. Just don't worry, we're going to make you well. Do you mind if Larry and I lay our hands on you and pray for you?"

To Grandma Presley, Elvis could do no wrong.

"That'll be fine, Elvis. You all do what you like."

The two healers consulted like specialists.

"We should begin," whispered Larry, drawing on his books, "by closing our eyes and relaxing, allowing our vital energies to flow. Then place our hands on Grandma's body, wherever seems natural. Your hands will know where to go. Feel the heat from your hands, and think of this heat penetrating her body, giving her energy."

Elvis nodded.

"Now," said Larry, "let us pray."

They prayed that God would give them whatever power they needed to help Grandma. And then they were ready.

"Grandma," said Larry, "close your eyes and relax."

They placed their hands on Grandma's chest, then her shoulders and head. For 30 minutes, as Grandma half-dozed, they visualized a healing light streaming from their hands into Grandma.

"You might see this blue light, Grandma, but I don't want you to get startled," Elvis said. "It only means you're getting healed."

Larry himself was startled that Elvis visualized a blue light, when he, Larry, had always meditated on a white light, as was the usual healing practice.

They all opened their eyes simultaneously.

Elvis looked at Grandma solicitously.

"Grandma," he said, "how do you feel now?"

Grandma sat up in bed. "Elvis," she said. "I do feel a little better. I would like to sleep now. I feel so relaxed." Elvis kissed her eyes shut.

Grandma could have been trying to please Elvis. But maybe not. Something seemed to have happened during the laying on of hands. Outside the room, Elvis reported with an excited ring to his voice, "I saw a light around you and Grandma, a circle of pulsation light."

Larry nodded. "I saw the same light. I felt a current of energy. I felt a transfer of this energy, and I felt she was being healed."

"Why," asked Elvis, "did we see the light? What did it signify?"

"We were tuned into our subconscious minds. This is far more sensitive than the conscious mind and sees far more. That light could have been a healing vibration, the very current of energy I spoke of."

It was all very new to Elvis. "I'll bet," he said, "that after Grandma sleeps through the night, she'll wake up feeling great."

The next day, Grandma was up and around for the first time in days. Elvis was in ecstasy. "It worked," he cried. "We healed her."

He smiled happily as he saw his beloved Dodger, as he fondly called her, moving around her room. He nudged Larry. "She's all right," he said. "She'll outlive me."

At 30, Elvis was strong and energetic. He vigorously flung himself into his healings, whenever the opportunity arose. One day, near Nashville, he was riding in a chartered bus when he noticed another bus traveling alongside. The bus abruptly pulled over to the side of the road. Elvis, who had been watching casually, saw the bus driver stand up in the bus, clutch at his chest, and stagger out onto the road and collapse.

Elvis commanded his driver to pull over. With Larry and the others, he raced over to the driver. He was sitting on the curb, holding his chest and gasping for air. The passengers had filed out by now and were looking down helplessly at the man. Nobody knew what to do.

"He is having a heart attack," somebody suggested.

The bus driver was about 50, with graying hair. His face was pasty, and his nostrils distended, his eyes bulging. He turned even paler at the remark and looked as if he were about to keel over.

Elvis bent down and put his arm around the man's shoulders, and said something reassuring. He placed his other hand on the man's heart, and said, with his customary politeness toward older people, "Just relax, sir. You're going to be fine."

The driver opened his eyes and looked up at Elvis in a dazed way. Then, as his eyes focused on the man kneeling over him, a look of astonishment, then joy, swept over his face. "You're Elvis, Elvis Presley," he cried. "I can't believe it."

Elvis tried to calm him. "Relax, sir, relax," he said, stroking his brow. The man forgot his attack. He struggled to his feet and grabbed Elvis' hand.

He peered into his face.

"I don't believe it," he kept repeating. "You're him ... you're Elvis." He shook his hand incredulously.

Elvis looked at him solicitously. "Are you all right, sir?"

"Oh, yes, Elvis," the man beamed, "I'm all right. I've had these spells before. But when I saw your face, I snapped right out of it."

Elvis put his arm around the driver and made him sit down on the curb. "I want you to take it easy, sir, and not get excited." He turned and made sure an ambulance was called, then put his hands on him once again before moving off. The driver waved goodbye from the curb.

"You're really Elvis," he cried, as if he still couldn't believe his good fortune.

Elvis and Larry climbed back into their bus.

"It was strange," said Elvis, "how that man came out of it after I laid my hands on him."

"Maybe your being Elvis had something to do with it," said Larry.

"Perhaps. As you said, Lawrence, the subject should have some rapport with the healer."

It would have been difficult to determine how much was Elvis' healing power and how much Elvis and his mystique. It was always possible the two were interwoven.

And Elvis' impact, particularly among the young, was universal. One day, he was driving along a Hollywood street when he saw four tough-looking teenagers brawling. "Look at those idiots," he cried out, "they're liable to kill themselves."

He stopped his car and bounded out into the street. He approached the young toughs and went into a fighting karate stance.

"Cut it out," he ordered, "or you'll have to fight me."

The brawlers turned angrily, ready to pounce on the intruder, when suddenly their eyes widened, and they cried in unison:

"Elvis!"

All thought of fighting vanished, and they scrambled around for pen and paper.

"We ain't going to fight anymore, Elvis," one said apologetically, "just give us your autograph, please Elvis?"

They shook his hand and weakly departed, comparing autographs.

Elvis was aware of the apparent paradox of believing in psychic healing, and then popping pills. But as he said, patting his traveling medicine kit, "It doesn't hurt to help nature a little."

He invariably came back to his childhood.

"You just know that Jesse Garon would have lived if my Mom could have gone to a hospital, instead of having us at home, without a doctor or nurse, without adequate care or facilities, without heat, running water. Nothing. Not even a drug to ease the laboring pains."

And yet he believed in the power of the mind.

"My mind," he told Larry, "tells me to take a pill."

Larry protested, "A person who is psychically healed essentially heals himself. That's what all healing is about. The body heals itself, given the chance."

"I agree," said Elvis, with a laugh. "But the pill makes you comfortable while you're being healed."

He was impressionable in almost everything.

He tried practically every remedy advertised on television. He would offer them to friends at the first sniffle or ache. He was a member of the school that felt if a little medicine is good, a lot is better.

At the same time, he practiced his healing devoutly and frequently volunteered his services. When his aide, Jerry Schilling, took a spill from a motorcycle, severely hurting his back, there was a knock on his door one night. It was Elvis in his robe.

"Jerry," he said, "I sensed that you weren't able to sleep because of the pain. Is that so?"

Jerry reached over and switched on a light. He had been lying in bed, groaning in his agony.

"I'm afraid so, Elvis."

"Get over on your stomach, Jerry, close your eyes, and relax, and leave the driving to me."

Elvis placed his hands on Schilling's back for a few minutes and prayed that he would be healed, visualizing a healing blue light beaming on his back. Before the meditation was concluded, Jerry had fallen asleep. He slept soundly through the night. In the morning, he felt refreshed. The pain had subsided and was almost gone. He felt healed.

"No question," he told Larry, "Elvis has healing powers."

Jerry was one of the few in the entourage to be receptive, believing with Shakespeare: "There are more things in heaven and earth, Horatio, than are dreamt of in your philosophy."

Elvis' healings were an expression of his love. They often began with a general discourse on metaphysics to a bevy of attractive young women. They always appeared interested. Elvis could have discussed the telephone book, and they would have been interested. He had been practicing healing a lot and considered himself quite adept. He decided that the healer was a channel, pulling a healing vibration out of the atmosphere and transmitting this energy, like a radio beam, to the person needing it.

On one occasion, sitting around the Holmby Hills house which Priscilla had recently vacated, Elvis was especially attentive to an airline stewardess of 25 or so. She had been listening avidly.

"Do you mean that anybody could lay his hands on me and cure me?" Her eyebrows came up incredulously.

Elvis laughed. "It's not quite that simple," he said. "The healing person would have to know what he was doing, and the other person would have to want it."

She placed a hand on a shapely leg. "I sprained my leg, skiing, and it's taken a long while mending." Her blue eyes widened. "Are you saying, Elvis, that you could heal me?"

Elvis smiled. "Let me try. Larry, here," he nodded at his mentor, "will work with me. What can you lose?"

She frowned ever so slightly, doubt clouding her lovely features. "It's contrary to what I learned as a child. We were taught not to trifle with the work of God. I was told that people who do these supernatural things go to Hell when they die."

"I know all about that," said Elvis. "I went to the same church. They pounded hellfire and brimstone into us all the time. But we create our own heaven and hell here on earth." His face grew scornful. "I don't see how anybody can be more Christian than Christ. He went around healing the blind, the crippled, the lepers, and he raised Lazarus from the dead." He wagged a finger for emphasis. "And didn't he say, 'Greater things shall ye do, with the help of the Father.' He used the power of healing and said we can do the same thing. Don't you see that?"

She looked at him, admiringly. "I do, Elvis, I do."

"There is nothing supernatural about it, no hobgoblins, or anything like that. It is the most natural thing in the world. Somebody said there is a cure for every disease man is heir to in nature, and I believe that." He thought of something and laughed. "I ought to know," he said, "I've tried about everything." He became serious. "Honestly, I think we can do something for you."

A tiny smile played over his lips.

"You have nothing to fear but fear itself."

"Oh, I trust you completely," she said. "I think it's great of you to offer."

She was ready to go upstairs, and in quiet seclusion mediate with Larry and Elvis. Her nervousness vanished.

"Know," he said, "that God made you perfect. Visualize a blue light around yourself and see it as perfection."

Elvis and Larry put their hands on her sprained leg and meditated. Her breathing became deeper and more rhythmic as they transmitted their energy into her level of consciousness. The healing process took a half-hour. She had almost dozed off. She sat up now, lazily rubbing her eyes. Then, remembering, she put her hand on her leg and shifted it gingerly. A look of astonishment spread over her face. "I swear to God," she cried, "my leg feels better. When you put your hands on my legs, I felt a tremendous soothing warmth. But I thought it was my imagination."

Elvis shook his head. "No, it was real."

The girl had moved off the bed now and was testing her leg on the floor. "It really is better." In a burst of emotion, she embraced Elvis, and thanked Larry as well.

"You were open," said Elvis. "You trusted us. You knew we weren't trying to get you alone in my bedroom for any ulterior motive. And that did the trick. Without your trust and faith, it wouldn't have worked."

If nothing else, meditation had a calming effect.

Some of the entourage meditated periodically with Larry and Elvis: Charlie Hodge, Jerry Schilling, Billy Smith, Ricky and David Stanley, and, of course, Linda Thompson and Ginger. Elvis regretted that the others showed little interest.

"I only wish the others would begin their spiritual search," he said. "That would make me happier than anything else."

Even the disbelievers in the entourage conceded that Elvis was remarkably intuitive. When anyone close to him was sick or troubled, he seemed to sense it. Investigation showed that he was invariably correct. Or if someone was about to call or drop by, he would mention it.

Again, he was invariably right. Often during a conversation, he would look up and anticipate what somebody was going to say.

Occasionally, when the pills didn't work, he would ask Larry for a healing. They would meditate together, and Elvis always claimed he felt better. But there was no lasting therapy. He preached energizing the body but depleted his own energy, without troubling to renew it. He was an enigma to everybody but himself.

"I will do what I have to," he said, "in the time I have to do it."

Elvis prided himself on keeping his father alive. During Elvis' last engagement in Las Vegas in December 1976, Vernon Presley had come up from Memphis to be with his son. He didn't look well. He had been suffering from palpitations, and his face looked pinched and strained. Suddenly, as he was talking to Elvis, his head fell to his chest and the color drained out of his face. His breath came in gasps. Elvis jumped up and threw his arms around him. There was a doctor in the dressing room, who immediately checked Vernon and ordered him into the hospital.

That night, Larry presided aver a healing service in Elvis' suite. Charlie Hodge and Ginger joined in. Elvis had found absentee healing could also work. It was not necessary to touch, or lay on hands, though contact seemed to help.

"I know," said Elvis, "that if we faithfully use our powers, we will heal Daddy. The doctors, God bless them, can only do so much. But we know how effective spiritual healing is, when all else fails."

The lights were turned off and candles lighted. Larry burned incense, adding a mystical flavor to the proceeding. The four sat in a circle, cross-legged on Elvis' giant-sized bed. They held hands, closed their eyes, and called aloud on Jesus to send his light to the ailing Vernon. A prayer by Elvis keyed their meditation.

"In the conscious realization of the oneness and unity of all life, let us be focal points through which God can manifest his divine healing. Let us visualize the blue light of healing and surround Daddy with its healing power."

They meditated silently for an hour, holding hands, keeping eyes closed. Then Elvis said softly, "Dear Lord, in your name, may others troubled and ill, wherever they are, receive Thy healing grace. Bless all those in dire need, according to Thy will."

As the session closed, Elvis enjoined the others: "Let us give thanks now that my daddy will be well tomorrow." He concluded, as usual, with three rapid amens.

The next day, Vernon left the hospital. The color had returned to his face, and he felt no pain. He said he felt wonderful. He stayed on for a few more days, then left for Graceland, looking like a new man. Elvis was sure the healing had turned the trick.

"We must give credit to Ginger," he said fondly. "She was new at this, but she entered into the spirit of it as if she had been doing it all her life."

Elvis had few health problems in his 20s and early 30s. He seldom caught cold, and when he did, he bounced back quickly. Because of his hyperactivity, he always had a sleeping problem and couldn't fall off to sleep unless somebody was next to him. Again, it could have been a relic of the symbiotic mother syndrome, clinging in adulthood to the mother he never gave up—his ideal woman being young and attractive, as his mother was when he was a child.

His appearance underwent no great change until after the breakup with Priscilla. He became puffy and languid, without buoyancy or animation. He had always had a weight problem, as had his mother. Normally 170 to 175 pounds, on a slightly under 6-foot frame, he would zoom to 200 pounds and more. He would look into a mirror, go on a crash diet, then quickly abandon it because he was concerned about losing weight too rapidly.

About Mario Lanza's premature demise. He compared his own situation to Mario Lanza's.

"It's dangerous to put on weight and lose it fast," he pointed out, overlooking his own dangerous eating habits. "It's too much of a strain on the heart. That's how Mario Lanza died. He would blow up to 280 pounds. And then go on a crash diet for a movie and lose 60 to 70 pounds in a month—too much for the body to handle that quickly."

During layoffs between movies, he ate everything in sight. The maids at Graceland prepared rich cream pies every night, loads of French fries and biscuits, and the junk foods he liked. He got heavier and heavier, until it was time to get back to Hollywood for another picture. He usually delayed dieting, and so the last few days resorted to diet pills. During the first week of filming, he was usually 10 to 15 pounds overweight, and as the movie progressed he would work back to his sleek self.

The diet pills frazzled his nerves and built up body fluids. "I hate them," he said, "they make me cranky."

But as the years went by, he took the pills in increasing numbers. Larry, a vegetarian, was horrified by Elvis' food intake and thought he was slowly killing himself. He tried to interest him in a balanced diet and finally induced him to visit Los Angeles nutritionist Wilma Minor. As she checked Elvis over, Larry stood by, to remember whatever she said. The examination took 45 minutes, with the nutritionist concentrating on the abdomen.

"Your intestines are inflamed," she announced. "'When I applied pressure, you tightened up. If this condition isn't dealt with, it will only get worse. You can get away with it now, you're only 31. But the toxins will accumulate, and in 10 years you will be in trouble, unless you start doing something about it now."

He threw up his arms. "I'll do whatever you say."

She gave him some pamphlets on nutrition and told him to stay away from diet drinks, sweets, starches, and meat, and advised fasting one day a week until the abdomen was no longer tender. "And no medications."

Elvis faithfully visited her once a week for three months, and periodically for a year. But eventually he reverted to the patterns of childhood. Wilma Minor thought it inevitable. She told Larry, "I don't think he will change. He's like a little boy. He listens, he promises, but he doesn't do as he should. The body doesn't lie." She touched on something that Elvis had indicated in his overview of the power of the mind. "I really feel that he believes that it doesn't matter what he puts into his body as long as he feels the mind controls all. But all those hamburgers and french fries, and all the sugar and salt, will catch up with him one day."

Wilma Minor's words were prophetic, or so Larry thought, as he sat with Elvis years later and examined the hands that Elvis held outstretched.

"Look at them," cried Elvis, in disgust.

They were twice their normal size and grotesquely discolored.

"The doctors don't know what is wrong. They haven't figured it out." Elvis stared at his hands, shuddering, as if they were something out of a horror movie.

"Press down on them," he said.

Larry pressed down, and his fingers made an indentation in the skin that remained for several minutes.

"My feet are the same way," said Elvis. "I can hardly put my boots on."

They went upstairs to Elvis' bedroom to meditate on his health. The table next to Elvis' bed resembled a drugstore. It was crowded with nasal sprays, eye pads, atomizers, digestive pills, sleeping pills, wake-up pills. There were enough drugs there, thought Larry, to kill a horse. How could any psychic healing survive such a bombardment?

Priscilla, though parted from Elvis, was also deeply concerned. "You should vary your diet, and be a vegetarian like Lisa Marie and myself," she urged Elvis.

She voiced her concern to Larry. "Elvis is so smart in many ways, he's such a beautiful soul. But when it comes to food and nutrition, he won't listen to reason."

Larry urged her to keep after Elvis, but it did no good. He reminded Elvis that the body was the temple of the soul. "It is our spiritual obligation to take care of our bodies. Don't you remember what Daya Mata told you?"

Elvis smiled good-naturedly. "I remember, and I appreciate everybody's concern. And I'm concerned myself. But, hell, man, I don't want to live forever."

"How would it be," said Larry, "if I brought you some books on health and nutrition?"

"Fine," said Elvis, "but keep those spiritual books coming. I don't have to tell you that man doesn't live by bread alone."

Larry brought him books by Adelle Davis and other nutritionists. Elvis seldom opened them. Nearing 40, his health problems reached crisis proportions. His kidneys and liver were functioning abnormally. The dark circles and puffiness under his eyes had aged him considerably. He quietly entered Baptist Memorial Hospital. He had additional surgery to relieve a blinding glaucoma in one eye. After every show, he put drops in his eyes and eye pads over them. His eyes constantly stung. His fans made it worse with their picture taking, which he tolerated because of what it meant to them.

"The moment I get onstage, all I see is hundreds of flashbulbs going off," he complained. "For the first 10 minutes, those flashes really get to me. Then after a song or two, the sweat drains into my eyes and they get so irritated I can't focus. Then, when I shake my head, my hair gets tangled in the sweat at the corner of my eyes. When I finally leave that stage, I can't see a thing and my eyes are burning up." He would give a quick smile. "I guess I should give myself a healing."

Larry trimmed his hair on the top and sides so that wisps wouldn't fall into his eyes. Meanwhile, he was prodded to exercise more by the group. But his one-time interest in keeping fit appeared to have waned. When he did exercise, it was sporadic. Not having worked out for months, he would throw on a gym suit and play strenuously at touch football or racquetball for hours at a time. He wanted to get in shape all in one day.

Formerly, he did his two shows a night, then sat up in his room for hours entertaining friends with his ballads. Now a single show drained all his energy. In his last two years his blood pressure shot up to 180, and he had trouble breathing.

It was obvious something was wrong. He seemed unsure of himself onstage, and his voice was raspy. The audience didn't mind. They would have applauded if he had read to them from one of his books. But the rumors spread that Elvis was on hard drugs. The papers ate it up. Anything on Elvis was news. The more outrageous the stories, the more newspapers were sold. Elvis was already an American folk hero, and people were hungry to know what he was like. They sensed a sweetness in him, a caring. The love in people, yearning for expression, reached out for the love he gave them. But the rumormongers didn't see it. It was not scandalous enough for them.

There were nights he had no vitality at all. He went onstage out of sheer fortitude. Sore throats were beginning to plague him. He was afraid he might lose his voice. He became panicky.

"My voice is my life," he told Larry. "That's what God gave me to make people happy. If that goes, it's all over."

In Orlando, on his last tour of Florida, he had a throat specialist flown in from Las Vegas, and he seemed to respond for a while. He would meditate, and he would take medication, but it was obvious he was getting no better. Each day there was something new. In Minneapolis, he called Larry to his hotel room.

"Lawrence," he announced, "my leg is killing me. I must have pulled a hamstring."

He sat on the bed and pulled down his trousers. On his thigh was a black-and-blue mark the size of a silver dollar.

"I can't take a painkiller (Percodan) before a show because they throw my timing off and make my voice fuzzy." He gave Larry an almost pleading look. "Put your hands on it, Larry. Give me a healing." Larry placed his hand on the sore leg. They meditated for a half-hour. Larry could feel Elvis relaxing, as the heat from his hand flowed over Elvis' body. He finally got up and walked around the room.

"I swear to God, it's really better," he said. "The sharp pain is gone. After the show, let's work on it some more."

His condition continued to deteriorate. In March 1977, in Baton Rouge, Louisiana, for the first time, Elvis felt too sick to go onstage. Larry had his first inkling of this at 10 that morning, when Ginger rang him, saying Elvis wanted to see him right away.

When he walked into the room, Elvis was sitting cross-legged on his bed, looking worse than Larry had ever seen him. His eyes were baggy and his nerves frayed.

He said, "Larry, I haven't been able to get any sleep. I feel terrible and think I should cancel the rest of the tour."

Larry was stunned. He had never seen Elvis totally deflated before.

"Why don't you try relaxing?" he said. "Just close your eyes, get under the covers, and rest. I'm sure you will fall asleep, if we just meditate a little." At 5 p.m., Elvis summoned him again. He had slept some but was still exhausted.

"Maybe I'll feel better after I get some food, it might give me some energy."

At 7 p.m., as showtime neared, he consulted with George Nichopolous, a Memphis physician who traveled with the troupe. He felt no better and decided to cancel the performance. He phoned his father in Memphis and told him he was entering a hospital.

There were only three days left in the tour. Urging him to hold on, some argued the newspapers would have a field day, blaming the cancellation on drugs.

Elvis shrugged. "Let them say what they want, I just can't make it." Joe Esposito, Charlie Hodge, and Tom Hulett, the tour agent, supported this view. "Your health is the important thing, Elvis," said Hulett. "Let's get you into a hospital."

In the midst of this discussion, Elvis motioned Larry into the bathroom with him, closing the door. He wanted to talk to him alone. He reached out both hands. They were shaking. His legs were wobbling.

"Larry," he said, "I'm really sick. I have no equilibrium. I can't walk straight."

That night, they flew back to Memphis and Elvis checked into the hospital. Dr. Nichopolous urged him to stay for two weeks and get a thorough checkup. The next day, as predicted, the newspaper headlines read. ELVIS ON DRUGS. CANCELS SHOW.

Elvis took some tests and left the hospital in a few days. He seemed improved. But in Baltimore, suffering a dizzy spell, he walked off the stage after 15 minutes, telling the audience: "Please excuse me, I'll be back."

Charlie Hodge took over the show, while Elvis tried relaxing in his dressing room. He was determined not to disappoint the thousands who had come to see him. He was still groggy when he walked back on, but he made a tremendous effort. Larry had never seen him more effective. The crowd rose to their feet, cheering wildly. But Larry, standing below, overheard somebody say, "Shoot, I'll bet he's on something."

Elvis was sicker than anybody knew. Yet, he kept stuffing himself. One evening, he ate five large banana splits, one after another. His system obviously craved sugar.

After the show, Elvis asked Larry to stay behind. He said in a tired voice:

"Larry, lay your hands on my body and use the blue light."

He perked up, but it was only temporary. His friends urged him to take a long vacation.

"Why don't you go to Hawaii for six months?" said Larry. "Rent a house in some secluded spot, eat a lot of vegetables and fruits, drink papaya juice, get into that ocean, and play on the beach. In a few months, you'll be a new man."

There were other places he could have gone, where he had felt at home and relaxed and had fun.

He loved Palm Springs, the desert spa a hundred miles from Los Angeles.

He had a beautiful home there, tucked away in the hills, with a secluded pool, a basketball court, two saunas, and a whirlpool bath large enough for 15 people. He would sit out by the pool late at night, look at the stars, breathe in the clear desert air.

"This is a healing place," he would say. "There is something magical in its vibrations."

But the magic had gone out of it for him.

Now, answering Larry, he smiled wearily.

"It sounds good," he sighed, "but I have to get out there and sing. That's what I was put here for, and that's what I will do, until I can't do it any longer."

CHAPTER 34

PROPHET

Elvis sees himself as a messenger from God.

He thought of himself increasingly as a messenger of God and spoke for Him, whenever he could. He always kept his cool when speaking for the Lord. But all somebody had to say was that they didn't believe, and the battle was joined.

"Why," he asked a lovely young thing, a self-proclaimed atheist, "do you boast about how much you are missing?"

He waved a hand at the great outdoors. "People who put down God don't realize there is an order in the universe: the seasons, the movement of the planets, the harmony of words and numbers. We have no order, unless it is by design." He smiled. "And no design, without a designer."

He was not impressed by the worldly and the wise, by the savants and the scholars, but by the simple and the pure who opened their hearts to the music of the universe. He understood their doubts and misgivings, more than those of the anatomist who looked at a corpse, and sneered: "Show me the soul."

What was that body, with the soul gone?

His faith removed many fears from his life: the fear of flying, the fear of living, and the fear of dying. Even the fear of being alone had begun to abate. He equated love with God now and wanted a wife united with him in this love. Not by chance did he choose *Where No One Stands Alone* for his gospel album.

CHAPTER 35

MORAL VALUES

If Elvis Presley saw life as an adventure, he also saw it as a search for knowledge, and religion was one of his central and most consuming interests. From the very beginning, he maintained a poignant awareness of the death of his twin brother, Jesse Garon, and was fascinated by the questions of life and death as they related to the scriptural teachings of the Bible. The experience of fundamentalist Christianity in his youth, which was strongly reinforced by his mother, had instilled in him a powerful feeling that he could go far in life if only he had faith in the Lord. If the meek could inherit the earth, then Elvis Presley, poor country boy, could be among the heirs.

When Gladys Presley died, Elvis's religious feelings took on an even more pressing importance, and while he would veer away from a conventional, churchgoing practice of religion, he always remained close to its meaning and power. The spirituals and hymns of his youth had imbued him with that power, and he came away from his early religious experience with all of the rudiments of Christianity intact. The traditional beliefs in the Trinity, the power of prayer, clear-cut notions of heaven and hell, and the promise of eternal grace and salvation. Many times, when discussing religion with Rick, he spoke of having prayed often and fervently on his way up. "Elvis always gave credit to the Lord for his success," he says. "He'd say, 'I just thank the Lord for what happened to me.'"

When Elvis was queried about his religion and his feelings about church-going, his stock response would be that going to church was simply too impractical because of the disturbance his presence would create. The more accurate reason, however, was that as he grew older, his own interpretations of religion may have left him in tune with the basic tenets of Christianity but out of tune with the typical master's interpretation. He was a Bible-toting, Bible-quoting man who probably never would have toted his Bible to church even if he could have. Elvis had his own ways.

"Elvis was not what you'd call a gung-ho Christian," says Rick, who often discussed religion with Elvis and prayed with him in later years. "In the situation he was in, it was pretty hard for him to lead a Christian life."

Religion in a conventional sense seemed to be a commitment to things not to do which Elvis, in his refusal to accept any limitations for himself, was unwilling to accept. The stern, authoritarian tenets of the "old-time" religion preached so emotionally throughout the South always dwelled heavily upon the promise of a better life in heaven after the troubled life on earth, of the need to control oneself in order to achieve that reward. Religion as Elvis knew it in his youth was preached through rules and maxims invoked from the Scriptures and handed down from the pulpits; the Lord often seemed a God of wrath and vengeance, terrible in his judgment when inveighing against the sins of man. Religion could easily seem an empty echo. It preached grace, salvation, and evoked universal brotherhood, but often stood for things like temperance, chastity, and maintaining the status quo.

In his position, it was easy for Elvis to take what he needed from his religious experience and discard what was inconvenient. "Elvis had seen a lot of religious phonies in his time," Rick adds, looking back on some of their discussions. "He was dependent upon himself when it came to interpreting the Scriptures and his relationship with the Lord." He could always maintain his religious fervor and the sincerity of his beliefs without worrying that they clashed with the lifestyle of the "King of Rock 'n' Roll." He was a true believer who made his own rules so that his beliefs could blend with the way he lived his life. "I think Elvis would have given anything he had for the peace of knowing God and living closely with him. He really wanted that and admired that strength."

He was fascinated by the image of Jesus. Apart from the Christian belief in Jesus as the Son of God and the Savior of man, Elvis was intrigued by Jesus as a historical figure, as a philosophical concept, as a force in people's lives, in every conceivable way he could perceive Him. "He had pictures of Jesus everywhere he went, which he carried," David says.

It was the power of Jesus that bowled Elvis over, says David, and it was the power that religion evoked in the lives of men that was at the root of his personal fascination. All of his favorite biblical passages, for instance, were the most vivid expressions of power in the Bible. "One thing that he liked to talk about was the parting of the Red Sea," says Pick, "or the plagues. He was really into the miracles, you know; the five loaves of bread and the two fishes to feed 5,000. Elvis thrived on impact. Strong things. That's why he liked the Book of Revelations. It's the Lord's testimony, the prophecy that tells what's going to be. Elvis looked into it because of its impact, because of the effect it had on people. See, that's what his claim to fame was; that's what he'd relate to."

"Raised up," as he was, to occupy such a position of magnitude, Elvis saw his own life as a miracle of true biblical intensity, and he sought religious knowledge to help him understand it. Within the confines of his sheltered and extraordinary life, he remained a passionately spiritual man. His world made it remarkable easy to set up his own rules of right and wrong, yet no matter what he did, he was still subject to the reproach of the same moral conscience instilled by his mother and the ways of his youth. "From the experience of his whole life," Rick says, "he knew the right way. That's why even when he did something that he knew was wrong and never let anybody know he felt guilty about it, he was his own worst enemy. He inflicted his pain on himself."

Religion demanded that he distinguish between right and wrong, but just as it sometimes filled him with guilt, it also allowed him to fall back on his Lord whenever things got rough. "Why me, Lord?" he would sigh in his many trying and painful moments.

Elvis was also interested in other religions, in spiritual powers of all kinds, looking for answers, knowledge, experience, and insights into himself and the world, for self-awareness. "The last 20 years of his life," says Rick, "Elvis was searching, constantly searching, trying to find himself through books and self-realization."

"He asked me once," remembers Billy, "there are so many religions, which one do you think is right? Now, that was one of the heaviest questions he ever asked me. I said, 'The only thing I can say is that I believe in God, Elvis.' And he said, 'Well, you've got your head screwed on right, that's the most important thing. You don't have to go to church or one certain church to prove that you believe in God.'"

"We were walking through the Hilton one time backstage and Elvis had a cross and a Star of David on the same gold chain," recalls Rick. "Someone saw it and asked him why. Elvis just looked at the guy and said, 'I don't want to miss out on heaven because of a technicality.'"

Ultimately Elvis' success and the fulfillment of his dreams had opened up many more troublesome questions than were answered. He began to think about the meaning of his life, about the universality of religion, about man's place in the cosmos, the question of life after death, and the relationship between God and man. He consumed ideas and information along with cars and jewels, and everywhere he went, he traveled with a couple of large portable bookcases in which he carried his favorite volumes along with his newly acquired books. His exposure to the sophistication of Hollywood had made him aware of what he lacked in formal education and of not being well-read, but it was a highly personal and specialized education that he now wanted to pursue.

"He would read all the time," says Billy, "whenever and wherever he had free time. He'd read before he went to bed; he'd read during the day; he was always reading something and underlining it, making sure he got the meaning." Sometimes Elvis would then turn the whole TCB group into a seminar, discussing the ideas in his latest books, getting reactions from the group, holding forth with his own opinions. "He was also really into words," notes Rick. "Elvis knew they were the building blocks for ideas." He gave dictionaries to his friends and soaked up any new word to cross his path—technical words, slang, everything. Even his well-known pride and ego were overpowered by his thirst. "If someone sprang something new on him, he'd inquire," Rick says. "It wasn't beyond him to say, "Hey, I don't understand that.""

Though he dabbled in many fields of interest, most of the subject matter had to do with what might give him an edge of enlightenment by teaching him something about himself or other people. He delved into the teachings of the Far East, particularly Buddhism, and looked into meditation and yoga. The place where he came to be buried on the Graceland grounds, the area out in back of the mansion known as Meditation Garden, was designated by Elvis to be a quiet place of contemplation and prayer. Medicine, psychology, and philosophy also fascinated him; he endeavored to find out as much as possible about how the human body and mind worked and how human thought had developed over the centuries.

In Kahlil Gibran, the great Lebanese poet, philosopher, and artist, Elvis found some of the most beautiful expressions of wisdom anywhere and a universalistic philosophy of life that blended many different religious ideas harmoniously. Islam was another religion that he wanted to learn about, and he enjoyed reading about the great mystics, spiritualists, and psychics. Psychic potentialities intrigued him, bringing about an interest in the questions of psychokinesis, telepathy, mind control, and other forms of extrasensory perception. The relationship between character and destiny sparked him to explore the meaning of numbers and the numerical vibrations in numerology (Elvis was a number "eight," known to be "alone at heart," to hide their feelings in life but do as they please) and to discover the astrological implications of having a sun in Capricorn.

The teachings of various gurus also found their way to him, although the only one he considered with any degree of seriousness was Yogi Paramahansa Yogananda, the founder of the Self-Realization Fellowship, with which Elvis carried on a correspondence. He did not see any of this as conflicting with his basic Christian beliefs, but rather as a way of "getting to know where your head is at" and of learning how to utilize that self-knowledge to more fully realize one's potential on many different levels. He also looked into Dianetics and Scientology, and many of the other offshoots of the Human Potential Movement, having been introduced to many of these ideas through his longtime buddy and hairstylist Larry Geller, who brought him literature and shared many of the same interests.

There have been reports to the effect that Elvis himself was known to manifest certain "special powers."

In truth, anyone who has ever seen him work his magic on an audience would be a fool not to recognize that Elvis was a uniquely powerful, charismatic person. "Charisma" is used here as the "special quality that gives an individual influence or authority over a large number of people," but the reference here is to powers psychic, spiritual, even "otherworldly." Rick says, "Elvis believed that people have mental power which is just as real as spiritual or physical power. He believed that his was pretty well developed and I do, too, but he wasn't a psychic by any means. He felt that he had mental power, mostly; he felt that he could read your mind, and that he'd know what you were thinking. Hell, sometimes he could! I mean, Elvis was very, very hip; he would blow me away with some of the things he would know. Sometimes, a second before I would ask him something, he would know my question, but it was more because of an "in-tune" relationship we had from being around each other all the tire." Rick is using the word "hip" here to mean "perceptive," and one thing that mostly everyone around Elvis will agree on is that he seemed to have been uncannily perceptive about people and about human behavior, which is why so many people have called him a genius when it came to just talking and being with people, at picking up a person's "vibrations."

Sometimes Elvis would like to play games with his "powers" just to see what he could and couldn't get away with. But no matter how perceptive he was, says Rick, he wasn't a mind-reader: "I just didn't believe that he could do it," he says, "and I'm being honest about it. Sometimes he was right, but sometimes he was in left field, too; a lot of people would go along with it even if it was a clear miss, just to keep from embarrassing him. They didn't want to blow him down in front of a bunch of people. You know, if anything continues for so long, it's like living a lie; you keep it up long enough, and you'll sincerely believe it. That's the way it was with him. It got to where he sincerely believed that he could. We had so much love for the man that we let him get away with it. It was just a kick, though he got away from it after he knew that some of the guys were just going along with him. See occasionally, when he wanted some recognition or something, he'd do something like that."

It seemed too frequent and too graphic to be merely coincidental. David recalls a particular karate exhibition in which he and Elvis were to put on a demonstration. In the karate studio, there were chains from which dummies were suspended as kick bags to practice with. When David and Elvis were introduced, they walked out onto seats and squared off, but one of these particular chains seemed to be dangling down in between them. In one graceful, slow-motion movement, Elvis reached upwards to punch it, and at the precise second that he made contact with it, says David, "lightning struck and it sounded as if the whole earth was enveloped in thunder! Everybody was freaked out, man. Things like that were happening all of the time. I remember driving out to Palm Springs once with him from Vegas. It was me, Elvis, Mindy Miller, and Steve Smith. We're driving along and we come right into one of those hellatious storms—you know, one of those god-awful West Coast storms—God! So we're driving along, and the storm is coming right for us. Elvis looks up and says, 'Don't worry; it's not going to get us. We won't even get one drop.' Minutes later, it's pouring rain right next to us, raining like a son of a bitch, but not where we're driving! Man, the sky looked like a holocaust, just all black and lightning, but we were cutting a path right through it! The whole way there it was like that, man, I swear. It was wild."

Similar to Elvis' interests in telepathy and the psychokinetic exertion of his will was a fascination with healing. Like most fundamentalist Christians, Elvis believed that men could heal by the laying on of hands through which the spirit of the Lord can work His power. The impressions conveyed by Red and Sonny West in *Elvis: What Happened?* were of a man firmly convinced that he had these powers and was imbued with special psychic knowledge. Well, say the boys, that's because sometimes, it was hard to tell the difference between when the Boss was kidding and when he wasn't. However, Red and Sonny say they were among the worst at being able to tell when Elvis was bullshitting and when he wasn't.

What is true is that Elvis was interested in the relationship between mind and body, in how the state of mind can affect the state of the body. His reluctance to be sick on a tour, for example, got him thinking about how the exertion of the human will can affect the health.

"If you think sick, you'll be sick," he would say. Whatever it was, say the boys, he could put it into a practice to a certain extent.

"I don't know what anybody else thinks, " says David, "but I personally believe that Elvis could heal. Elvis was the most spiritual man I've ever seen. Now, I don't mean he could heal you if there was something radically wrong, like cancer, but he had a way of getting you to relax and stay calm and feel better. Dean Nichopoulos hurt his knee in Vail once—a real bad sprain—and he was in a lot of pain. Elvis just talked to him and put his hand on it, and you could almost see the vibration. He just helped Dean bring himself down to where he was feeling better."

Rick elaborates on this: "To a certain extent, Elvis believed that if you have enough faith, you can be healed by the laying on of hands. See, the Bible tells you that you can. I've witnessed healings by hands and I know Elvis believed in it, but I don't believe that Elvis thought that he was the one, that it could be the Lord working through him. He believed that through the Lord he could do things like that if it was the Lord's will."

The Boss believed in reincarnation: The deja vu in his life convinced him that he had not only been around many times before but was surely returning, as he told Billy, "in the spirit and body of somebody else." Many of these interests were outgrowths of Elvis' preoccupation with religion, but they also reflect, once again, the question of limits in his life. Reincarnation was the ultimate expression of eternity to him. Elvis loved the idea of being able to do something extraordinary, to test himself to see if perhaps he did have the ability to transcend the norms of human existence. If anyone was "special," it was he. "Elvis' mind was so far advanced and different from the everyday person's," David says. "He was almost like an alien—the closest thing I've ever seen to a true 'leader.' He could have been a leader in any field."

Finally, Elvis Presley had a deeply ingrained fascination with death, which became the underlying curiosity for his search for knowledge about life. He wanted to "understand" it and turned to thanatosis—the contemplation of death—as a natural interest after his own mother's death, which was the key emotional experience of his life. His curiosity led him into mortuaries, where he learned about embalming, and through volume after volume on the subject.

The evangelist Billy Graham has called death "the most democratic institution in the world" and something to look forward to because when we die, we go into the presence of the Lord. The promise, inherent in Christianity, of peace and salvation in death removed much of Elvis' fear of dying.

"Only when you drink from the river of silence shall you indeed sing," wrote Gibran in *The Prophet*. "And when you have reached the mountaintop, then you shall begin to climb." Reflecting on his own life, Elvis contemplated those words very carefully. "He read about the cases of people dying and being brought back to life, and how beautiful it was to die," says Billy. "He called death the best thing that could happen you." "Elvis often said how glad he'd be to see his mom when he got to heaven," adds Rick.

Death was the last, most powerful and pronounced expression of the driving individualism that inclined Elvis Presley to follow his own road, to be free to do things his way, no matter the cost. Somewhere, in those moments thinking about it or when he came closest to it, Elvis must have recognized that the one place he hadn't been held the most answers for him. Death was the riskiest risk, the most challenging challenge, the final definition of limits and limitlessness, where the limits he could never accept in life rubbed against the limitlessness of the ultimate unknown.

The more boring, lonely, unhappy, and meaningless life would seem in the years to come, the more he felt that he had done everything he wanted to do, the closer Elvis would come to the experience.

"Well, I never been to heaven," he sang passionately when he did Hoyt Axton's *Never Been to Spain,* "...but I've been to Oklahoma...."

It is said, he firmly believes he is a prophet who was destined to lead, designated by God for a special role in life.

He believed that only strong people who show they have power on earth will be reincarnated. He would often say, "If you are powerful enough on earth and are strong enough, you will come back. Weak people can't bring themselves back from the dead. Only strong people."

On the album *Elvis Country,* subtitled (*I'm 10,000 Years Old*), Elvis sings the song of immortality, adapting and arranging this spiritual complete with Bible references. The song ran the entire length of the album, preceding and following all of the other songs. The song seemingly had meaning for somebody; however, it was never considered a hit by Presley standards.

The name "Elvis" apparently stems from an old Norse name, "Alviss," which means "all wise."

CHAPTER 36

NAMES, NUMBERS, AND LETTERS

As Elvis got into the spiritual, he felt there was some subconscious significance to his name, even if his parents were consciously unaware of it.

He combed through metaphysical books and the Bible, to find some special meaning to his name or its individual syllables, El and Vis. El, he discovered to his delight, was a common contraction of El-ohim, the God of the ancient Hebrews, and Vis, an Orientally derived word for the Force or Power. He had the power of God working for him.

In his obsession with names, he was intrigued that Jesse, the father of David, for whom twin Jesse Garon was named, was the lineal root of Jesus, and Aaron, Elvis' middle name, was the high priest of Israel. He was born under good auspices; a blue light was said to have blazed over the humble Presley home at the moment of his birth. It was almost an omen...

Elvis' beliefs in words, numbers, and resurrection.

The word "man" intrigued him. He discovered its roots in the Sanskrit word *manes,* meaning "to think." "And that is what distinguishes man—his power of thought. He is the only creature on God's earth who knows from the beginning that he is going to die." He smiled knowingly. "And by the same token, the only one to have any idea what happens after that." He considered himself.

"Take my own name, Elvis. If you scramble the letters, as in an anagram, you come up with what?"

Larry was puzzled.

"L-I-V-E-S--lives....Elvis lives." He smiled with satisfaction.

Elvis studied numbers, but not numerology, an art as complex as astrology or palmistry. His interest in numbers was simply derived. He believed that nothing happens by chance. People were born into a certain family for definite reasons, at a specific time. He was influenced by Cheiro's *Book of Numbers,* and by Cheiro's ability to impress people like Sarah Bernhardt and Mark Twain with his insight into their lives.

It was elementary. If you were born on the first of the month, you were a 1; on the second a 2, and so on up to 9. Double digits were added together to arrive at the person's number. If a person was born on the 29th, the digits added up to 11, and these added together formed a 2. This was the person's number.

Born on January 8, Elvis was an 8. Priscilla, born May 25, was a 7, like his mother, born April 25; and Ginger Alden, born on November 13, was a 4. Numbers 8 and 4, he was to read, had a special magic together. Linda Thompson, born May 23, was a 5. Fives were friendly, alert, and bounced back fast. That seemed to fit Linda.

Elvis was baffled, at first, seeing Priscilla as a 7. She showed no interest in the metaphysical, and yet Cheiro plainly stated:

"These people (7s) usually have remarkable dreams and a great leaning to occultism. They have the gift of intuition, clairvoyance, and a peculiar magnetism of their own that has a great influence over others." But afterward, when Priscilla's occult interest began to develop, he was ready to credit Cheiro:

"Number 7 people have very peculiar ideas about religion. They dislike to follow the beaten track; they create a religion of their own, but one that appeals to the imagination and based on the mysterious."

Elvis glowed proudly. "That's Priscilla, just a late bloomer."

Whenever he liked anybody, Elvis inquired about their birthday, and would refer to Cheiro's book or Corinne Heline's *Sacred Science of Numbers*.

He was pleased that Larry, like himself, was an 8, born on August 8. He felt this had to do with their common interest. He marked off Cheiro's passages and read them back to Larry:

"These people (8s) are invariably much misunderstood in their lives, and perhaps for this reason they feel intensely lonely at heart. They have deep and very intense natures, great strength of individuality. They generally play some important role on life's stage, but, usually, one which is fatalistic, or as the instrument of fate for others. These number 8 people are either great successes or great failures. There appears to be no happy medium in their case."

He would smile. "That's me, either great success or great failure. No happy medium. I've always known my success was a matter of fate or destiny."

One side of 8 represented upheaval, revolution, eccentricities; the other side, a leaning toward occult studies, religious devotion, zeal for any cause espoused, and a fatalistic outlook.

Some of Cheiro was prophetic:

'All persons who have the number 8 clearly associated with their lives

feel that they are distinct and different from their fellows, and they seldom reap the reward for the good they may do while they are living. After
their death, they are often extolled, their works praised, and lasting trib-
utes offered to their memory.'" These passages convinced Elvis.

"I'm certainly into philosophy and religion," he said. "And I've always felt
different. When I was in high school, I was an oddball and a loner. I didn't
understand it then, but in class I would always be daydreaming and be
looking out a window. I have always known loneliness, even when Mom
was alive. It had something to do with my brother. I would never have
felt alone, had he lived. How could I? He was my twin. He was me."

He drew other parallels:

"I'm always being misunderstood. They never understood me in Hollywood. They never had the slightest idea of what I was all about. They
wanted me to conform to their ridiculous movies, the same damn movie,
every one of them. All they did was change the titles and my name. They
even used the same extras and dancers. It got so they thought I was the
guy they were putting on the screen." He was fascinated with his own
number 8. And he would discuss it with every girl he was close to, and
some he knew only casually. At the same time, he would ask their birthday, then describe what their number meant, comparing their qualities
with his own.

In one of these philosophical moods, he read from the *Sacred Science
of Numbers,* which appeared to accent the spiritual more than Cheiro's
book. "Those who come under the leadership of this number," he read
aloud, "rise easily above the material and claim their own the things of
the spiritual. Eight is the number of the resurrection into a higher consciousness and a new manner of living. It offers truly an exodus from the
old, the finite, and the personal into the promised land of the New Age,
wherein freedom, equality, soul companionship and cosmic knowing, all
of which are key words of 8, will be generally realized."

PART VII
MEDICAL FACTORS

CHAPTER 37

AUTOPSY DEFENDED

*Autopsy: Inspection and dissection of a body after death, as for deter-
mination of the cause of death; postmortem examination*

It is art, as well as science, the autopsy. There are findings and there are
interpretations.

Jerry T. Francisco, M.D., a board-certified specialist in forensic pathology, has been analyzing autopsies for 23 years, and he takes a historical
view.

"The autopsy dates from the British coroner system," Dr. Francisco patiently explains. "William the Conqueror brought it to Britain back in
1066. In the early days of Britain, the only purpose of the coroner was
to distinguish for the Norman King the death of Saxons from the death
of Normans. If Saxon, nothing more need be done. If Norman, the king
would extract a tribute from the villagers where he died. British coroners
have evolved to our current system of medical examiners."

For Dr. Francisco, medical examiner of Memphis, Tennessee (Shelby

County), since 1961, the "Norman" in this case is Elvis Aaron Presley, but as a tribute, some people seem to want Dr. Francisco's head.

Two years after Elvis collapsed and died at age 42 in his Memphis mansion, his memory lived on to make money for countless entrepreneurs.

Within hours of Presley's death, it was Dr. Francisco who told a press conference that the death was due to "cardiac arrhythmia of undetermined cause." Two months later, he concluded his investigation by describing the death as "HCVD associated with ASHD," hypertensive cardiovascular disease associated with atherosclerotic heart disease.

At that time, he acknowledged to a press conference that autopsy toxicological studies indicated the presence of up to 11 drugs in the singer's blood, but he stated that "Elvis Presley died of heart disease and prescription drugs found in his blood were not a contributing factor. Had these drugs not been there, he still would have died."

When Elvis' personal physician, George Nichopoulos, M.D., was charged by the Tennessee Board of Health with improperly prescribing 5,300 pills for Presley in the seven months before his death, and when ABC-TV charged on its *20-20* news broadcast that Elvis was a "medical drug addict" and that his drug-induced death had been "covered up," Dr. Francisco held a third press conference. Presley died of a weak heart, not a drug overdose, the medical examiner repeated.

The combination of the charges against Dr. Nichopoulos and the allegations of coverup against Dr. Francisco had their effect. Although everyone wants to "let the man rest in peace," a change in public attitude seemed to be setting in. Bartenders know it. Cab drivers know it. Real estate agents know it. Everything points to drugs.

But does it, really?

Because of the exceptional interest in Presley and the everyday issues posed to medical examiners, Dr. Francisco gave the only interview he has ever granted to discuss the Presley autopsy to American Medical News.

His views are these:

Presley died of heart failure and heart failure alone. "This is based on the totality of the medical record—Elvis' medical history, the detailed autopsy, including the toxicological findings, and the circumstantial evidence at the death scene."

Drugs were present, but neither caused nor contributed to death. "There is no proof that the level of drugs found in his blood would cause death."

Restrictive Tennessee laws regarding medico-legal cases preclude an open discussion of the case. "In Shelby County, an autopsy can only be ordered by the county district attorney, although the county medical examiner can recommend one. The DA can order an autopsy only if he suspects a homicide or foul play. None was suspected in Presley's death. Had not the family requested a private autopsy, it is unlikely there would have been one at all."

The crux of the controversy is that Dr. Francisco's medicolegal finding was based partially on a private autopsy protected by confidentiality statutes. Dr. Francisco offers his reasoning for a finding of heart failure, but disbelievers claim the suppressed autopsy argues for death by drugs, or "polypharmacy."

To many, the cause of death is irrelevant. Nothing can bring Elvis back. But a principle is involved. In many ways, Dr. Francisco's dilemma is common to all medical examiners bound by a law as pro-privacy and anti-autopsy as the one in Tennessee.

For a medical examiner, it is a Catch-22. Dr. Francisco is in many ways a victim of circumstances. First, the Presley family, for reasons all their own, ordered a private autopsy through the singer's attending physician, Dr. Nichopoulos. (A rumor that would later surface claims that the late Vernon Presley feared his son had been poisoned and that he was actually relieved to find only prescription drugs in the body.)

Since the singer's death was sudden and the medically unattended body was found dead, the death was a medical examiner's case. By statute, the medical examiner, Dr. Francisco, would have to pinpoint a cause of death—only one cause—but the crucial evidence to that determination, the autopsy, was entirely out of his control.

This is the law—then and now.

The bare outline of Presley's death is summarized in Dr. Francisco's *Report of Investigation by County Medical Examiner,* a single-page public document that entrepreneurs have, astoundingly, hawked by the thousands to fanatical fans of the entertainer.

Presley was found dead in the bathroom of his Memphis mansion by a female companion, Ginger Alden. It was 2 p.m. on August 16, 1977. At 3:30 p.m., he was pronounced dead by Dr. Nichopoulos, who with the family's consent requested an autopsy. The Memphis Police Department was notified at 3:30 and promptly began its investigation. Dr. Francisco was attending an educational seminar at the time of death, but his office was notified by 4 p.m. At the request of the family, the body was taken to Memphis' Baptist Hospital for autopsy. Dr. Nichopoulos' report to medical investigators of conditions for which Presley was under treatment stated "hypertensive cardiovascular disease/colon problems."

At 5:30 p.m., some 30 people gathered under tight security in a room at Baptist Hospital to conduct the "most meticulous autopsy this hospital has ever done. I doubt if a single hair on Presley's body was lost." There were 10 physicians participating in the procedure, including eight Baptist Hospital pathologists under the direction of E. Eric Muirhead, M.D., plus Drs. Nichopoulos and Francisco.

Both Dr. Francisco and spokesmen for Baptist Hospital say that relations between the hospital and the medical examiner's office have always been smooth. The hospital and Dr. Francisco's office are within a block of each other in Memphis' medical center.

"The hospital contacted me," Dr. Francisco said, "and we agreed that because of the crowd forming outside Baptist and the danger in trying to bring the body across the street to my labs, the autopsy would be performed at Baptist. Furthermore, I do not see how that without bending the law, I could have taken control of the autopsy and/or requested the district attorney to take control of the autopsy. There was no suspicion of foul play.

"I decided that I would, instead, participate in the Baptist autopsy, make sure that it was performed correctly, and use the autopsy findings as part of my record in determining the cause of death and completing the medical examiner's report."

The autopsy was concluded within three hours. "The pressure for some sort of a statement to the press was incredible," Dr. Francisco said, "and the autopsy team decided that it was my role to be the spokesman. With their knowledge, I said that based upon the results of the gross autopsy, the death was due to cardiac arrhythmia of undetermined cause."

Explanations from this point on become blurred.

Officially, only Dr. Francisco is empowered by law to sign a medical examiner's report and a death certificate.

In October 1977, Dr. Francisco listed death as natural due to hypertensive cardiovascular disease. Contributing cause was coronary artery disease. He signed the death certificate (under Tennessee law, a death certificate is a private document for 50 years and then it becomes a public record).

At that time, Dr. Francisco held a press conference to explain his determination of the cause of death. The detailed toxicological reports, he said, detected as many as 11 prescription drugs in Presley's blood, but these were not related to the cause of death. A weak heart—period—killed the singer, the forensic pathologist concluded.

Officially, that should have been the end of it. But the doubts persisted. The Memphis Commercial Appeal published portions of a contraband copy of a report of one of five laboratories involved in the autopsy. "Near toxic levels of drugs reported in Presley's blood," said the headline.

ABC-TV apparently obtained the lab report. The network's documentary charging a "cover-up" of a drug-induced death consisted of five elements:

The drug levels reported by the Memphis newspaper were again reported. The laboratory in question, Bio-Science of Van Nuys, California, stated that it always stands behind its findings, although it specifically refused to discuss the Presley case. Various Presley intimates told stories of how the singer abused drugs. A former Baptist hospital pathology resident, Noel Florendo, M.D., who was present at the autopsy, stated that the gross autopsy did not in his opinion indicate severe heart disease; and two "expert witnesses" concluded from toxicology data alone that the drugs in Presley's blood had proven fatal.

A sixth element that gave the show added impact was the accusation of Presley's physician, Dr. Nichopoulos, with indiscriminate prescribing of pills in the seven months before the singer's death.

Both the newspaper story and the television show strongly implied that the autopsy team at Baptist Hospital did not agree with the findings of the medical examiner but was by law precluded from explaining why.

Unraveling the story is somewhat like Plato's description of interpreting the shadows on the wall of a cave.

On the one hand, Dr. Francisco discussed at length—and for the first time anywhere—his findings for heart failure.

On the other, Baptist Hospital says it is bound by law to respect the privacy of the autopsy. The drug labs used as consultants by Baptist, Bio-Science and its two subcontractors, the forensic toxicology lab in the Orange County (California) coroner's office and the Center for Human Toxicology Studies in Salt Lake City, Utah; the lab at Memphis Methodist Hospital; and the forensic toxicology lab at Memphis' U of Tennessee Center of Health Sciences are bound by consultant-client privacy agreements.

Only the executors of the Presley estate, essentially his ex-wife, Priscilla Presley, can release the autopsy for discussion. Attorneys for the estate say this is not going to happen.

So be it, says Dr. Francisco. The 46-year-old pathologist is the only medical examiner Shelby County has ever had since the state abolished the old coroner system and in 1961 approved a post-mortem examination law. For 18 years he has been the Shelby County medical examiner; for the past nine years, he has also served as the Tennessee chief medical examiner, a salaried position.

His roots are as deep in Tennessee as those of Elvis: born in Huntingdon, Tennessee, medical school at the U. of Tennessee Center for Health Sciences, Memphis, and internship and residency at the City of Memphis Hospitals.

"I am not involved, and never have been involved in a cover-up," Dr. Francisco said. "I have my own reputation to protect without worrying about somebody else's reputation. "

Whenever Elvis is involved, motives are suspect, but even Dr. Francisco's doubters say it is unlikely he would cover up for his mother. Some imply, however, that he is mistaken about his finding of a fatal heart attack. "Okay," the forensic pathologist says. "Let's look at the entire record, the totality of the record upon which I base my decision.

"First, there was cardiac hypertrophy. The heart was enlarged to double its normal size. There was severe coronary artery disease. The arteries were 60% clogged. In reviewing his (Presley's) medical records, I found a pattern of abnormal electrocardiogram readings.

"Second, he had a history of high blood pressure, as much as 160/110. He also was treated over the years for diabetes, depression, insomnia, overweight."

"Third, the circumstantial evidence. This was a sudden death. His body was found in a flexed position in the bathroom. There was a pressure point upon the side of his head. Had he died of drugs, the body would have first gone into a coma and it would have most likely been found in a comfortable, reclining position. Had he suffocated by falling into the bathroom carpeting, the pressure marks would have been on the nose and chin.

"The evidence of cardiovascular disease found in the detailed autopsy, the medical and family history disclosed in the medical charts—his mother died at 42, too—and the circumstantial evidence all point to a heart attack. (Speculations abound as to what might have triggered the fatal attack, but Dr. Francisco says, "We do not know. It could have been many things. Medical examiners do not deal in speculations." One speculation is that an anxious Presley, worried about the concert tour he was to begin the day he died, was fasting to get down his weight. The fasting, combined with a history of constipation, might have led to "straining at stool" and stress on the heart. A valid basis for such a hypothesis, Dr. Francisco said, can be found in the medical literature.)

"As for the drugs, there were four drugs found in significant or therapeutic concentrations (expressed as micrograms per 100 milliliters of blood); Ethinamate, or Valmid, 100 micrograms; methaqualone, or Quaalude, 600; codeine, 100; and unspecified barbiturates, 800. Four drugs were found in trace levels: chloropheneramine, an antihistamine often used to control hay fever; Demerol; Valium; and morphine, which may have metabolized from the codeine.

"Based on my study of the toxicology reports from the five labs, I believe these eight drugs were present. The Bio-Science report also listed 500-700 micrograms of ethchlorvynol, or Placidyl, and specified three barbiturates—pentobarbital, butabarbital, and phenobarbital—at a level of 1,940 micrograms.

"Even assuming the highest concentrations, it is my opinion, supported by advice from two forensic pathologists and three forensic toxicologists with whom I consulted, that these drugs neither caused death nor contributed to death.

"He died of heart failure."

The medical examiner's critics are pushing for a finding of a drug-induced death. Interpreting the toxicological numbers is complex.

One thing can be said with certainty. There is no possible medical indication for the number and levels of drugs found in Presley's body. The AMA Department of Drugs says that any patient using these 11 drugs—all central nervous system depressants—clearly has a drug abuse problem and is putting his health at risk.

But did this list of drugs kill Elvis Presley?

Probably not, informed sources say. The reason, ironically, is the tolerance undoubtedly developed by Presley, who for almost two decades reportedly abused prescription drugs.

Forensic toxicology, like forensic pathology and forensic psychiatry, is art as well as science. Estimates for lethal doses of prescription drugs can vary widely, a hundredfold in some cases, even without the factor of tolerance.

For the five drugs found in significant levels in Presley's blood, the breakdown would be as follows: Valmid at 100 micrograms is well within the therapeutic range of 500-1,000, furthermore, it almost never occurs in lethal concentrations. Quaalude at 600 micrograms is near the therapeutic range of 500 and below the lethal dose of 2,000 (source for this and others is the Southwestern Institute of Forensic Sciences Toxicology Laboratory consulted by Dr. Francisco; the barbiturates at either 800 or 1,940 compare with a therapeutic range of 2,500 for slow acting agents to 400-870 for the intermediate agents and lethal range of 7,500 or the slow-acting to 3,000 for the intermediates. (Two of the barbiturates identified by Bio-Science are slow acting and one is intermediate); Placidyl at 500-700 compares with a therapeutic level of 200 and a lethal level of 10,000.

The principal offending drug appears to be codeine, which at 100 micrograms is 33 times the therapeutic dose of 3 and one-fifth the lethal dose of 500. A key potential synergistic agent—alcohol—was apparently seldom used by Presley and was not in his blood at death.

Theoretically, the high levels of codeine, ethchlorvynol, and barbiturates, all CNS depressants, could interact to induce death.

This was the interpretation advanced on ABC-TV by two physicians, Cyril Wecht, M.D., Pittsburgh, Pa., and Matthew Ellenhorn, M.D., Beverly Hills, CA. Both physicians—Dr. Wecht is a board-certified pathologist specializing in forensic pathology, and Dr. Ellenhorn an internist specializing in clinical pharmacology—had access only to the toxicology reports. Both said the drugs Bio-Science reported to be in Presley's body could kill.

Dr. Wecht has a national reputation for appearing as a witness in controversial medico-legal cases. While ABC-TV identified Dr. Wecht as "one of the foremost forensic pathologists in the entire country," it did not mention that he was embroiled in a local controversy. Pittsburgh newspapers charged Dr. Wecht with using his office as Allegeheny County Coroner for private financial gain. The county controller and a grand jury sought a court order to obtain the morgue's financial records. Dr. Wecht's response, the newspapers reported, was to claim confidentiality. County officials petitioned the state supreme court to open the records so that a finding could be made before Dr. Wecht's bid for election as a county commissioner—he was chairman of the Allegeheny County Democratic Party—was made in that November's general election.

In a one-hour special show alleging a medical examiner's cover-up in Tennessee, ABC-TV produced only three professional witnesses: Dr. Wecht, who was involved in his own medical examiner controversy and whose defense—confidential records—is the very principle ABC-TV attacked in its Tennessee suit to release the Presley autopsy.

Dr. Ellenhorn, who ABC says was paid a fee to render an opinion.

Dr. Florendo, who now refuses to discuss the case, saying, "my role in the autopsy, really, was rather limited." The rest was subjective footage outlining how Presley abused drugs. That abuse—and the tolerance it built up—is, ironically, the factor that leads many to think the drugs did not kill the singer.

One physician-toxicologist said, "If the case went to court with the autopsy findings as outlined by Dr. Francisco, the medical examiner would win hands down. If only one choice can be made, heart failure is that choice."

Fueling the controversy is the unavoidable implication that the Baptist Hospital autopsy team, headed by Dr. Muirhead, opted for polypharmacy. Dr. Francisco said, "I understand many people are upset about the number of drugs found in the blood. But the medical examiner is neither concerned with lifestyle nor compelled to comment on drug abuse. He is concerned only with cause of death. I accepted the findings of the autopsy—the factual material—but I did not necessarily accept the interpretation of the autopsy, the opinion.

"It is my responsibility to decide the cause of death. I made that decision based upon my education, experience, and ethics. The autopsies I have done are in the thousands, the drug deaths in the hundreds. Sure, anything can happen. The drugs could have killed him. Bananas can cause cancer. That's a little strong, but when you're obligated by law to take the responsibility for making your best judgment, you look at the entire record. You look very carefully.

"I feel very comfortable with my decision."

Dr. Francisco had been through it all before. "When Martin Luther King was killed back in 1968," he said, "I handled the investigation. There were people who refused to believe he'd been shot, although the bullet holes were there to see. Some people refused to believe it was really him. I learned a long time ago that I do not have the ability to convince everybody of everything I do.

"The Presley case proves two things: medical examiners are always going to be in the public spotlight, and they are always going to be second-guessed."

CHAPTER 38

THE PRICE OF HEALTH CARE

The Price of Health Care, reprinted in its entirety from *Elvis, Portrait of a Friend* by Marty Lacker, Patsy Lacker, and Leslie S. Smith.

Doctor George Nichopoulos is a Memphis physician who became Elvis Presley's doctor some years prior to the singer's death. Doctor Nick, as the guys called him, was one of the group. He is a short, well-dressed, distinguished-looking man with silver-gray hair who often traveled with Elvis and became the family doctor for most of the guys and their wives. The doctor's wife, Edna, was a friend of many of the guy's wives, and his son, Dean, worked for Elvis during the later years.

Doctor Nichopoulos was a partner of Elvis, Joe Esposito and one Michael McMahon in a racquetball venture in Memphis which seems to have turned sour toward the end. The doctor is well liked by many of the guys who feel he always had Elvis' best interest at heart.

Memphis public records reveal that George C. Nichopoulos and Edna S. Nichopoulos borrowed from Elvis A. Presley the sum of two hundred thousand dollars as evidenced by a non-interest bearing promissory note of either July 29, 1975 or July 29, 1976. The deed of trust, as recorded, carries both dates.

A second deed of trust is recorded which shows that on March 3, 1977, George C. Nichopoulos and Edna S. Nichopoulos became indebted to Elvis A. Presley for an additional fifty-five thousand dollars. This deed of trust states that the promissory note is interest bearing and payable in installments with a final maturity of March 1, 2002.

From these public records it appears that Doctor Nichopoulos was indebted to Elvis Presley for a total of two hundred and fifty-five thousand dollars. Two hundred thousand dollars of that amount was non-interest bearing.

An interesting side light of these financial dealings is that the Executor of the estate of Elvis Presley, Elvis' father Vernon, lists on the inventory of the assets belonging to the estate the following:

Promissory note dated March 3, 1977, in the face amount of 25,000.00, secured by Trust Deed on Lot 40, Section A, Eastwood Manor Subdivision, payable to the order of Elvis A. Presley and bearing interest in the amount of 7% per annum.

Lot 40, Section A, Eastwood Manor Subdivision is the home of George C. and Edna S. Nichopoulos. Either the trust deeds are filed incorrectly in regard to interest, or the executor's inventory report to the probate court is incorrect.

Repeated attempts were made to communicate with Doctor Nichopoulos regarding his association with Elvis Presley. Messages were left with his secretary requesting that he return the telephone calls, and explanations were given for the reason for the calls, but they were never answered. It is, therefore, impossible to include any comments by Doctor Nichopoulos in this manuscript.

Patsy Lacker speaks harshly of George Nichopoulos. She remembers the pain of the drugs and blames him for being the source. It would be difficult to find fault with her reasoning. During one forty-six month period, January 24, 1973, through October 28, 1976, Doctor Nichopoulos prescribed the following medication for Marty Lacker: 6,464 Placidyl, 3,204 Darvon, 1,508 Hycomine, 708 Empirin Codeine #3, 500 Dalmane, 400 Valium, 216 Darvocet, 200 Valmid and 91 other assorted pills which are not important.

The total number of pills prescribed by Doctor George Nichopoulos for Marty Lacker, and consumed by Marty Lacker, during that forty-six month period was thirteen thousand two hundred and ninety one (13,291). The average per day was ten.

Placidyl is an oral hypnotic used for insomnia. According to the Physicians Desk Reference the following warning is to be considered when prescribing Placidyl: Prolonged use of Placidyl may result in tolerance and psychological and physical dependence. Prolonged administration of the drug is not recommended.

Valmid is a sedative-hypnotic. Dalmane is a hypnotic for insomnia. Hycomine is a cough suppressant and respiratory tract decongestant. Valium is a tranquilizer. Empirin Codeine #3 is a narcotic analgesic painkiller. Darvon is an analgesic painkiller containing phenacetin which has been reported to damage the kidneys when taken in large amounts for a long period of time. Propoxyhene, also found in Darvon, has been known to cause cardiac arrhythmias.

The reason for isolating those forty-six months is that we have certified copies of the records from the pharmacy which filled the prescriptions. Unfortunately they did not preserve records prior to that period, and we have only Marty's and Patsy's word that the average amounts were approximately the same for the six years prior to January 24, 1973.

Marty Lacker has no anger against Doctor Nichopoulos. "There were times when he was very nice and tried to do everything possible for you, but there were other times, and his son was worse than he was, when you would ask him something and he would come out with a smart remark to try to show off.

"That's the only thing I feel toward Nick in a negative way. I don't have any grudge or feel bad toward him because of the pills or any of that. It may sound funny, or stupid, but I just don't have it."

"When Elvis wanted something, nothing was going to stop him from getting it. Nick used to come to the house just about every night to check Elvis and see if everything was all right. He would bring his medical bag along and when he was finished with Elvis he might set it down, and go into another room to talk with some of the guys. The first time I remember this happening Nick had left the bag by one of the doors and Elvis saw it. He walked over to the bag and tried to open it, but Nick had locked it. Elvis started cursing under his breath and I started laughing. It happened again the next day. Elvis called Nick into the room, aimed a pistol at the bag and said, 'If you keep locking this thing I'm going to blow it open.'

We all took it as a joke but I guess Nick realized what Elvis was saying to him, so, he later said, he began leaving a prescription drug bottle full of non-drug capsules in the bag and not locking it so Elvis would think he was getting something he wanted.

"There's no question Nick was writing prescriptions for what Elvis wanted. He was Elvis' doctor. He treated him. But the drug prescriptions came from other doctors too. Nick wasn't the only one. That's why I keep saying that Nick was the lesser of all evils, he tried to control it. He knew Elvis was getting it from other people, so he limited and controlled what he gave him. But he knew what Elvis was getting and he knew what Elvis was capable of doing. Every one of us told Nick, especially Joe who was real close to him. Joe would tell Nick, "Elvis will just go to another doctor to get what he wants if you don't give it to him or make him think he's getting it by giving him a limited amount, he'll go to another doctor."

"We've all said it and Elvis would go to another doctor whether he knew him or not. He would have thought nothing of going to a doctor's house and knocking on his door. You know when a doctor saw Elvis Presley there he would be thrilled and either call his nurse or his wife to meet Elvis, and Elvis would sit there and con him into giving him exactly what he wanted. He was an actor, he could sit there and say, 'I'm having a problem sleeping,' or 'I've got a pain here' and the doctor would believe him.

"He would act like he didn't know anything about medicine and the doctor would believe him and tell him, 'I'll take care of you. There's nothing for you to worry about.'

"When Elvis left he would have exactly what he wanted, and the doctor would think he had done a real service for Elvis Presley.

"I picked up prescriptions for Elvis or had one of the other guys do it when that was part of my responsibility as foreman of the guys. We used a lot of different pharmacies to keep too many prescriptions from being on file at one place.

"We've often talked about the pills when Elvis wasn't around, all of us have. Mostly we joked about them and there was always the question of how he was going to be when he got up. That is, what kind of mood he was going to be in, which really meant, was he going to be on the pills?

"If he stayed upstairs late and called down on the intercom you could tell if he was on the pills, and if he was, someone would say, 'Oh hell, he's out of it again.'

"Of course we used to say that about each other too. But I have to say this, most of the guys did not use anything during the day. I did, but most of them did not. I was the fool.

"Occasionally, we had serious conversations about the pills but most of us thought it was futile. There was no way we could change things. There was also the thought which ran through my mind and, I'm sure, some of the others', and that was I didn't believe anything would harm Elvis. It didn't matter what he did, nothing would harm him. I know how scared I use to be about flying but when Elvis was along I never worried. I just didn't believe anything would happen.

"It's a strange thing to say, but I had the feeling that regardless of how many he took nothing was going to happen to him. I don't know what it was that made me feel that way.

"There were times when we talked about it as a group. Mostly after Elvis yelled at somebody or did something which we felt he wouldn't have done had it not been for the pills. Lamar use to say things, but he never did anything about it. Sometimes Red or Sonny or Joe would say something. Joe and I talked about it a lot, just the two of us, but the conversation usually ended by one of us holding up our hands and saying, 'What the hell can we do about it?'

"There was no way we could really do anything about it. There were times when it was a real problem for me or Joe. We were in a position of responsibility and had to get things done, but sometimes we couldn't because Elvis wouldn't talk about something. If he was irritable because of something he was taking, or something he wanted to take, he would just cut you off. He would say, 'I don't want to talk about it,' and there was nothing you could do.

"Joe and I got mad many times when he would act like that, but the next minute he would come in with that smile on his face and wipe all the anger away, until the next time.

"There was never a real conference, as such, of all the guys to talk about Elvis' problem. You didn't know Elvis. You had to know him to understand the situation. Elvis would get what he wanted. If Nick had said, 'No', to something Elvis wanted, he would have said, 'Get the hell out of here and don't come back.'

"He would have gotten another doctor who probably would have given him anything he wanted, and not cared what happened. Nick was able to control things by being there. I know of times, and Sonny says the same thing, that Nick would substitute sugar pills, or vitamin pills, for all the other junk. He cared about Elvis and I honestly think he knew that if he left, things would have been much worse than they were. He could, at least, partly control what happened, but if he wasn't there someone else would have been.

"It would not be right to lay all the blame on Nick. If he was wrong, we were all wrong, including the public. We all contributed to Elvis' life and death. You have to know Elvis to understand. He was going to have his own way about what he wanted.

"The fault lies with all of us. Every single one of us, including the public who really didn't know him, that they thought they did, but they didn't. I'm speaking of the people who met him once or twice and sat and talked with him, because that was his nature, but they didn't get to know him. We, who were around him all the time, really didn't know him. I don't know if he even knew himself.

"Elvis was so damn dynamic he would overpower anyone, and he wouldn't listen. If that was really what he waited to do, we could sit and talk until we were blue in the face, but it wouldn't do any good.

"We knew that, at least some of us did, it would be like talking to a wall. Elvis did what he wanted to do. There had to be times when he knew he shouldn't be doing what he was doing, and there had to be times when Nick knew he shouldn't be giving him what he gave him, but most of the fault lies in Elvis' abusing, really abusing the prescription medications.

At one time Nick tried to combat that by having someone hold the prescription drugs and giving Elvis only the right amount. It was easy to abuse the drugs, especially if he didn't fight it too much.

"Part of the fault was the pressure of his life, his lifestyle, the disappointment, the split with Priscilla, his mother's death. I know those kinds of things happen to a lot of people, but we're not talking about a lot of people, we're talking about one individual, and how it affected him.

"Elvis was a lonely person. That's why he had to have companionship all the time, female and the guys. He knew we loved him, he knew that even though natural doubts crept into his mind about all of us, but deep down he knew we loved him.

"Where the fault lies? You've got to put it on all of us, including him. He probably was his own worst enemy. Most of us are."

CHAPTER 39

THE DOCTOR AS PUSHER

The medical doctor is the number one drug pusher in the United States, according to drug abuse authorities. It is not the street junkie, who is selling to maintain a habit, who does the lion's share of the damage, but rather the family physician in terms of his careless prescribing practices.

The doctor is overloaded with patients and often overworked. There are not enough doctors available, according to those in the profession who are concerned with the unethical practice of this minority and the careless practice of the majority. The conscientious segment of the medical profession, though opposed to the free and easy dispensation of drugs, explains the practice by pointing out that almost 80% percent of the patients who came to their office are affected with nothing more serious than hypochondria.

Doctors get very impressive printed material from the pharmaceutical companies, with promises of instant relief of pain and pressure for their patients, and they all too often fall to the temptation of solving an undiagnosed malady with a prescription for one of the magic drugs. Valium, for example, is the most prescribed, and over-prescribed, drug in America.

There are more admissions to hospital emergency rooms for Valium complications than for any other drug, not heroin, not alcohol, not cocaine. Valium is the drug of choice. It is the most abused drug in the country. Valium is meant to be, and is quite effective as, a muscular relaxant, but now it is being prescribed as a calmative agent for men, women, and children who are unable to define that which is bothering them. Valium is the doctor's friend, the pill which allows him to write a prescription. He knows the patient will not be satisfied unless he receives a prescription which must be filled by a pharmacy. But Valium is a self-elevating drug; if one is good, two is better, and the Valium patient all too often ends by abusing the drug. The doctor who pushes pills will argue that the patient demands more than advice and will not accept anything less than a drug prescription.

Unfortunately, even the most scrupulous doctors seem to fail to realize that the 80% whom they think of as hypochondriacs are seeking a cure for something. It may be an unnamed disease brought about by the stress of a family argument, a flat tire, or a broken refrigerator, but it is nevertheless a very real disease to the sufferer, and a prescription for addictive drugs is not the answer.

There is a cartoon showing a bewildered patient standing before a doctor who is handing him a prescription and saying, "Take two a day until addicted."

It's funny to everyone except those who have lived through the terror of trying to get off a drug habit.

Pharmacists seem to tend to be more cautious than doctors. They often ask a patient if the doctor knows how many times a prescription has been refilled, but this, of course, is not the responsibility of the pharmacist. The cautious doctor will not write a prescription which may be refilled, although under the law he can usually allow up to five refills from one prescription. In the perfect world of sound medical practice, the doctor would require the patient to return for a consultation or physical check-up prior to allowing a prescription for an addictive drug to be refilled.

The temptation may be great for the doctor to write a prescription for Valium and get on to something more important. It may satisfy the doctor's need to do something and, in fact, it may make the patient feel better, but it does not solve the problem and may well create a new and far more serious problem by being the first step to an addiction. The physician should be honest with the patient. If he is unable to find a cause for the patient's distress, he should say exactly that.

The people who do the most intensive research on the drugs are the pharmaceutical companies, who are also the manufacturers. The profit motive is obviously the base line for these companies which are, of course, commercially oriented, and yet there exists a very incestuous relationship between the doctor and the pharmaceutical company. This relationship is fostered by the Bible of the medical profession, the *Physicians' Desk Reference,* which contains the names and descriptions of every drug on the market. The drug descriptions are written by the manufacturing firms which, thereby, tell the doctor what to prescribe for the patient. To add to this love affair, the pharmaceutical companies supply free samples to the doctors to use on their patients. Prescribing patterns, therefore, are not based on well-thought-out research and experience, but by the education brought to the doctor by the pharmaceutical companies. Promotional expenses for brand-name drugs amounted to more than 350 million dollars last year.

There are thousands of prescription drugs, but only hundreds of formulas, so the difference comes in the packaging, the way they're put together. The companies bombard the doctors with so much promotional literature they can't possibly keep up with all the new information. The doctors, then, are dependent upon the pharmaceutical companies for what they prescribe for their patients.

The danger of abuse is ever-present. Mixing one drug with another can be deadly, and alcohol is included in the drug category. Perhaps the most dangerous is the mixture of alcohol and any drug in the depressant category like the barbiturates, tranquilizers, opiates, and narcotics. The mixture of any of these with alcohol can be lethal, especially alcohol and barbiturates. According to the Shelby County Medical Examiner, Dr.

Jerry Francisco, the following drugs were found in therapeutic levels in the body of Elvis Presley during the autopsy performed at Baptist Memorial Hospital:

Ethinamate, trade name Valmid, is a sedative-hypnotic. The *Physicians' Desk Reference* says the concurrent ingestion with other central nervous system depressants, especially in overdosage, will increase the potential hazards of these agents. Methaqualone, trade name Quaalude, is also a sedative-hypnotic. A hypnotic (sleep-inducing) dose should be taken only at bedtime, immediately before the patient retires, since Quaalude may produce drowsiness within 10 to 20 minutes. Care should be used during administration with other sedative, analgesic, or psychotropic drugs because of possible addictive effects. Quaalude acts on a different central nervous system site than barbiturates or glutethimide.

Large overdoses have been accompanied by cutaneous edema, bloating of the fluid in the skin, and renal insufficiency. Shock and respiratory arrest may occasionally occur.

Quaalude should not be used continuously for periods exceeding three months. Barbiturates are used as hypnotics for anxiety, and sedatives for anxiety and tension. They are central nervous system depressants, and are also used as anti-convulsants.

Codeine is a narcotic analgesic or painkiller. Patients receiving other sedative hypnotics or other central nervous system depressants concomitantly with codeine may exhibit an additive central nervous system depression. When such combined therapy is contemplated, the dose of one or both agents should be reduced. In severe overdose, circulatory collapse, cardiac arrest, and death may occur.

The medical authorities with whom this case has been discussed state unequivocally that there is absolutely no medical reason for mixing the above drugs. No doctor, in other words, should prescribe Quaalude, Valmid, barbiturates, and codeine for use at the same time. There would simply be no medical reason for prescribing these drugs in combination.

The following drugs have been reported as being used by Elvis Presley in addition to those four found in therapeutic levels during the autopsy:

Hycodan is a cough tablet or syrup. It contains a codeine derivative.

Ritalin, methylphenidate hydrochloride, is used on children with minimal brain dysfunction.

Percodan, oxycodone hydrochloride, is a sedative and semisynthetic narcotic analgesic.

Demerol, meperidine hydrochloride, is a narcotic analgesic.

Dilaudid, narcotic analgesic.

Drug abuse means the taking of drugs beyond the amount necessary to affect the cure of, or alleviate the distress from, a physical or mental disorder. Drug use simply means the taking of prescribed drugs in the proper amounts.

A person may be a drug abuser without manifesting the visible signs of having a drug problem. A drug problem exists when the use of drugs interferes with the accepted normal social functions of an individual. A person who takes two Valium or two martinis, or two Quaalude, or two shots of heroin a day, may or may not have a drug problem. There are as many types of drug problems as there are people who abuse drugs.

There are thousands of people who have two or three alcoholic drinks with lunch and several more with dinner and, according to most authorities, these people are alcoholics. If, however, they are able to function properly, they may not have a drug problem, for the time being anyway, as far as our society is concerned.

Tolerance means that a user of a given drug will need larger and larger amounts of that drug as time passes, to achieve the same effect once gained from a small quantity. Toxicity is the degree to which a drug is lethal. The toxic, or lethal, dose of a drug may remain constant while the tolerance level increases. For example, five milligrams of drug X may be lethal to a given individual who originally was able to achieve the desired high from one milligram. As tolerance increases, the drug abuser may find he needs two, three, or four milligrams to achieve the same euphoria. If or when tolerance increases to five milligrams, which is also the lethal dose, this individual will overdose and probably die as a result of so doing. A polydrug user is a person who uses more than one type of drug. Usually these people are comfortable with everything from aspirin on up and often mix drugs to achieve a desired sensation.

The sedative-hypnotic or tranquilizer type drugs such as Placidyl, Quaalude, Valium, Valmid, and Dalmane, are considered psychoactive or mind-altering drugs. The high comes from resisting the intended effect of the drug.

One forces himself to remain awake while the drug is trying to induce sleep. The high, or feeling of intoxication, is usually described in very sexual terms of tingling sensations, feelings of complete relaxation, and the sensation of being asleep while actually being awake. Drug experts say that approximately 2% of the 500,000 doctors who are authorized to write prescriptions in the United States are involved in the practice of supplying drugs for other than medical needs. This means that there are 10,000 legal pushers plying their trade in this lucrative field of medical malpractice with virtual immunity.

The same experts feel that illegal traffic in prescription drugs is now greater than the trade in the hard drugs, such as heroin and cocaine. During 1977, over 2 million doses of legal drugs were sold for improper use. The estimated income to the sellers for these painkillers, stimulants, and sedatives was in the hundreds of millions of dollars. One Dilaudid tablet, for example, may cost only a few cents at the pharmacy, but on the street it will bring as much as thirty to forty dollars.

Dilaudid has become known as drugstore heroin and others are blended, mixed, and combined to produce heroin-like trips, at one-third the price of heroin, by knowledgeable addicts. Valium, Ritalin, Quaalude, and Percodan are also popular on the street. Prescription pads are stolen or copied, and the unwary pharmacist becomes a link in the chain of illegal drug traffic. Addicts and pushers with some medical knowledge find it easy to feign a variety of diseases that respond to one of the many desired drugs, and the careless doctor writes a prescription for the sought-after substance.

The less honest doctor finds the trade in legal drugs a very lucrative business. When a doctor teams up with a pharmacist, and they split the profits, it is almost impossible to prove any wrongdoing. Making a criminal case against a physician is a difficult and time-consuming task. Law enforcement officials generally prefer to direct their efforts against the pusher of hard drugs, who is more often a stereotype criminal, because the authorities have found that doctors are reluctant to testify against other doctors. Because of this, it is difficult to obtain a conviction in other than the most flagrant cases of abuse.

The mission of law enforcement officials is made even more difficult by the scarcity of complaining victims. Drug abusers seldom come forward and report cases of being given, or sold, excessive drug prescriptions. More often than not, the doctor literally buries his mistake, or his greed, with the body of the overdosed abuser. For as long as he is alive, the abuser is in the clutches of the physician who has become his source of the needed drug, and when he is no longer alive, his friends and relatives are reluctant to mention his drug habit. Society for many years has frowned upon the drug abuser as something dirty or less than human.

Such is the case with Elvis Presley. Had Elvis suffered from cancer, whether or not it was the cause of his death, those who knew and loved him would not hesitate to talk about the disease, if by so doing they could help prevent others from contracting it. Because the disease was drug abuse, some now feel they would be soiling Elvis' image by talking about it.

There is a weakness in the human race which makes us seek heroes and sometimes create them if they are not readily found. We try to make our heroes into beings which they are not. We seek advice on politics from famous artists and advice on art from politicians. We often fail to understand that it is possible to love and respect someone for what they can do without making them all-powerful. Our heroes become gods by our doing, and our making gods from heroes destroys, too often, those we claim to love, and who from the beginning were really only human and subject to human frailties.

Tales told by doctors involved in the treatment of drug abuse are shocking. Men who actively seek arrest and enforced abstinence from heroin, to be able to feel again the thrill of the first fix when they are released, are commonplace. Children who make pill salads from their parents' uppers and downers, and anything else they find in the medicine chest, and wind up in the hospital, or the grave, are far more numerous than most of us know.

People jump from windows or off bridges, shoot themselves or shoot others, wreck their cars and the cars of others, murder strangers or their own families, steal, cheat, and riot under the influence of drugs and alcohol. We die like flies from lung cancer and fill the hospitals with addicts and alcoholics, and there is little reason to believe that any major change of our national habits will take place in the foreseeable future. As a people, we've mostly ignored the warnings against cigarette smoking, and we will undoubtedly ignore the warnings against drugs.

If, however, we can understand that even a man like Elvis Presley can become addicted to drugs, if we can understand how easily the disease can be acquired, and how difficult it is to cure, than perhaps there is a chance of preventing its continual spread. There is absolutely no chance if we hide from it and pretend it does not happen. Drug addiction is not a disgrace, it is a disease and should be recognized as such by all of us, including the most devoted fan of Elvis Presley.

We need education. We need to understand drugs and drug abuse. We need to learn to question the necessity of a drug prescription and refuse it if the prescribing doctor can possibly provide an alternative. The medical profession also needs education. Those who simply err in their judgment concerning the dispensation of prescription drugs must be made to understand the potential danger which they dispense at the same time. Those who use drugs as a means for their own gain should be held responsible for their acts, and controls should be instituted to make the acquisition of prescription drugs more difficult.

None of this is any more intended as a wholesale condemnation of the medical profession than it is a condemnation of the behavior of Elvis Presley. Those who are, or who know, sincere dedicated physicians are aware of their concern for the health and well-being of their patients. The vast majority of doctors are honest and seek only to help those who call upon them for assistance. To believe otherwise is as absurd as feeling that Elvis Presley was less talented, or less good, or less lovable, or less generous because he was afflicted with the all-too-common disease of drug addiction.

Elvis would have been a greater man had he been able to come out and say, "I have a drug problem."

Elvis would have been a greater man had he been able to do that, but the fact that he could not, or did not, does not make him less than he was. Any who love him less for the knowledge they now have, loved him little to begin with. To love a brother, a father, a son, or a friend less because he is ill speaks little for the person with that feeling.

If Elvis Presley was one-tenth the man that those who claim to love and know him say he was, there is not one single doubt possible that he would now want the young people about whom he cared so much to profit from the knowledge of his misfortune. If Elvis Presley were able to say, "Look what it did to me, don't let it happen to you," he would say it.

If a forthright, honest admission of the drug problem by the friends who now hold back would prevent just one young man or woman from following the same path, then their silence and denials do Elvis no favor. If only one out of the millions who thought he was the greatest understands that if this horror could happen to Elvis Presley, how easily it can happen to them, then, in fact, they were right, he was the greatest.

CHAPTER 40

SCHIZOPHRENIA: A SOCIAL CREATION? (TURNING PEOPLE INTO WALKING ZOMBIES AND PONCE DE LEONS)

"Among the various aspects of the hypnotic state (*or any other emotional state*) interest is drawn to 'suggestion' and its physiological response. Suggestion provides conditioned stimuli, which are as real as any unconditioned stimuli (*physical reality*). Suggestion provides stimuli, which exceed in richness and many-sidedness any of the others, allowing comparison neither qualitatively nor quantitatively with any unconditioned stimuli. Suggestion because of the preceding life is associated with all the internal and external stimuli which reach the cortex, signaling and replacing all of them. They bring forth all the responses contingent on the touchable stimuli. 'Suggestion' is the simplest form of a conditioned reflex. — Pavlov

Several researchers have revealed that schizophrenia may well be viewed as a social creation generated to deal with and label people whose actions are not up to standard to others who are socially more powerful.

While there is little reservation that some individuals, on circumstance, perform in ways that others would call mad or psychotic, this in no way proves or establishes as a reality that this behavior is due to a brain disease. The kinds of behavior that diagnosed "schizophrenics" show prove to be so wide-ranging, and the patients' actions so particular to their individual life histories, that one researcher declared:

"The notion of a common cause for such an assortment of human actions can be entertained only if... we reduce the interesting array of polymorphous [various or varied] actions to a small number of categories, for example, delusions, flattened affect, and hallucinations, and further, if we arbitrarily redefine the categories as 'symptoms' of to-be-discovered disease entity."

The same researcher asked 15 knowledgeable therapists to name the most noteworthy item of behavior used to diagnose schizophrenia. Every one but three listed hallucinations, and many added that hallucinations indicated an underling thought disorder. These results were in agreement with a prior 1965 assessment of 346 English psychiatrists. Their survey established that a thought disorder was considered to be the most significant feature of schizophrenia. For the next few years this researcher studied "hallucinations" in the laboratory, in the clinic, and in the library, publishing a number of papers on the subject matter. Following the account of the notion from the 16th century to the present revealed that conduct described as hallucinatory was constantly based on the self-report of imaginings.

The expression "hallucination" belongs, in behavioral language, to a family of words that includes daydreaming, imagining, fantasy, fictions, inventions, and fabrications. Hallucinations or false perceptions are much more widespread. Entirely sane and ordinary people have these on occasion and are in no way threatened with involuntary detention or a diagnosis of schizophrenia. The imaginings that are constructed by so-called normals—imaginary companions in childhood, adult dreams of glory, imaginary contacts with pop idol figures, religious encounters, playful or romantic fantasies—all are the same sort of topics covered by psychiatric patients. Normals also declare their imaginings are "real." In a 1966 experiment, volunteer college students were induced to imagine (suggested) they tasted salt solutions and were so sure they were that they were prepared to testify in court. Actually, they tasted only distilled water.

It is well known that people have experiences in which they give an equal amount of trustworthiness to their imagining as to verifiable perceptions. When religious figures and theologians say that God spoke to them and told them to spread His word, few church members and believers consider such reports hallucinations. Strangely, the identical account coming from a street person or a drunk would swiftly lead to a diagnosis of schizophrenia from a psychiatrist. In one researcher's language,

"Social status considerations may insidiously insert themselves into the clinician's diagnostic matrix. The frequency of schizophrenia diagnoses among persons who are poor and black supports the claim that social structural features of the diagnostic setting supply a readiness for professionals to employ pejorative interpretations of atypical conduct."

If the person's distinctiveness has not been besmirched previously, then the imagining may be considered as a creative, mystical, or transcendent experience.

In the therapeutic setting, even the most commonplace statements of hopes, fears, desires, and imaginings can be misinterpreted by the therapist as obvious indicators of pathology. This is shown by Seth Farber in his book *Madness, Heresy and the Rumor of Angels.*

As Farber observes, the mental health expert's approach to people whose behavior is dissimilar is to presuppose routinely that the behavior is psychopathological. Then they take for granted the behavioral symptoms are due to a malfunctioning psychophysiological system enclosed in the body. If the individual is unhappy, this is seen as brain damage or something off beam in the neuronal pathways, and all situational and environmental influences are disregarded.

Whether a particular belief is branded as delusional has zilch to do with the reality. Beliefs held by preceding generations of scientists and later proven to be untrue are not generally considered delusional. The method of constructing images and beliefs is the equivalent for supposed schizophrenics and supposed normals. People using the expressions *hallucinations* and *delusions* in no way seem to be engrossed in determining what these things mean in the life of the person having them. Whenever such things are investigated in depth, it is typically revealed that the patient's hallucinations and delusions, as the patient's way of making sense of their world, play a very major position and purpose in the patient's adjustment, world-view, and ultimate recuperation.

Research has revealed that the majority of the theories of schizophrenia in the early 1970s were supported on the foundations of only one or two experiments. When these experiments were replicated, the outcome did not support the theories. The rise and fall of early schizophrenia theories—none of which exists today—led researchers to conclude the theories, both somatic (physical) and psychological, all have a half-life of about five years.

Following this early work, researchers reviewed each research article on schizophrenia published in the *Journal of Abnormal Psychology* for the 20-year period beginning in 1959, as well as an all-embracing review of chosen articles from psychiatric journals. A total of 374 reports of experiments dealing with schizophrenia were reviewed. All the reporters were looking for "a reliable diagnostic marker, psychological or somatic, that would replace the subjective (and fallible) diagnosis." The finding of such a indicator undoubtedly would establish the long sought-for soundness for the postulated thing "schizophrenia."

Each of the studies compared the *average* responses of "schizophrenics" on experimental tasks with the *average* responses of "normal" people. Hundreds of experimental tasks were calculated to illustrate that schizophrenics were cognitively or linguistically lacking, perceptually incompetent, affectively dysfunctional, and psycho-physiologically impaired. It was understood schizophrenics would perform defectively.

After analyzing the 374 studies on more than a few dimensions, researchers concluded the criteria for selecting subjects for the studies were defective and undependable. To get their study up-to-date, these same researchers performed the same analysis on the *Journal of Abnormal Psychology* reports for the 10-year period of 1979–1988. These experiments followed the identical model discerned in the previous analysis.

Even though about 80% of the studies reported the schizophrenics performed weakly when compared with the controls, high usability in performance was the rule, and the reported mean differences were minute. There was a substantial overlap of the distributions of the experimental and control groups. At the same time as many theorists took these minute mean differences to sustain the credibility of the schizophrenia hypothesis, this measure of reliability dissolved when it was revealed that a great number of the experimental subjects were on neuroleptic medication, and there were great differences in addition present in the socioeconomic standing and education. Mean differences in presentation could well be associated to cognitive skills, a correlate of schooling and socioeconomic standing. Furthermore, just submissive patients were recruited. Any of the numerous concealed variables would account for the small mean differences observed.

Researchers affirmed, "One conclusion is paramount: in 30 years of psychological research covered in our analyses has created no indicator that would ascertain the authority of the schizophrenia disorder." Subsequent to studying these results, some theorists argued that psychological variables are too rough to recognize the disease development and that biochemical, neurological, and anatomical studies would in all probability disclose the definitive indicator for schizophrenia. Nevertheless, those studies using somatic-dependent variables have proven to be no different and disparity is, once more, the rule. Arguments such as (1) dimension of the hemisphere brain ventricles; (2) disorder of neurons in the hippocampus; (3) encephalitis; (4) focal infections; (5) hemodialysis to relieve patients of pressured schizotoxins; (6) too much dopamine; and (7) defective genes have all been propounded as the origin of schizophrenia. A high degree of unpredictability marks all of these measurements, and no decisive indicator has been established to date.

These specifics have, in no way, dispirited the biopsychiatric believers. Representative of the biopsychiatric viewpoint is Dr. Irvin Gottesman's *Schizophrenia Genesis: The Origin of Madness.* His wide-ranging examination of schizophrenia covers early accounts of the disorder.

As physicians, psychiatrists are supposedly bound by the Hippocratic Oath, which stipulates, "first, do no harm!" However, it is nearly impossible to practice psychiatry without doing considerable harm. How, for example, can a psychiatrist validate his identity as a psychiatric doctor without labeling others as mentally sick—that is to say, without dehumanizing others and thoroughly destroying their identities?"

Tardive Dyskinesia: A Treatment Worse than Schizophrenia

The world's leading antagonist to the use of neuroleptic medications has been Dr. Peter R. Breggin, who, for over a decade, has protested decidedly in opposition to their use. Gathering a remarkable quantity of information, Breggin has persuasively made known that the neuroleptics cause severe harm to the highest centers of the brain, producing unending mental dysfunction, tardive dementia, and tardive psychosis. The most serious of the drug-induced disorders is a chronic neurological disorder identified as tardive dyskinesia, is characterized by erratic, abnormal movements of the voluntary muscles. Nearly all cases are enduring, and there is no recognized treatment. TD strongly mimics Parkinson's disease, Huntington's chorea, and lethargic encephalitis. Drug damage to the higher brain centers, considered the mental equivalent of TD, also occurs. The use of neuroleptics to take care of schizophrenia is nearly total in psychiatry, and most psychiatrists use them as the original line of management. This is done in spite of the reality that various researchers have known that the neuroleptics have no explicit ameliorative result on any mental disorder and that they are imprecise brain-disabling agents that execute a chemical lobotomy to a certain extent in the course of the disturbance of dopamine neurotransmission in the limbic and frontal lobe pathways. The drugs do not alleviate anything. In its place, they crush the emotions, create indifference and lack of interest, and impose submissiveness. Rather than helping schizophrenics, in a controlled study researchers established that practically all patients having their first schizophrenic experience can be treated more effectively devoid of neuroleptics than with them. TD can show up after a few weeks or months on medication, but more often than not occurs after six months to two years of medication. If the state is detected near the beginning and medication is stopped, an expected 20 to 50 percent of the patients can get better. Because numerous cases go unreported or are covered up, it is not easy to establish the entire number of TD cases in the nation at present. Breggin estimates that the sum exceeds 1 million. The predicament is so grim that both the American Psychiatric Association and the Food and Drug Administration have issued warnings about neuroleptic use. In Breggin's terminology, "It is no exaggeration to call tardive dyskinesia a widespread epidemic and possibly the worst psychiatrically-induced catastrophe in history."

How to Construct a Schizophrenic

Schizophrenics, according to the chemical model, may not exist; instead, they are "human beings who have undergone terrifying, heart-breaking, and damaging experiences, usually over a long period of time, and as a consequence are emotionally disturbed—often to the point of incapacitation." Adolf Meyer, the originator of contemporary American psychiatry, argued schizophrenia is not a disease but is instead due to a breakdown of habits of feeling and thinking.

Studies completed on the families of schizophrenics have revealed that the disorder cannot be contained in a single individual but is simply a part of a larger pattern of distressed family interactions. Looking at a quantity of unambiguous family examples, it was seen that schizophrenia is a learned response to troubled family relations and communication failures. Most remarkable has been the unearthing that every one of the families of the schizophrenics were more neurotic and distressed than the schizophrenic him/herself.

Researchers have revealed exactly how parents create schizophrenia in their children by placing them in a no-win quandary called a double bind. In a double bind situation, for illustration, the mother acts like an affectionate mother, but as quickly as the child responds to her, she instantaneously withdraws and expresses antagonism to the child. In the mother's outlook, the child's very being arouses her angst and resentment. Nevertheless, she continues to make loving overtures to the child, then reject him as soon as he responds. Such a state of affairs, unrelenting over a period of years, is unquestionably enough to drive anyone over the edge. Such personality disorders as the mother evinced above may well cover three or four generations and project a dread of going insane from generation to generation. When the parents project their personal trepidation onto the patient and care for him as if he were by now insane or approaching the state, a self-fulfilling foretelling is fashioned in which the parents' horror produces anxiety at first and then a psychotic panic. Schizophrenia, it appears, is transmitted in the course of the *belief* that madness is hereditary rather than by heredity itself.

Another researcher who studied patients whose mental troubles were organic, i.e., caused by brain lesions, toxic poisoning, and metabolic disorders, rapidly concluded that schizophrenics were a dissimilar variety completely. They did not undergo the disorientation, memory loss, and intellectual erosion that marked the brain-damaged. Studies of the families of schizophrenics over a period of years demonstrated every one of them to be schizophrenic—either one or both parents were so self-centered they were powerless to disconnect their own desires and thoughts from those of their child. Additionally, in those families identified as schismatic—those that are marked by open marital conflict and rivalry for the child's allegiance—the child is trapped in a double-bind in that attempting to satisfy one parent causes rejection by the other. In the second kind of family, called skewed, one parent seeks completion through the child and is incapable of viewing the child as something other than an expansion of his/herself. Sadly, the children who develop into schizophrenics are the ones closest to their parents sensitively, and if they have any defects, it is in their love for these imperfect parents, for whom they have sacrificed their individualism and, in due course, their sanity.

As a consequence of existing in these malfunctioning families, schizophrenics misrepresent reality in harmony with their parents' requirements rather than their own. This makes such children predominantly vulnerable to a schizophrenic breakdown. The significance of the loss of ego defenses and the resemblance involving the schizophrenic's thinking and the thinking of normal people has shown schizophrenia occurs when the individual's safekeeping operations, upon which he depends to preserve his self-esteem, stop working completely.

When this happens, the individual suffers from an extreme condition of panic and, in this state, has a petrifying visualization of himself as someone of no importance, like becoming a Walking Zombie. Such panic states—which are the most abysmal and destructive experiences any person can endure—are utterly disorganizing. These panic states can be induced in a number of diverse ways. One of the most frequent is being subjected to exceedingly harsh and frequently malicious belittling by people who are deemed important and on whose good estimation the individual is fundamentally reliant for his self-worth. This type of treatment typically has a long record.

A second sort of panic begins with the psychological immaturity of the sufferer and the stunting of his development by his subservience to and alteration of reality in agreement with his parents' requirements. His/her lack of ability to function as an adult can activate emotional crises, and then schizophrenic episodes, when he/she encounters job promotions, leaving home for the first time, marriage, or parenthood. A third source of fear is the invasion into the person's consciousness of objectionable cravings, feelings, or thoughts, i.e., homosexual, incestuous, or homicidal impulses or ideas. These can cause an extremely unnerved loathing and the dread that one must be subhuman to have them. Such experiences unaided will not bring on schizophrenic attacks, save the individual's ego resistance in addition has broken down. Once the panic situation has happened, five things then transpire as a consequence: (1) a splitting of the personality; (2) a harsh tightening of interests; (3) sleeplessness; (4) the return of the split-off piece of the personality which invades and takes over the ego; and (5) the development of an unambiguous delusional system.

According to one researcher, "Far from being a disease, schizophrenia is actually a very purposeful and meaningful attempt by the individual to cope with a catastrophic loss of self-esteem." When defensive measures of the individual's ego fail, he then distorts reality in order to regain the feeling of worth.

One of the personality splits that come from the panic condition is the consequence of a parent's excruciatingly malicious behavior. In order to feel psychologically protected, the child will view the parent through rose-tinted glasses and deceive him/herself by believing his parent's vindictiveness is in reality his/her own responsibility so all he needs to do is change, "be good," and then he will be appreciated. A second characteristic of the splitting is the circumstances following an especially harrowing panic-producing experience in which the individual emotionally withdraws from external reality into a secure inner world. This leaves the conscious ego confused and missing, sapped of feeling, awareness, and liveliness. In this condition, the whole lot seems illusory, and the individual also feels deadened and immersed in a contracted loop of recurring thoughts to the omission of everything else.

Because the future seems impossible, the individual retreats further from reality into the inner world and recollections of a more contented earlier period. It is as if they have found the Ponce de Leon fountain of youth. At this point, we can discover the individual reading, thinking, and identifying with a superhuman person or escalating on striking religious ideas. These things take his brainpower off panic-producing thoughts. If he/she is thinking about Buddhism, Jesus, or Kennedy, the abhorrent sexual or murderous feelings are kept back.

Such thoughts also ward off the feelings of deadness, like a "Walking Zombie"—feelings of separation from others and even him/herself. These obsessive thoughts strengthen his vacillating sense of uniqueness and, at the identical point in time, defend him against anxiety and panic. As a consequence, the thoughts turn out to be exceedingly addictive, and the individual is literally unable to discontinue thinking. And as long as he is thinking, he is powerless to sleep. This cascade of unrelenting thought will persist 24 hours a day, seven days a week. According to one researcher, "prolonged sleep deprivation has been the pattern in every schizophrenic I have ever talked to and is mentioned in the autobiographies of various schizophrenics." This was undoubtedly correct in one sufferer's case, who said, "I myself was virtually unable to get any sleep in the six or seven weeks immediately prior to the onset of my psychosis." The reasons for this are well acknowledged. When a panic experience occurs, catecholamines (adrenaline, noradrenaline, and dopamine) are created in superabundance, causing a hyper-aroused condition, which leads to protracted sleeplessness. It unaccompanied is adequate to construct illusions, visual hallucinations, and additional psychotic symptoms. Once the borders sandwiched between sleep and waking are gone, the individual's field of attention is further narrowed, the withdrawal into the inner world is enhanced, and his customary reality orientation fades. It becomes progressively more complex to detach fact from fiction, imaginings from reality, and constantly in the background are "internal persecutors" (imagined accusers that occur from feelings of responsibility). As the individual's reality-orientation fades, the persecutors come to appear more authentic and are harder to keep out of his field of consciousness. When this happens again, the individual panics, narrows his focal point of interest further to keep the persecutors from consciousness, and the vicious loop continues. The ego retreats more into the world of unreality.

In one recovered schizophrenic's language,

"As individuals . . . proceed into a panic state, terror floods their entire being as they view themselves as loathsome, inhuman creatures whom nobody could possibly respect. In this profoundly demoralized and despairing state, these individuals desperately clutch at any idea or notion which would provide them with a feeling of dignity or self-respect."

Schizophrenic Etiology

The longest part of one schizophrenic's work describes in detail his own family history, his mother's beliefs in genetic determinism, his father's aversion to children, his numerous and wide-ranging guilt trips, his religious mystification and brainwashing, seven weeks of extended sleep deprivation, his delusion that he was John the Baptist, his hallucinations, and lastly, his complete recuperation. One of the most moving statements in the book points out that being labeled a schizophrenic causes a hundred times as much misery as the illness itself:

"Since recovering my sanity in 1961, I have spent decades struggling to gain some measure of self-understanding and self-esteem. In this regard, I never fully recovered from what psychiatry and my parents did to me until I finally realized I had never been ill in the first place."

This ex-schizophrenic furthermore shows the insufficiency of the psychiatric model to deal with the cause and nature of his symptoms. He shows plainly that his hallucinations were due to psychological rather than psychiatric causes and are understood in terms of the events that preceded them: the personality splitting, extended sleep deprivation, his considerably narrowed focus of consciousness, and his religious obsession. In addition, with regard to hallucinations, researchers have found that auditory hallucinations happen in three stages: (1) the individual projects his own thoughts of self-disparagement onto the outer world— he even feels hostility in the air, believing others are talking with reference to him, (2) he at that time puts himself in "the listening attitude"; (3) in conclusion, he/she hallucinates; he/she hears voices for the reason that he/she expects to hear them. Even though it is universally believed that hallucinations are for the most part auditory, visual hallucinations are in addition especially widespread.

With regard to hallucinations per se, normal people can furthermore hallucinate without judged psychotic. Another researcher, in studying normal people who lost their mates, found that 50 percent of the women and 66 percent of the men hallucinated. A survey of normal college students found that between 15 to 25 percent of them have had sporadic auditory hallucinations; 35 percent of the relatives of psychiatric patients hallucinated, 34 percent of non-psychotic psychiatrically ill patients have hallucinated, and 58 percent of unselected psychiatric students in addition reported having hallucinated. In view of the fact that typical people hallucinate under pressure, hallucinations may be an expression of humanity, not an indicator of a disease.

The fact that an individual religious belief is bogus does not automatically indicate suffering from a brain disease or that he/she could not think rationally and sensibly. Often such people are capable of both. The simple fact that schizophrenic delusions are frequently irrational or peculiar is not corroboration that schizophrenics cannot think realistically. It is also essential to keep in mind that delusions—false beliefs—in the general populace are as well exceptionally widespread:

"For instance, in our culture the most ordinary people have the most extraordinary delusions of grandeur: they believe that after they die they will become demigods, and live forever in a beautiful mansion in the sky. There are also large and growing numbers of people, many of them well-educated and sophisticated, who believe their lives are controlled by the stars, and who are incapable of making decisions without first consulting an astrologer [one such person was president of the United States]. Moreover, with the advent of the so-called New Age movement many delusions and superstitions once confined to schizophrenics, borderline schizophrenics, and other marginal people are now becoming almost the norm. There are millions of people who firmly believe that little green men from outer space are going to land *en masse* on this planet and usher in a New Age—just as tens of millions of other people firmly believe that Jesus Christ is going to return and usher in a thousand-year Reich. There are also hundreds of apparently normal and well-adjusted people who sincerely believe they have been kidnapped by alien creatures and taken aboard UFOs where they had undergone complicated and often painful psychiatric examinations. The ability of ordinary people to delude themselves is virtually limitless. Delusions are so common that their absence rather than their presence should be taken as an indication of abnormality." (Baker)

This typical patient's delusions were a derivative of Protestant fundamentalism and a disease does not, in any way, cause them. In the psychiatric analysis, schizophrenics are biologically substandard persons made of fundamentally second-rate material—poor brains, bad chemistry, or faulty genes.

In probing this observation, this recovered schizophrenic comes into his own as a satirist. In response to the statement, "The natural history of the disease [schizophrenia] is one of deterioration . . .the assumption that schizophrenia is a brain disease is 'a giant step backward' " resulting from three trends: ideological, economic, and political.

When Thomas Szasz claimed schizophrenia was a sham disease and psychiatry fraudulent medicine, psychiatry panicked and repudiated its total psychological tradition and conducted a considerable propaganda movement to prove to the public the "illnesses" its practitioners care for are every bit as genuine as diabetes or cancer.

The monetary need to classify schizophrenia as a disease was owing to psychiatry being susceptible to competition from other nonpsychiatric psychotherapies—clinical psychology, clinical social work, etc. all taking clients away. It became essential to persuade the public that every mental disorder is of an organic nature and can only be appropriately treated by psychiatric professionals.

As a final point, as the political climate of the nation became more conservative, both political and psychiatric reactionaries revealed their belief in biological determinism. If biological determinism is right, the poor are poor for the reason that they are intrinsically stupid and substandard. Inequality of the sexes, the races, and the social classes are biologically determined. Funds committed to social programs or to serving schizophrenics is a waste! In the same way, "until psychiatric science discovers a cure for schizophrenia sometime in the future, people afflicted with this disease are totally beyond help."

To give reason for this view, schizophrenia was attacked on a broad assortment of fronts: as a brain blemish, a biochemical deficiency, and a genetic shortcoming. An ex-schizophrenic looked at these points of view in turn and refuted them with a wide sequence of data.

The Pavlovian (Hypnotic) Explanation of Schizophrenia
THE CONDITIONED REFLEX

"In general, it should be pointed out that in experimental disorders of the nervous system almost always separate phenomenon of hypnosis (suggestion) and conditioned reflexes (associated responses) are observed, which give the right to assume that this (hypnosis or conditioned reflexes) is a normal physiological remedy . . .." (Pavlov, 1994)

When the developing animal world reached the stage of man, an enormously important addition was made. In the animal, reality is determined almost entirely by the physical cues of the environment, which come through receptors of the creature. This is how we acquire original impressions of the world. These cues represent the natural—with the omission of words. This is the original set of cues of reality.

However, words represent a suggested system of reality, being the suggestion (conditioned stimuli) CS of the (unconditioned stimuli) UCS or original impression. Because of this, words or suggestions of ideas have, to some extent, separated us from reality. Therefore, we must always keep in mind suggestion in order to be modest in our understanding of reality. Yet, it is predominantly words which make us human. The fundamental laws ruling the first cueing system must also rule that of the suggested system or words, because it is influencing the same physiology.

Conditioned Reflexes (CR) or hypnotic responses have shown that the phenomenon of our objective and subjective world has combined and that it is very difficult, for our bodies, to distinguish them. This was demonstrated by experiments with conditioned reflexes (CR), or hypnotic suggestion and responses, reproducing pathological states of the human—including what has been called neuroses and certain psychotic symptoms.

Breakdowns according to Pavlov

Normal brain activity is a balance of participating processes. Imbalance is a pathological state. Often there is a temporary imbalance in a normal person. The difficult conditions, which stress the nervous system, include: 1. Overload, of the brain, by intense activation suggestion such as food, sex, and optimism, 2. Overload, of the brain, by suppression like famine, sexual expression, and fear, and, 3. A direct collision of the opposing processes; that is, both activation and suppression simultaneously.

Pavlov identified three stages of emotional/mental breakdown in his experiments. The first stage he called the "equivalent" phase of brain activity. In this phase, all stimuli produce the same amount of a physiological change. This is comparable to normal people under severe stress. There is little difference between their emotional reactions to significant or insignificant experiences. This may well represent cases of schizophrenia. The symptoms may have derived from this phase of breakdown. Along with other emotional sensitivities, this may be due to conditioned stimuli associated with repeated memorization and similar techniques used in early education.

Excitation of the brain by an original impression, as discovered by Pavlov (such as light, smell or sound) causes physical parts like the autonomic nervous system (ANS), the involuntary muscles and/or the body chemistry to change. The counterpart is suppression where an original impression causes a nervous impulse that suppresses or inhibits a physical reaction. (Todes, 2000)

When stronger stressors are applied, the "equivalent" phase is followed by a contradictory or "paradoxical" phase, in which an insignificant suggestion produces livelier responses than a significant suggestion. The more significant suggestion now only increases suppression of the brain, while the insignificant suggestions still produce noticeable physiological responses.

Pavlov's dog refused food when it was preceded by an unconditioned stimulus but accepted the food when the unconditioned stimulus was suggested. This paradoxical phase occurs in human behavior when the emotional or physical stress becomes more intense. On such occasions, the individual's normal behavior is reversed to a degree that seems quite irrational, not only to a separate observer, but to the individual him/herself—unless either of them have studied Pavlov's experiments on suggestive influences via conditioned reflexes leading to nervous breakdowns.

The third stage of emotional/mental breakdown or "protective" inhibition Pavlov called the "ultra-paradoxical," meaning increased suggestive inconsistency. Positively suggested responses suddenly switch to negative and negative to positive. For example, Pavlov's dogs would, after the stress had been sufficiently increased and/or prolonged, attach themselves to a laboratory assistant whom they had, until that time, disliked. Also, they would try to attack the master they had previously loved. Their behavior became exactly the opposite of all their earlier conditionings.

Pavlov showed that a human could be suggested or conditioned to hate what it formerly loved, and love what it formerly hated. In the same way, imposing unendurable strain on a normal person can momentarily replace one set of behavior patterns with another.

When the third stage of mental/emotional breakdown called transmarginal inhibition begins, a state comparable to humans is an atypical suggestibility, or distractibility. Clinical reports, according to Pavlov, of people under hypnosis proliferate in descriptions of abnormalities matching those in the "equivalent," "paradoxical," and "ultra-paradoxical" phases of nervous breakdown.

Summary of Above Findings

1. Dogs, like human beings, respond to imposed stresses or conflict, both real and imagined or suggested.

2. A dog's, like human beings', reactions to normal stress depends on environmental influences or suggestions to which it has been exposed.

3. Dogs, like human beings, break down when stresses, including suggested stressors or conflicts, become too immense for their nervous system to master.

4. At the point of collapse, their behavior begins to diverge from earlier suggestion and conditioning.

5. The quantity of nervous tension or conflict that a dog or human can master without breaking down varies with its physical condition. Exhaustion, tedious repetition, fevers, drugs, and glandular changes can bring about a lowering of resistance.

6. When the nervous system has been stimulated by physical stimuli and suggested stimuli further than its ability to respond normally for extended periods, a dog's or human's responses eventually become inhibited.

7. This "transmarginal" inhibition or hesitation of involuntary or spontaneous responses is self-protective and results in changed performance. Three obvious phases of increasingly more uncharacteristic behavior take place:

   a. The so-called "equivalent" phase, in which the organism gives the same response to both the original physical stimuli and merely its suggestion.

   b. The so-called "paradoxical" phase, in which the brain responds more actively to mere suggestion (the conditioned stimuli) than to the actual original stimuli (unconditioned stimuli).

   c. The so-called "ultra-paradoxical" phase, in which conditioned responses to suggestion and behavior patterns turn from positive to negative or from negative to positive.

8. When stresses, suggested or physical, are imposed on the nervous system of dogs and humans, the result is transmarginal "protective" inhibition, which is comparable to hysteria, and heightened suggestibility, in humans.

Pavlov told an American physiologist that this circumstance convinced him that each dog or human had its "breaking point" — provided that the fitting stress was correctly applied.

Pavlov thought that his research could explain the breakdown that could lead to various forms of schizophrenia and a secular explanation of the religious phenomenon called possession.

PART VIII

CONCLUSION

THE CONCLUSION

Lyndon Johnson's last years, as described in the book *Lyndon Johnson and the American Dream* by political scientist Doris Kearns Goodwin, were filled with disappointment and frustration. Deprived of power and influence, the retired president was judged harshly for his Vietnam policy, even by former associates and admirers. Discussing the Nixon administration's efforts to cut off funds for his domestic programs, Johnson compared his "Great Society" to a starving woman. "And when she dies," said Johnson, who served as a president despite a heart attack in 1955, "I will die."

President Nixon was inaugurated for a second term on January 20, 1973, and the next day his administration announced plans for the complete dismantling of the Great Society. The following day—January 22—Lyndon Johnson dies of a heart attack. A coincidence? Perhaps. Still, one cannot help wondering whether the death of a man of Johnson's political passions might have been brought on by this final blow...

During the late 1960s, a number of clinicians began to describe patients with heart disease who had suddenly died after coming to what seemed an impasse in their lives or being at the "end of their rope." The reports were in accord with work being done by Arthur Schmale, William Greeneard, and George Engel at the University of Rochester. Their studies suggested that illness is more likely to develop at those times when people are having difficulty coping with changes in their lives and are inclined to give up. They had encountered instances of people who suddenly died unexpectedly—usually from cardiac arrest or brain hemorrhage—under such conditions...

For example, the obituary noting the sudden death at 51 of the newly appointed president of CBS stated that he was on the way to attend the funeral of his father, who had died the day before. A prominent British tycoon, prematurely forced into retirement after a bitter dispute with his company, was reported to have collapsed and died at the airport as he was leaving the country for a "well-earned rest." At a memorial concert honoring the late Louis "Satchmo" Armstrong, his widow was struck with a fatal heart attack as she played the final chords of "St. Louis Blues."

Of the life circumstances surrounding 275 deaths, "the most common" (135 deaths) was an exceptionally traumatic disruption of a close human relationship or the anniversary of the loss of a loved me.

Some (of those about to die) actually seem to conclude at one point that it is no longer worthwhile to change the situation. Instead, they seem to expect death and wait for it calmly. While many different emotions may be exhibited immediately before sudden death, the most frequent seem to be those of giving up and hopelessness.

Biorhythms were plotted involving the period just prior to the death of Elvis. According to his biorhythm, he had what is called a doubly critical day just two days before his death, the anniversary of his mother's death. Both intelligence and the physical biorhythms were considered to be at their most critical stage, and his emotional state was considered to be at its lowest without being critical.

Concerning heart attack and sudden death, Herbert Benson, M.D., in his book *The Mind/Body-Effect,* states that "The probable physiological mechanism of sudden death is a disruption of normal heart functioning. Death, which occurs suddenly or unexpectedly, within a period of several minutes, in a person with apparently good or stable health, is almost invariably due to cessation of the circulation of blood. Such sudden death is due to malfunctioning of the circulatory system. Death which is due to alterations of normal function in other organ systems usually is preceded by ill health and occurs much more slowly. Therefore, the sudden deaths related to very intense psychological states such as hopelessness-helplessness, overwhelming fear, and other extreme emotions are almost certainly related to circulatory events."

One electrical component of the heartbeat can be markedly affected by emotions. When you become emotionally upset, your heart rate increases due to increased stimulation of the sympathetic nerves. Fainting, which is frequently associated with fright or emotional distress such as the sight of blood, is often due to unbalanced responses of the sympathetic and parasympathetic nervous systems. Immediately prior to fainting, there is a sudden decrease in blood pressure and an inappropriate slowing of the heart rate. The normal compensatory mechanism, which produces increased blood pressure by increasing the heart rate, does not occur. Blood flow to the brain is interrupted, and fainting results. Then, since the person is lying down, blood flow to the brain almost invariably increases within several seconds and the person rapidly regains consciousness. Although fainting may result in injury from the fall itself, it is usually not a serious or dangerous occurrence if it is not a frequent event.

However, when fainting is caused by a sudden dangerous irregularity of the heartbeat, adequate blood flow cannot occur even when the person is lying down, and permanent damage or death often occurs. The extreme emotional disturbances, which have previously been described in the cases of sudden death, probably caused a dangerous irregularity of the electrical component of the heartbeat. The subsequent inadequate blood flow would account for many of these sudden deaths.

The absolute truth is something we may never know. Even if Elvis was alive and this analysis was being considered by him, we must deal with subjective truth, both his and mine. An analysis, however, of this sort should never be given as fact. The one being analyzed would too quickly reject the hypothesis. A cautious therapist would only use it to give himself a tentative handle on the situation, and as new facts arise, he must be open to another direction or twist in the analysis. The analyst should still maintain his ground, for the subconscious mind, because of its needs to repress these sorts of ideas and feelings, would divert the analyst's thrust in an effort not to reveal itself.

A physician in ancient times once said that a healer has three methods to elicit a cure: the word, the herb, and the knife. The first is the word. We have perhaps fallen too much into the use of the latter two. What our society may need in all respects is more in-depth verbal intercourse on all levels.

An analysis of Elvis Presley is used because, if I used the people who would come to my office, I may have all of the factors present in Elvis' case, except of course the death. Relating private case experience does not, I believe, give the public a novice and experienced analyst the chance to compare his or her abilities at discovery. By using a person with such public awareness, the information is available to everyone.

If indeed my analysis is correct and had I dealt with Elvis, it is my belief and experience that suggests to me that his time of death could have been altered. Even though there are many factors contributing to his death, the primary one seems to be emotion.

Before the age of modern medicine, it was more commonly felt that one could die of a "broken heart." Heart attacks, etc., are often associated with emotional trauma. Depressions, etc., are often seasonal. There may even be something to the science of biorhythm. By this measuring of human factors, Elvis' physical and emotionally critical days were just days prior to his death.

I may be wrong in my theories, etc. But as Benjamin Franklin said as he wrote the dissenting report in Franz Anton Mesmer's conviction for practicing mesmerism, "Although his theories may not lead us to the goal of discovery, certainly there is something about his cures we should investigate further." Mesmer, the father of hypnosis, had practiced suggestive therapy without knowing it. He called it "animal magnetism." He had many elaborate theories concerning his work, which were soon discarded. However, we must keep in mind that they did work. The science of hypnosis and psychology must advance, as in any other science, such as physics. It may first originate and be understood on a limited and primitive scale. Through experiences, openness, objectivity, and acceptance of the "facts" as we now know them. We may not be exactly on the absolute right track, but we are moving and if we continue to search, we may find answers. If not, we have lost nothing.